PATERNOSTER THEOLOGICAL MONOGRAPHS

The Holy Spirit in African Christianity

T0385275

PATERNOSTER THEOLOGICAL MONOGRAPHS

The Holy Spirit in African Christianity

An Empirical Study

Chigor Chike

Copyright © Chigor Chike 2016

First published 2016 by Paternoster

Paternoster is an imprint of Authentic Media
52 Presley Way, Crownhill, Milton Keynes, Bucks, MK8 0ES

www.authenticmedia.co.uk
Authentic Media is a division of Koorong UK, a company limited by guarantee

09 08 07 06 05 04 03   8 7 6 5 4 3 2 1

British Library Cataloguing in Publication Data
A catalogue record for this book is available from the British Library

ISBN 9781842278413

Printed and bound in Great Britain for Paternoster
by Lightning Source, Milton Keynes

To Chinyere

PATERNOSTER THEOLOGICAL MONOGRAPHS

Series Preface

In the West the churches may be declining, but theology—serious, academic (mostly doctoral level) and mainstream orthodox in evaluative commitment—shows no sign of withering on the vine. This series of Paternoster Theological Monographs extends the expertise of the Press especially to first-time authors whose work stands broadly within the parameters created by fidelity to Scripture and has satisfied the critical scrutiny of respected assessors in the academy.

Such theology may come in several distinct intellectual disciplines—historical, dogmatic, pastoral, apologetic, missional, aesthetic and no doubt others also. The series will be particularly hospitable to promising constructive theology within the evangelical frame, for it is of this that the church's need seems to be greatest.

Quality writing will be published across the confessions—Anabaptist, Episcopalian, Reformed, Arminian and Orthodox—across the ages—patristic, medieval, reformation, modern and counter-modern—and across the continents. The aim of the series is theology written in the twofold conviction that the church needs theology and theology needs the church—which in reality means theology done for the glory of God.

Series Editors

Trevor A. Hart, Head of School and Principal of St Mary's College, School of Divinity, University of St Andrews, Scotland, UK

Anthony N.S. Lane, Professor of Historical Theology and Director of Research, London School of Theology, UK

Anthony C. Thiselton, Emeritus Professor of Christian Theology, University of Nottingham; Research Professor in Christian Theology, University College Chester; and, Canon Theologian of Leicester Cathedral and Southwell Minster, UK

Kevin J. Vanhoozer, Research Professor of Systematic Theology, Trinity Evangelical Divinity School, Deerfield, Illinois, USA

ACKNOWLEDGEMENT

I am indebted in this work to many people who have supported me all the way through. I would like to thank Dr Mark Cartledge, for his guidance and support when I did the research work. I greatly appreciate the work done by Jane Freeman and Agata Jezak who patiently proofread the completed work and suggested many corrections. I want to thank Revd Dave Wade for his support during my curacy at St Luke's Church, the period most of the work was carried out. I am also very grateful to the Church of England for their financial support during the time this research was conducted. I am greatly indebted to my wife, Obi, and my children for their patience and understanding whilst I was conducting this study. Finally, I want to thank the Almighty God for making it all possible.

Chigor Chike 2015

CONTENTS

ABBREVIATIONS

AIC	African Initiated Church
ESRC	Economic and Social Research Council
FGBMFI	**Full Gospel Business Men's Fellowship International**
KICC	Kingsway International Christian Centre
KJV	King James Version
RCCG	Redeemed Christian Church of God
UCC&S	United Church of the Cherubim and Seraphim
WCC	World Council of Churches

CHAPTER 1

Introduction

I came to live in the United Kingdom from Nigeria in 1992 not aware that my move was part of a very wide trend. A study has shown that the number of people who came to settle in Britain in the 1990s was unprecedented[1]. The factors behind this trend have been the growth of international students, the rise in asylum applications, the increase in family reunification and economic migration[2]. Even though a significant number of those immigrants were white people, a high percentage came from Asia or Africa. Hence, Somerville and Cooper in their study of immigration trends in the United Kingdom note that "since 1990, sustained immigration flows have diversified the ethnic, linguistic, and religious composition of the British population".[3]

One result of this trend has been the large number of African Christians in Britain. Africans in the African continent have often been described as a very religious people.[4] It would appear that they have brought this religiosity with them to the UK and perhaps passed it on to their children.[5] Many British cities can boast of a large church either founded by an African or having a congregation that has Africans in the majority. In London, there are well known churches like Kingsway International Christian Centre (KICC) founded by the Nigerian Pastor Matthew Ashimolowo, which is now believed to be the largest single congregation in Western Europe.[6] Others include, Glory House, led by two Nigerians, the Odulele brothers; Trinity Baptist Church led by Francis Sarpong, a Ghanaian; El-Shaddai Ministries led by the Zambian, Dr. Ramson Mumba; New Covenant Church led by Paul Jinadu; Bethany Fellowship International led by John Blackson; Lighthouse Chapel International led by Bishop Dag Heward-Mills and Christ Faith Tabernacle led by Apostle Alfred

---

[1] W. Somerville and B. Cooper "United Kingdom: Immigration to the United Kingdom" in Uma A Segal, Doreen Elliott, Nazneen S. Mayadeas (eds.) *Migration Worldwide: Policies, Practices and Trends* (New York: Oxford University Press, 2010), 124.

[2] Somerville and Cooper, *Migration Worldwide*, 124.

[3] Somerville and Cooper, *Migration Worldwide*, 124.

[4] O. Kalu "Preserving a Worldview" in *Pneuma* 24.2 (Fall, 2002), 122.

[5] A. Adeogame, "Engaging the Rhetoric of Spiritual Warfare: The Public Face of the Aladura in Diaspora," *Journal of Religion of Africa*, 34.4, (2004), 505.

[6] R. Burgess, "Nigerian Pentecostal Theology in Global Perspective," *Pentecostudies*, 7.2 (2008), 32.

Williams[7]. Perhaps even more significant are the hundreds of small congregations spread across the country meeting in community centres, school halls or church buildings belonging to other denominations. These are often set up and led by men and women who have a day job, but work as pastors in the evenings and at weekends. In addition to churches set up in this country, many well established churches in Africa have branched out in a major way into Europe, including here in Britain. These include the Victory Bible International Church, the Redeemed Christian Church of God (RCCG), the Praise Valley Temple, the Mountain of Fire, the Gospel Faith Mission International, the Deeper Life Christian Ministry, the International Central Gospel Church, the House on the Rock and the Church of Pentecost.[8] These churches have successfully set up several congregations around the country and are continuing to grow.

This trend is reflected in the growth of the African membership of the traditional denominations. In East London, where I carried out the fieldwork of this research, I noticed that many congregations of Church of England, Roman Catholic and Methodist churches have a sizeable African proportion and a good number of these churches have Africans in the majority. There has also been an increase in the number of Africans in the leadership or exercising a recognised ministry in those congregations. The most high profile of these is the current Archbishop of York, Dr. John Sentamu, who is originally from Uganda. These high profile positions, in addition to the numerous priests and ministers of African origin, are making Africans a more significant force in those denominations here in Britain. This reality makes it important to understand the nature of African Christianity.

The Aim of the Study

The present study aims to understand the nature of the belief held by African Christians, focussing on what they believe about the Holy Spirit. "Pneumatology", which is used several times in this study, technically refers to the study of spirits or the Spirit – ("Pneuma" means "spirit" and "logos" means "word" or "study"). However, it is common practice in Christian theology to use the term "Pneumatology" to refer to the doctrine or study of the Holy Spirit and this is the way I use the term in this study. The doctrine of the Holy Spirit is an important subject in the context of African Christianity because churches founded by Africans often put emphasis on the person and work of the Holy Spirit.[9] The wider aim of the study is to promote the understanding of African

---

[7] I. Olofinjana, *Reverse in Ministry and Mission: Africans in the Dark Continent of Europe* (London: Author House, 2010), 38-41.

[8] Olofinjana, *Reverse in Ministry and Mission*, 38-41.

[9] A. Anderson, *Introduction to Pentecostalism* (Cambridge: Cambridge University Press, 2004), 103; J.K. Asamoah-Gyadu, *African Charismatics: Current*

Christianity by non-Africans. In my view, a greater understanding of the nature of the faith of Africans would reduce the suspicion and feeling of uneasiness some people have towards African Christianity.

Terminology

It is necessary to clarify the terms and concepts I use in this study. Firstly, I am going to explain my use of the words *Africa* and *African*. To begin with, Africa north of the Sahara Desert is predominantly Muslim whereas sub-Saharan Africa is mainly Christian. The latter is what I focus on in this study, and it is what is being referred to when *Africa* is used. As regards *African*, clearly in addition to the people who originate from the continent of Africa and currently live there, there are many people of African origin who live in different parts of the world. It is therefore my view that everybody who can trace their ancestral roots to Africa, no matter how long ago their forebears left that continent would be right to regard themselves as Africans. This would include many who live in or have links with the Caribbean or those living or linked to America. However, for simplicity of language, I use the term *African* to describe those born in Africa and who still live there or have emigrated to other parts of the world or the children of those immigrants. If the need arises, I use the term African-Caribbean and African American to describe those Africans with links to the Caribbean and those in the Americas, respectively. Other terms to describe ethnic background are explained as they occur.

The concept of *African Christianity* can be problematic for some and so deserves words of clarification. It is worth noting that Christianity has a long history in Africa. As far back as the New Testament, one can note that the man who helped Jesus to carry his cross (Mt 27: 32) was from Cyrene in what today is Libya; the people who gathered to hear the disciples on the day of Pentecost (Acts 2: 5-11) included many from African cities and the man riding on the chariot whom Philip was led to share the gospel with (Acts 8: 26-40) was from Ethiopia. Some of the earliest and most prominent Church Fathers were also Africans. Tertullian, the second century Father, and the first to describe God as Trinity was from Carthage which is in present day Tunisia.[10] Athanasius, the fourth century Church Father, sometimes referred to as Pope Athanasius, Augustine, easily the most prominent of the Church Fathers, Clement, Justin Martyr, Origen and Donatus were all North Africans.[11] But this flourishing of Christianity in North Africa was brought to an end as Islam swept through that region. The result is that much of the Christianity in present day Africa has been due to the missionary work of Europeans in the last few hundred years.

Developments within Independent Indigenous Pentecostalism in Ghana (Leiden: Brill, 2005), 341.

[10] J. Mbiti, *Bible and Theology in African Christianity* (Oxford: Oxford University Press, 1986), 1.

[11] Mbiti, *Bible and Theology*, 1.

Christianity had a "re-entry" into Africa.[12] It is that modern phase of Christianity in Africa that I am primarily concerned with.

One would imagine that most Africans are grateful for the work of European missionaries who had to battle immense odds and break new grounds to bring Christianity to many parts of the continent. But there has also been the widespread feeling that many things went wrong and needed to be corrected. It is fair to say that for about the last one hundred years many Africans have been involved, more or less consciously, in the task of correcting the errors made by the missionaries. At the heart of the matter is the feeling that some missionaries had imposed western culture on Africans with their brand of Christianity. This left many Africans in a deep internal conflict. It was as though the Christian religion clashed with their African cultural heritage. This feeling set off the search for a way of understanding and practising the faith which resolved that conflict and left the Africans at ease. As Kwame Bediako put it, Africans sought to:

> achieve integration between the African pre-Christian religious experience and African Christian commitment in ways that would ensure the integrity of African Christian identity and selfhood.[13]

This search, in my view, has gone along in two independent streams. One stream, more conscious and academic, is the work of African Christian scholars, such as Bolaji Idowu and John Mbiti. These two pioneers have lamented the conflict described above and led an army of African scholars to search for an African Christian theology that would put their people at ease. Much of the work in this stream comes through publications and conferences.[14]

The second stream searching for a truly African Christianity is made of churches set up by Africans. Within this are what has been termed the African Initiated Churches (AICs). (The terms "instituted" or "independent" are also sometimes used.) These include churches like the Aladura in Nigeria, the Arathi in Kenya, the Sunsum Sore in Ghana and the Zionists in South Africa. These churches have been formed since the 1910s by people who broke away from missionary churches out of disillusionment. Also within this stream are the African Pentecostal Churches which have exploded into the African religious landscape in the past forty years. Despite the activities of this group, the new Pentecostal churches tend to be driven primarily by their belief in the Bible and reliance on the Holy Spirit, rather than by intellectual outrage or political considerations. However, the analyses of their Christian beliefs and practices have shown that they have been strongly influenced by their African

---

[12] A. Amanor, "Pentecostal and Charismatic Churches in Ghana...", *Journal of Pentecostal Theology* 18 (2009), 123.

[13] K. Bediako, *Jesus in Africa: The Christian Gospel in African History and Experience* (Carlisle: Editions Cle and Regnum Africa, 2000), 49.

[14] A. Anderson, *Moya* (Pretoria: University of South Africa, 1991), 20-25.

worldview. For example, Kwabena Amanor has noted how Pentecostalism "has ridden on the back of the African religious worldview" to grow in Ghana.[15] Hence the emergence of these African Pentecostal Churches has given more energy to this second stream.

The Significance of the Study

The intention of this study is to add to the existing studies of African Christianity. Even though there has been a number of studies of African Initiated Churches, such as Afe Adogame's study of the Celestial Church of Christ, J.A. Omoyajowo's study of the United Church of the Cherubim and Seraphim, M.L, Daneel's study of Zionism in Rhodesia and H.W. Turner's study of the Church of the Lord, there are fewer extensive studies of the new Pentecostal churches or of African Christians in the historic denominations.[16] Asonzeh Ukah's study of the Redeemed Christian Church of God, J.K. Asamoah-Gyadu's study of Charismatic churches in Ghana, Richard Burgess's study of the Pentecostal movement in Nigeria since the 1960s and Ogbu Kalu's study of African Pentecostalism are some of the welcome contributions in that regard[17]. The intention is that the present study contributes to the understanding of this new group of African churches.

Secondly, it is noticeable that many studies of African Christians and their churches focus on aspects other than their theology. In some cases, a chapter or less is devoted to theology. One of the few exceptions to this trend is Allan Anderson's *Moya*, a study of the doctrine of the Holy Spirit among African Initiated Churches in Southern Africa. The present study, by focusing on the doctrine of the Holy Spirit among the new African Pentecostal churches and the historic churches, seeks to add to the understanding of the theology of African Christians.

By carrying out the field study in Europe, it seeks to complement the research on African Christians undertaken in the African continent. It seeks to add to the few existing studies of the nature of the faith of African Christians

---

[15] Amanor, "Pentecostal and Charismatic Churches in Ghana...," 123.

[16] A. Adogame *Celestial Church of Christ* (Frankfurt: Peter Lang, 1999); J.A. Omoyajowo, *Cherubim and Seraphim – The History of an African Independent Church* (New York: Nok, 1982); Daneel M.L. 1993, 1970, *Zionism and Faith-Healing in Rhodesia: Aspects of African independent churches* (Paris, Mouton, 1993); H.W. Turner, *African Independent Church II – The life and faith of the Church of the Lord (Aladura)* (Oxford: Clarendon, 1967).

[17] A. Ukah, *A New Paradigm of Pentecostal Power: A Study of the Redeemed Christian Church of God in Nigeria* (Trenton: Africa World Press, 2008); Asamoah-Gyadu, *African Charismatics: Current Developments within Independent Indigenous Pentecostalism in Ghana*, (Leiden: Brill NV, 2005); R. Burgess, *Nigerian Christian Revolution: The Civil War Revival and its Pentecostal Progeny (1967-2006)* (Oxford: Regnum, 2008); Ogbu Kalu *African Pentecostalism: An Introduction* (New York: Oxford University Press, 2008).

living outside Africa, such as studies by A. Adogame, H. Harris and R. Gerloff.[18] It also continues my previous work on the doctrines of God, Christ and Salvation among African Christians in Britain.[19]

Key Sources

The key sources of the study are the African Christians living in the United Kingdom whom I interviewed. Data was also gathered during several visits to the churches these participants belong to. These included my observations during these visits and the written data I collected from the churches. In the search for relevant literature, I made use of several search engines, including the ATLA Religion database, the University of Birmingham database and the British Library database. My primary literature sources were the academic writings on the subjects of African Christianity and Pneumatology. I also drew on the publications by African Christian ministers on the Holy Spirit as a secondary source of information. This latter group of work, which is often based on practical experience of ministry, includes works by such prolific writers as Enoch Adeboye, Chris Oyakhilome, Lawrence Tetteh, Albert Odulele and Gilbert Deya.

Structure

This book is laid out in seven chapters. Following this introductory chapter, Chapter 2 deals with the methodology employed. In addition to that, explanation is given for why this study consists of two phases, as well as the reason behind the choice of methodology for each phase. Chapter 3 is devoted to the fieldwork undertaken in the first phase of the study. Chapter 4 is a literature review carried out to clarify and expand the findings of the fieldwork. Chapter 5 is a description of the fieldwork carried out in the second phase of the study. Chapter 6 is where I attempt to give an account of the findings. In that chapter, I articulate the make-up (anatomy) of African Christian Pneumatology. Chapter 7 is my Conclusion, summarizing the main points from the study as well as proposing areas for further study.

---

[18] A. Adogame, "Engaging the Rhetoric of Spiritual Warfare" and A Adogame, "Raising Champions, Taking Territories: African Churches and the Mapping of the New Religious Landscape in Diaspora" in Theodore Louis Trost (ed.), *The African Diaspora and the Study of Religion* (New York: Palgrave Macmillan, 2007), 21-46; H. Harris, *Yoruba in Diaspora: An African Church in London* (New York: Palgrave Macmillan, 2006); R. Gerloff, "Theology on Route: The Inner Dynamics of the Black Church Movement in Britain," *Mission Studies* 10.1&2, 19&20 (1993), 134-147. See the Bibliography for other works by Gerloff in this area.

[19] C. Chike, *African Christianity in Britain* (Milton Keynes: Author House, 2007).

CHAPTER 2

Methodology

The purpose of this chapter is to describe the methodology applied in the carrying out of this research. I will describe the philosophical issues I had to consider in the process of choosing a methodology and the stand I take in each of those issues. Then I will describe the process I will follow for the whole study and its constituent parts. In that section, I will describe what was done in the field and give the rationale for each step. Finally, I will discuss the interpretive framework which I adopt and end with a summary of the main points.

Philosophical Considerations

Before conducting a research project, a researcher faces a number of philosophical considerations or assumptions. Creswell has identified five of these:

> The philosophical assumptions consist of a stance toward the nature of reality (ontology), how the researcher knows what she or he knows (epistemology), the role of values in the research (axiology), the language of research (rhetoric), and the methods used in the process (methodology).[1]

I will follow these five areas (in a different order from that above) to describe the consideration I have made leading to my choice of approach in this research project.

Methodological issues raised by the project

The technical meaning of "methodology" is the science or study of methods.[2] G. Payne and J. Payne write, "The term 'methodology' in a literal sense means the science or study of methods. . . . Methodology deals with the characteristics of methods, the principles on which methods operate, and the standards governing their election and application."[3] In practice, however, the term is used not only in this technical sense but to refer to the grand "scheme of ideas

---

[1] J. Creswell, *Qualitative Enquiry and Research Design: Choosing Among the Five Approaches* (London: Sage, 2007), 16. See also, P. Corbetta, *Social Research: Theory Methods and Techniques* (London: Sage, 2003), 13.

[2] G. Payne and J. Payne, *Key Concepts in Social Research* (London: 2004), 150.

[3] Payne and Payne, *Key Concepts in Social Research*, 150.

orienting researchers' work" or in an even less abstract sense, as the "pathway" of social research.[4] Methodology is not to be confused with method because while the former is about process or strategy of research, the latter, which I later discuss in more detail, is about the specific tools employed in the research process.

Methodology is seen as important in research because it forms the bridge between theory and fieldwork.[5] The methodology one employs would depend on the nature of the research question. For example, M.Q. Patton notes that not all questions lend themselves to numerical answers.

If you want to know how much people weigh, use a scale...If you want to know what their weight *means* to them, how it affects them, how they think about it, and what they do about it, you need to ask them questions, find out about their experiences, and hear their stories.[6]

The first method referred to by Patton, involving the use of a weighing scale, is a quantitative approach to research. In a quantitative methodology, there is the tendency to use a standardized measure and the validity of the findings usually depends on the careful construction and use of the measuring instruments. The idea in a quantitative approach to research is to fit a variety of responses into predetermined categories.[7] This methodology usually deals with a large number samples and facilitates comparison between the samples to give a broad, generalised finding.[8] There is the tendency in quantitative research to isolate and focus on specific factors rather than looking at things in context and taking seriously their relationship and interdependence with other things.[9]

The second approach in Patton's example above, which involves interviewing the participants to find out what their weight means to them, is the qualitative one. Qualitative methodologies enable issues to be studied in a greater depth and detail.[10] Because fieldwork is usually done without predetermined categories of analysis, there is greater openness on the part of the researcher.[11] Unlike the quantitative methodology which produces broad information from a large sample set, the qualitative methodology produces

[4] Payne and Payne, *Key Concepts in Social Research*, 150.
[5] Payne and Payne, *Key Concepts in Social Research*, 2.
[6] M.Q. Patton, *Qualitative Research and Evaluation Methods* (London: Sage, 2002), 13.
[7] Patton, *Qualitative Research and Evaluation Methods*, 14.
[8] Patton, *Qualitative Research and Evaluation Methods*, 14; M, Denscombe, *The Good Research Guide* (Buckingham: Open University Press, 2007), 248-49.
[9] M. Denscombe, M., *The Good Research Guide* (Buckingham: Open University Press, 2007), 249.
[10] Creswell, *Qualitative Enquiry and Research Design*, 4.
[11] Patton, *Qualitative Research and Evaluation Methods*, 14.

detailed information about a smaller sample.[12] The researcher is the instrument and the credibility of the work depends on his or her skill, competence and rigor.[13] I took a qualitative approach to the present enquiry because, firstly, my quest is exploratory by nature so I had no predetermined categories and, secondly, it was my hope to present a detailed view of the topic and not a panoramic one.

Another methodological decision that had to be made is related to the "inductive" and the "deductive" approaches to research. This decision also often depends on the nature of the research questions. For example, when investigating a new area where there is not much existing knowledge or where a researcher's real interest is in generating new theories, a research approach which begins with data gathering, followed by the analysis of the data for a discernable pattern is preferred. This is the inductive approach to research.

A. Bryman writes, "With an inductive stance, theory is the outcome of research. In other words, the process of induction involves drawing generalizable inferences out of observations."[14] He goes on to illustrate this with a research work by K Charmaz who examined the experiences of chronically ill men. For this, the researcher interviewed twenty men suffering from this condition:

> The bulk of her data derive from semi-structured interviews. In order to bring out the distinctiveness of men's responses, she compared the findings relating to men with a parallel study of women with chronic illness. She argued that a key component of men's responses is that of a strategy of preserving self.[15]

On this case study, Bryman notes, "the inductive nature of the relationship between theory and research can be seen in the way that Charmaz's theoretical ideas (such as the notion of 'preserving self') derive from her data rather than being prior to the data."[16]

A more common kind of relationship between theory and research is where the researcher begins with the theory and uses the research data as a means of testing that theory. This is the deductive approach to research. Bryman writes:

> The researcher, on the basis of what is known about a particular domain and of theoretical considerations in relation to that domain, deduces a hypothesis (or hypotheses) that must then be subjected to empirical scrutiny. Embedded within

---

[12] Patton, *Qualitative Research and Evaluation Methods*, 14; Creswell, *Qualitative Enquiry and Research Design*, 4; Denscombe, *The Good Research Guide*, (2007), 249.

[13] Patton, *Qualitative Research and Evaluation Methods*, 14; Creswell, *Qualitative Enquiry and Research Design*, 175.

[14] A. Bryman, *Social Research Methods* (Oxford: Oxford University Press, 2004), 9.

[15] Bryman, *Social Research Methods*, 10.

[16] Bryman, *Social Research Methods*, 10.

the hypothesis will be concepts that will need to be translated into researchable entities.[17]

An example of this is a research project, also described by Bryman, which began with the hypothesis, that a religious environment of a nation makes a major impact on the beliefs of its citizens. After surveying people from fifteen countries the research concluded that this was the case.[18] There was a clear movement from theory/hypothesis to data collection and then to findings, leading to corroboration (or falsification) of hypothesis (or the possibility of revising the theory).[19]

In the present study I adopt a research process which combines both the inductive and deductive approaches. This is discussed more fully in a later section.

Ontological issues raised by the project

Ontology is the branch of metaphysics concerned with the nature of being. In social research, however, it tends to be concerned with the nature of reality. "It addresses the question: when is something real?"[20] As there are a number of possible answers to this question, it means that any piece of social research has "an ontological question".[21] Or, in other words, a social researcher would need to state what ontological assumption underlies his or her work. An established ontological position and one which can underlie research is realism. This is the view that "entities in the world exist independently of the human mind".[22] A further qualification of "realism" is what has been termed "naive realism". Naive realists hold that "there is a direct relationship between the external world and human perception, so that 'reality' can be perceived directly".[23] Naive realism tended to be the assumption underlying research in the scientific field. However, many are convinced that this approach is not appropriate for social research because of the complexity of the subject matter (i.e. people). C. Robson writes:

> People, unlike the objects of the natural world, are conscious, purposive actors who have ideas about their world and attach meaning to what is going on around them. In particular, their behaviour depends crucially on these ideas and meanings...Their behaviour, what they actually do, has to be interpreted in the light of these underlying ideas, meanings and motivations.[24]

---

17 Bryman, *Social Research Methods*, 8.
18 Bryman, *Social Research Methods*, 9.
19 Bryman, *Social Research Methods*, 9.
20 Creswell, *Qualitative Enquiry and Research Design*, 248.
21 P. Corbetta, *Social Research: Theory Methods and Techniques* (London: Sage, 2003), 12.
22 A. McGrath, *Christian Theology: An Introduction* (Oxford: Blackwell, 2001), 230.
23 McGrath, *Christian Theology*, 230.
24 C. Robson, *Real World Research* (Oxford: Blackwell, 2002), 24.

Hence, social phenomena should be seen as existing in people's mind and should not be treated as if they exist "out there".[25]

This awareness of the complex nature of social reality has moved some researchers to the opposite pole, from realism to a position called "relativism". There are many variants, but in its extreme form philosophical relativism is the view that "there is no external reality independent of human consciousness; there are only different sets of meanings and classifications which people attach to their world".[26] (Relativism in this context, that is, with regards to consciousness of external reality, is related to its more common usage in the context of moral values, where it is understood as opposite to absolutism). A joke about three baseball umpires illustrates the difference between naive realism and relativism:

> . . . three umpires having a beer. One says "There's balls and there's strikes and I call 'em the way they are." Another responds, "There's balls and there's strikes and I call 'em the way I see 'em. The third says, "There's balls and there's strikes and they ain't nothing until I call 'em".[27]

Whereas the first umpire is not only confident that there is an external reality but, also that his perception corresponds to that reality, the third umpire does not think there is any reality beyond his perception – "they ain't nothing until I call 'em", that is, they do not exist until I say so. This position corresponds to relativism. It gives a key place to the human observer in the issue of the nature of social reality. In my view, however, it overstates the case. As Robson points out, such a position is at odds with commonsense knowledge of the world. He writes,

> he standard counter-example is the fall of a tree in a forest where there is no person to hear it. Do you believe it makes a sound while falling? Or does the event require a hearer?[28]

To suggest that the tree does not make any sound unless there is a hearer, and hence that there is no "mind independent" world is to run the risk of absurdity.[29]

A more nuanced position than the two outlined so far is what has been termed critical realism. Critical realism is essentially realism in the sense that critical realists hold the view that there is an external world independent of their perception. As Roy Bhaskar, one of the leading thinkers in this area, writes, there is within critical realism the recognition that there are "enduring

[25] Robson, *Real World Research*, 23.
[26] Robson, *Real World Research*, 22.
[27] J.R. Middleton and B.J. Walsh, *Truth is Stranger Than it Used to Be* (London: SPCK, 1995), 133.
[28] Robson, *Real World Research*, 22-24.
[29] Robson, *Real World Research*, 24.

structures and generative mechanisms underlying and producing observable phenomena and events".[30] In other words, there is a level of reality which is beneath and precedes the events we observe. Elsewhere, he illustrates the point by pointing to how scientists use laboratory experiments to reach conclusions about natural structures and laws that are invisible:

> What is so special about the patterns deliberately produced under meticulously controlled conditions in the laboratory is that it enables them to identify the mode of operation of natural structures, mechanisms or processes which they do not produce.[31]

This "mode of operation" or "causal laws" is the real object of scientific enquiry, not the observable patterns produced by the scientist.[32] Critical realists do not deny the reality of events rather they hold the view that events can only be understood if we understand the structures that generate them.[33] The structures and laws that are "embedded" in those structures thus constitute a deeper layer of reality for the critical realist. In their philosophical ontology, something is regarded as real if it brings about material consequences (i.e. it is causally efficacious). (Critical realism has been discussed in other fields. One example is in the Biblical studies where Wright, 1992 has advocated this by highlighting the role stories play and should continue to play in the perception of reality.)

Critical realism is represented in the second umpire in the above illustration who said "There's balls and there's strikes and I call 'em the way I see 'em." In other words, I may not always see them as they really are. Unlike the naive realist, critical realists do not think their perception always corresponds to the reality. This restraint from certitude is because critical realists believe the process of perceiving the external world is always mediated through models and analogies.[34] Hence, like relativists they take the perceiver's conceptual frameworks seriously. However, unlike relativists who believe one conceptual framework is as good as another, because there is no external reality to conform to, critical realists believe some frameworks are better than others in getting close to the external reality. In this way, critical realism combines the strengths of both realism and relativism while avoiding their weaknesses.

Critical realism is the position I take with regard to the nature of reality in this research work and there will be more discussion about it in the following section.

---

[30] R. Bhaskar, *Reclaiming Reality: A Critical Introduction to Contemporary Philosophy* (London: Verso, 1989), 2.

[31] R. Bhaskar, *Possibilities of Naturalism: A Philosophical Critique of the Contemporary Human Sciences* (Hemel Hempstead: Harvester Wheatsheaf, 1989), 9.

[32] Bhaskar, *Possibilities of Naturalism*, 9.

[33] Bhaskar, *Possibilities of Naturalism*, 9.

[34] McGrath, *Christian Theology*, 230.

A related philosophical issue raised by this research project is that of epistemology. Epistemology is the branch of philosophy that studies the nature and basis of knowledge.[35] The term "epistemology" comes from the Greek word *episteme* meaning knowledge or science.[36] It is about the way in which people know what they know. In academic disciplines, it would be concerned with acceptable ways of knowing within the particular discipline. In social research, one can speak of an "epistemological question".[37] This is the question regarding "the knowability of social reality and, above all, focuses on the relationship between the observer and the reality observed".[38] In discussing the epistemological basis of our research project, I will no doubt encounter similar issues as I considered in the discussion of ontology. However, instead of looking at the issues from the point of view of the nature of reality, I will be looking at them from the point of view of the nature of knowledge.

An issue we have already encountered is the question of the extent to which social researchers can adopt natural science approaches. In epistemological terms, the question can be phrased as follows: to what extent should social researchers adopt the epistemological traditions of the natural sciences? In the natural sciences, the world is viewed as external to the observer. The emphasis is on using "scientific methods" to investigate and know that external world. It is the scientific nature of these methods that guarantees the reliability of the knowledge gained. Natural science methods are typically quantitative (i.e. rely on quantification or measurements), involve the testing of hypotheses and the search for explanations, causes and reproducible results.[39] This way of understanding knowledge has been called Positivism.[40] Social researchers who adopt it tend to see the social world as external to the observer and consisting of phenomena that can be observed.[41] The observer makes "theories" that describe phenomena and then devises ways of testing these theories.[42] Knowledge is demarcated from feelings because, unlike knowledge, feelings are not based on the senses.

At the opposite pole of this epistemological position is what is sometimes called Interpretivism. "It is predicated upon the view that a strategy is required that respects the differences between people and objects of the natural sciences

---

[35] E.D. Cook, "Epistemology" in S.B. Ferguson and D.F Wright (eds), *New Dictionary of Theology* (Leicester: Inter Varsity Press, 1988), 225.

[36] Cook "Epistemology," 225.

[37] Corbetta, *Social Research*, 12.

[38] Corbetta, *Social Research*, 12.

[39] Payne and Payne, *Key Concepts in Social Research*, 172-73.

[40] Payne and Payne, *Key Concepts in Social Research*, 170.

[41] Payne and Payne, *Key Concepts in Social Research*, 171.

[42] Payne and Payne, *Key Concepts in Social Research*, 173.

and therefore requires the social scientist to grasp the subjective meaning of social action".[43] Unlike Positivism, which operates on the basis that the social world is external to the observer, Interpretivism sees a less clear cut separation between knowledge gathered and the social circumstances being observed. Rather, knowledge is regarded as coming from "culturally determined preconceptions".[44] For this reason it gives greater weight to the mental process that determines knowledge and understanding. [45] Knowledge gathering is seen as having more to do with the interpretation of other people's meaning. Unlike the Positivist approach, which tends to translate to methods emphasizing detached observation, this philosophy of knowledge emphasizes the need to empathise with those studied. Against the primacy of the external world found in Postitivism, this view emphasizes "actor's interpretation" of their world.[46]

Even though these two positions exist in theory, in real life the situation is much less clear-cut. Advocates of Positivism are increasingly willing to accept that interpretation plays a role in the process of knowing. This has led to the emergence of what has been termed "post positivism", which combines aspects of both positivism and interpretivism. Hence post positivists, like positivists, will take a scientific approach to research, have a tendency to be logical, emphasise empirical data collection, and operate on the basis of cause and effect.[47] Yet, unlike positivists and more like those working within Interpretivism tradition, they would accept that what is observed can be influenced by the researcher's background knowledge and values. Whilst like positivists they maintain that one reality exists, they believe "that it can be known only imperfectly and probabilitstically because of the researcher's limitations".[48]

A separation of ontology and epistemology, as I have done in this chapter, can be difficult because both ontology and epistemology are about reality and its knowability. Naive realism in ontology corresponds to positivism in epistemology. In the same way, relativism corresponds to interpretivism. As it happens, many writers discuss critical realism under epistemology, such as Wright referred to above. [49]

Critical realism is the epistemological assumption underlying this research project. It coheres with my position on the nature of social reality which is discussed in the Ontology section. In my view, what people accept as social reality begins with what obtains in the external world, but is mediated to them by their own conceptual framework, which are specific to time, culture and

[43] Bryman, *Social Research Methods*, 13.
[44] Bryman, *Social Research Methods*, 172.
[45] Bryman, *Social Research Methods*, 172.
[46] Bryman, *Social Research Methods*, 172.
[47] Creswell, *Qualitative Enquiry and Research Design*, 20.
[48] Robson, *Real World Research*, 27.
[49] N.T. Wright, *The New Testament and the People of God* (London: SPCK, 1992).

situation. It is a position that has the potential to emancipate because the awareness of the historical and social factors in conceptions of reality is the first step to criticising them. This is, in fact, how Robson uses the term *critical* in "critical realism". In his view, the awareness of the social factors involved in the conception of reality "provides a rationale for a critical social science" which "criticizes the social practices that it studies".[50] I will not be working under the extreme interpretivist position, the most common of which is known as constructivism. Social constructivism holds that individuals in seeking understanding of the world they live in "develop subjective meanings of their experiences" which are "varied and multiple, leading the researcher to look for the complexity of views rather than narrow the meaning into a few categories of ideas".[51] This epistemological tradition is related to the relativist view of reality which I have rejected.

Axiological issues raised by the project

Axiology deals with the philosophical consideration of value.[52] In social research, the axiological consideration is about how the researcher's values influence the research project. Creswell writes, "All researchers bring values to a study, but qualitative researchers like to make explicit those values. This is the axiological assumption that characterizes qualitative research."[53] These values and the social location that shapes them are important in qualitative research:

> How we write is a reflection of our own interpretation based on the cultural, social, gender, class, and personal politics that we bring to research. All writing is positioned and within a stance. All researchers shape the writing that emerges, and qualitative researchers need to accept this interpretation and be open about it in their writing.[54]

The researcher's openness about their social location and values has been termed reflexivity and it is increasingly common, especially among qualitative researchers. M. Denscombe writes:

> Reflexivity concerns the relationship between the researcher and the social world. Contrary to positivism, reflexivity suggests that there is no prospect of the social researcher achieving an entirely objective position from which to study the social world. This is because the concepts the researcher uses to make sense of the world are also a part of that social world.[55]

---

[50] Robson, *Real World Research*, 34.
[51] Creswell, *Qualitative Enquiry and Research Design*, 20.
[52] K. Geach, *Axiology: A Theory of Values* (Walton-on-Thames Ken Geach, 1976), 2.
[53] Creswell, *Qualitative Enquiry and Research Design*, 18.
[54] Creswell, *Qualitative Enquiry and Research Design*, 179.
[55] M. Denscombe, *The Good Research Guide* (Buckingham: Open University Press, 1998), 240.

An example of this is in the growing area of visual ethnography, which is where a researcher investigates and documents the life and activities of a culture-sharing group using photographs, video recording and other visual media. Attention has been drawn to the way information about the researcher, such as their age, gender and academic background, influences what is photographed and how the resulting image is composed.[56]

The concept of reflexivity thus redefines the researcher's goal with regards to objectivity. Rather than seeking the impossible (i.e. complete objectivity) the researcher's focus becomes one of balance. S/he seeks to understand and depict the world in "all its complexity while being self-analytical, politically aware, and reflexive in consciousness".[57] This does not mean the researcher's work degenerates into pure subjectivism. Rather the intention is to promote self-awareness and self-questioning even during the research process. Such a reflexive approach to research also means that researchers can take responsibility for their work and findings and ownership of their perspective. Hence a researcher should ask himself or herself, what are his or her political values that need to come into the report, has he or she backed into a passive voice and "decoupled" their responsibility for interpretation?[58]

I take up such reflexive approach in this research. As regards me, I would like to state that I am an African and a Christian. I am at present a minister in the Church of England, though I have at different times worshipped at other denominations. This has given me both an insight into and sympathy for Christian ideas, particularly the slant that fellow Africans put on them. All these have epistemological significance. Also significant is the sympathy I have for the philosophical/cultural phenomenon that has been termed "postmodernity"; specifically, its suspicion of the modernist metanarrative and the attendant naive realist metaphysics. I stand with J.R. Middleton & B.J. Walsh in their recognition of the dangerous link between metanarratives and the epistemological systems behind them:

> Post-modern suspicion about the violent and homogenizing nature of all epistemological totality claims is well founded. We do tend to construct perspectives, worldviews and metanarratives that erase difference and marginalise whatever does not fit.[59]

It is therefore necessary to expose the constructed nature of metanarrative:

> Claims to moral universality, whether rooted in systems or metanarratives, can be deconstructed in such a way that they are seen to be little more than the

[56] Bryman, *Social Research Methods*, 312.
[57] Patton, *Qualitative Research and Evaluation Methods*, 41.
[58] Creswell, *Qualitative Enquiry and Research Design*, 180.
[59] Middleton and Walsh, *Truth is Stranger Than it Used to Be*, 170.

legitimation of the vested interests of those who have the power and authority to make such universal pronouncement.[60]

It is noteworthy that the people who think they have found an absolute tend to be the same ones who consider themselves superior to others.[61] Hence, the deconstruction process also involves pointing out to those concerned that what they experience as natural is, in fact, cultural. It involves undermining any totalising vision of reality and opening up space for "free play of difference".[62] It has the potential to clear "the ground for the possibility of doing justice to the marginal, for the liberation of those excluded or oppressed under the hegemony of modernity".[63] This tendency towards the liberation of those oppressed under modernity is what attracts me to postmodernity.

Rhetorical issues raised by the project

My fifth and final philosophical consideration is rhetorical. Out of the five areas, this is perhaps the most likely one to be ignored or overlooked, mainly because of the different ways the word "rhetoric" is understood. For example, a question contained within a speech, asked not for an answer but for effect, is often described as "a rhetorical question". This follows the traditional understanding of the word which goes back to the Greek thinkers Socrates, Plato and Aristotle. In that understanding "rhetoric" was associated with speech, and in everyday usage, with artistic devices used to persuade an audience. In more recent time, "rhetoric" has broadened in meaning to include not only oral but written material. It also now includes the way the content and form of texts (such as the ordering of arguments) and even the medium of a presentation work together to present a particular perspective. Hence, "the modern rhetorician identifies rhetoric more with critical perspective than with artistic product".[64]

This modern meaning is the best way to understand the point that there is a rhetorical assumption underlying the work of research and the reporting of its results. Rhetorical assumptions underlying research would contain assumptions about the theses that are already acceptable to the listeners or readers on which the speaker or writer would base their argument.[65] Creswell gives the example of the use of "I" in the reporting of qualitative research:

> Qualitative researchers tend to embrace the rhetorical assumption that the writing needs to be personal and literary in form. For example, in the use of metaphors,

[60] Middleton and Walsh, *Truth is Stranger Than it Used to Be*, 71.
[61] K. Mannheim, "Theology and Sociology of Knowledge" in R. Gill (ed.), *Theology and Sociology* (New York: Cassell, 1996), 80.
[62] Middleton and Walsh, *Truth is Stranger Than it Used to Be*, 36.
[63] Middleton and Walsh, *Truth is Stranger Than it Used to Be*, 36.
[64] P. Geotz, (ed.), *Encyclopaedia Britannica* (Chicago: Encyclopaedia Britannica), 15th edition (1985), 26.804.
[65] Geotz, (ed.), *Encyclopaedia Britannica*, 26.804.

they refer to themselves using the first-person pronoun, "I," and they tell stories with a beginning, middle, and end, sometimes crafted chronologically, as in narrative research.[66]

In addition, qualitative researchers avoid such quantitative terms as "generalizability" and "objectivity", preferring instead to use terms such as "transferability" and "credibility".[67]

This qualitative rhetorical approach is what I follow in conducting and reporting this research. As an approach, it puts into practice the philosophical positions that I have espoused above. For example, by adopting the personal pronoun "I", I am admitting the personal (what would have been called the "subjective") nature of my observation and accepting that others may see or do things a different way. The personal pronoun "I" also enables me to take responsibility for my research approach and findings. It coheres with the position I have taken in the different aspects of my philosophical consideration. Ontologically, it coheres with the idea of multiple "realities", because what I recount as reality might not be what another person in the same position would recount; epistemologically, it coheres with the local, temporal nature of knowledge, because "I" is short for "I, at this place at this time"; axiologically, it is value laden, because "I" is not a disembodied reference but short for "I, Chigor Chike, with all the facts about me and values I have disclosed about myself"; and it coheres with my methodological position, because there is no pretence of "objectivity" or "universality", rather there is a commitment to be fair, balanced and credible as far as this is possible.

The research process

The Empirical Cycle

The fieldwork was carried out in two phases. The first phase involved undertaking an inductive study of an African Pentecostal Church to derive some theories on Pneumatology. The second phase, which was deductive, involved testing out the theories derived from the first phase on African Christians from various denominations. This pattern of starting with an inductive enquiry, establishing theories from that enquiry and then testing the theory or theories on a fresh sample, is known as the empirical cycle.[68] It is widely used by empirical researchers because it has the benefit of employing in the research process a cycle that is used in the natural process of human learning.[69]

---

[66] Creswell, *Qualitative Enquiry and Research Design*, 18.

[67] Creswell, *Qualitative Enquiry and Research Design*, 18.

[68] De Groot, *Methodology: Foundations of Inference and Research in the Behavioural Sciences* (Paris, Mouton, 1969), 1.

[69] De Groot, *Methodology*, 4; J.A. Van der Ven, *Practical Theology: An Empirical Approach* (Kampen: Kok Pharos, 1993).

Following A. De Groot, J.A. Van der Ven applied the empirical cycle approach to theology.[70] For van der Ven, the empirical theological cycle is the basis of the methodology employed in empirical theology. He notes that this is a cycle because at the end of the deductive process, after the result is tested and its significance evaluated, the outcome could become the beginning of the process all over again. He also notes that unlike in science, empirical theology does not rule out the use of intuition. In the inductive phase, the researcher uses not only his or her five senses but "all available intuitive and associative apperceptive capacities in order to let the data speak for themselves and to do them justice".[71] He also notes that empirical theology does not give "exclusive" power to empirical data because at the end of the process, the data is put in a broader theoretical frame.[72]

In the present study, I have broadly used the empirical cycle in its basic form. That is, I have an inductive phase, where I carried out an open-minded field study of a church. This is followed by a theory phase, where I relate the findings of the study to existing literature and then a deductive phase, where the theories that arose from the first two phases were tested. All the fieldwork, both the inductive and the deductive phases of the present research, took place in East London, with the participating churches situated within two miles of each other.

In the following section, I will give the reasons for choosing particular methods, churches and participants.

Phase One (Inductive): Case Study of an African Pentecostal Church

A case study in the field of social research has been defined as "a very detailed research enquiry into a single example (of a social process, organisation or collectivity) seen as a social unit in its own right and as a holistic entity".[73] The case being studied is usually located in one physical place and would also have clear boundaries, that is, a way of knowing what or who is part of the case or not. Robert Yin distinguishes case studies in two ways, namely, single or multiple case studies and holistic or embedded case studies. A single case study is where a single unit such as a school or classroom is studied, whereas in a multiple case study, it is a number of schools or classrooms. R. Yin's distinction between holistic and embedded has to do with what is being analysed in the case study.[74] In a holistic case study the focus of analysis is the whole case, but in an embedded case study, the focus is a subunit or process

---

[70] De Groot, *Methodology*.

[71] Van der Ven, *Practical Theology*, 114.

[72] Van der Ven, *Practical Theology*. See also, M. Cartledge, *Charismatic glossolalia: An Empirical-Theological Study* (Farnham: Ashgate, 2002); idem, *Encountering the Spirit: The Charismatic Tradition* (Maryknoll: Orbis, 2007).

[73] Payne and Payne, *Key Concepts in Social Research*, 31.

[74] R. Yin, *Case Study Research – Design and Methods* (London: Sage, 1984).

within the case.[75] "In an organisational study, the embedded units also might be 'process' units, such as meetings, roles, or locations."[76] Yin describes this as a 2x2 matrix because both single and multiple case studies can be holistic or embedded. This stage of my study is an embedded case study, because I am studying a church and how it understands the Holy Spirit. I do not approach it holistically as the study does not involve the whole of the church, with all its activities, processes, structures and beliefs.

A case study offers me a number of advantages. It can be contrasted with a "cross-case" study like a survey, in that while a case study investigates one case intensively, a cross-case study would look across many cases often in a more superficial way. John Gerring gives this helpful illustration of that contrast:

> There are two ways to learn how to build a house. One might study the construction of many houses — perhaps a large subdivision or even hundreds of thousands of houses. Or one might study the construction of a particular house. The first approach is a cross-case method. The second is a within-case or *case study* method.[77]

The concentration on one case would allow me to do very detailed work on it and to dig very deeply. This would give me the opportunity to uncover links and internal dynamics within the case which would be missed by a survey because of the superficial nature of surveys. It is for these reasons that I have chosen a case study in this phase of my research. Since there is little study of the Pneumatology of African Christians in Britain, this case study allows me to adopt an inductive open-minded approach that in turn enables my understanding to develop from the research itself.

The case study will be of a church I have called Mount Zion in order to protect their identity. Mount Zion is based in East London. It is led by Africans and has a membership that is predominantly African. Mount Zion started about twenty years ago with a handful of people mostly from Nigeria. It currently has a membership of several hundreds. These characteristics mean that I can expect the church to be a rich source of data for study. It also fits the characteristics discussed above. For example, it is a social unit with clear boundaries. It is also at a single location. The data gathering phase of this research lasted over a year. I was interested not only in the worship but in other church activities, including weekday activities. But as this is an embedded study and not a holistic one, my interest in these activities was in how they shed light on the church's Pneumatology.

---

[75] Yin, *Case Study Research*, 41.
[76] Yin, *Case Study Research*, 41.
[77] J. Gerring, *Case Study Research: Principles and Practice* (New York: Cambridge University Press, 2007), 1.

Methods

Three methods were employed in this case study, namely, participant observation, interviews and documentary analysis.

(a) Participant observation

This entailed visiting the church and recording my direct observation of the church activity. My observations were those of a participant, hence the term "Participant-observation":

> Participant observation is data collection over a sustained period by means of watching, listening to, and asking questions of people as they follow their day-to-day activities, while the researcher adopts a role from their setting and partially becomes a member of the group in question.[78]

Participant observation is vital in researching a new group such as this. It allowed me to blend in with those whose profile I studied and enabled me to experience their world "from the inside". I was able to observe this church, as far as possible, in its natural form without being obtrusive.

(b) Interviews

I chose interviews rather than a survey in line with the philosophical basis of the research discussed in the previous section. This method enabled me to engage with a cross-section of people, even though they were at different levels in terms of their ability to articulate their understanding of the Holy Spirit. It allowed me to probe deeply where necessary and so avoid the impossible task of predicting how and where people might see the Holy Spirit at work in order to put it in a questionnaire. I used open-ended questions in line with the inductive nature of this stage of my research. Thus, rather than exercising tight control over the interview, I gave room for the interviewees to develop their own ideas and pursue their own thoughts. This approach is sometimes described as an "unstructured interview", as opposed to a "structured interview" whereby tight control is exercised by the interviewer.[79] Both the members and the leaders of these churches were interviewed to ensure that the doctrine of the Holy Spirit that came across was shaped from both ends of the church hierarchy.

(c) Documents

Examination of data related to the organisation was my third research method. Usually, this would include organisational records, memoranda and correspondence, official publications and reports, letters, minutes of meetings, art works, photographs, newsletters and websites. In this church, I had access mainly to the training booklet for church members and the church's website. I

---

[78] Payne, and Payne, *Key Concepts in Social Research*, 106.
[79] M. Denscombe, *The Good Research Guide* (Buckingham: Open University Press, 1998), 113.

also studied books and other publications written by members/leaders of the church or by other people about the church. The great advantage of documentary sources is their accessibility. However, it is important that they are not always taken at face value because they can sometimes be selective in terms of what they report and their content can be a particular interpretation of what happened.[80]

By using multiple methods, I ensured that data collected by means of one method is compared with other data. Hence this use of multiple methods, methodological triangulation, ensured the corroboration of the data collected.[81]

Study outcome and relation to existing literature

The fieldwork carried out in the case study generated much data. There is a variety of ways these can be analysed, but Yin has described the steps simply as examining, categorizing, and tabulating "or otherwise, recombining the evidence to address the initial proposition".[82] In spite of this simple description, in practice it is never straightforward deciding where one stage ends and another begins, or how many sub-stages there are in, for example, the categorising stage. The first thing I did was to formulate the data into a case record, which pulls them together "into a comprehensive, primary resource package" and "include[s] all the major information that will be used in doing the final case analysis".[83] In approaching the analysis, I was armed with what Yin calls a "general analytic strategy", the role of which is "to help the investigator choose among different techniques and to complete the analytical phase of the research successfully".[84]

Yin describes two types of these analytical strategies. The first relies on theoretical proposition.[85] It involves simply looking to see whether the original proposition that started off the research has been answered, and presenting the data to make the case. The second entails developing a case description. This involves developing "a descriptive framework for organising the case study" and is used when the original intention of the research is to describe and there is no propositional statement at the outset of the research.[86] This second strategy fitted this phase of my research, because I did not set out with a propositional statement about the nature of the understanding of the Holy Spirit among this group of African Christians. Rather, I looked out for patterns with which I could make "theoretical" statements about the subjects. These "pattern theories" do not have the kind of causal links one finds in quantitative studies,

---

[80] Denscombe, *The Good Research Guide*, (1998), 162.
[81] Denscombe, *The Good Research Guide*, (1998), 85.
[82] Yin, *Case Study Research*, 102.
[83] Patton, *Qualitative Research and Evaluation Methods*, 440.
[84] Yin, *Case Study Research*, 103.
[85] Yin, *Case Study Research*, 103.
[86] Yin, *Case Study Research*, 104.

but contain concept and relationships that reinforce each other.[87] In other words, I looked for relationships that made sense and not for causes and effects.[88]

It is noteworthy that at this phase the "theory" from my case study emerges at the end, fitting the inductive approach I have taken for this phase of the project. For that same reason (i.e. the inductive nature of my approach) I will introduce existing literature at this point. In general, the use of literature in a study has the following purposes:

(a) it shares with the reader the result of other studies that are closely related to the study being reported...(b) It relates a study to the larger, ongoing dialogue in the literature about a topic, ...(c) It provides a framework for establishing the importance of the study...[89]

If I introduced existing literature earlier, I would have risked being overly directed in my research questions by that literature. Since the subject of interest, that is, the Pneumatology of African Christians in the UK, is relatively unexplored, such influence would have narrowed my work in an unhelpful way. However, by introducing the literature at this stage I ensure that it deepens my understanding of the theories. These "theories" contextualized in relation to existing literature are tested in the second phase of the empirical cycle.

Phase Two (Deductive): Testing the findings

This phase involves testing the theories arising from Phase One on other groups of African Christians. Now, apart from the Africans belonging to churches set up by Africans, a significant number of Africans belong to the "historic" churches like the Church of England, the Roman Catholic Church, the Methodist Church, the United Reformed Church and the Baptist Church. Since these people are Africans as well as Christians, a study of African Christian Pneumatology which takes them into account would offer a fuller picture. However, unlike the African Pentecostal Churches or the African Initiated Churches where the founders, leaders, and majority of the members are Africans, this group of African Christians tend to be in the minority in their church, and so would not have the kind of influence their fellow Africans have in shaping church life in the churches set up by Africans. Their influence is also hindered by the fact that these denominations tend to have long standing traditions. For these reasons, a case study or participant observation of their church would not reveal as much about their own beliefs as with the participants at Mount Zion. Therefore, even though I visited these churches and participated in several services, I put more emphasis on the interviews I conducted among the members.

[87] J. Creswell, *Research Design: Qualitative and Quantitative Approaches* (London: Sage, 1994), 94.
[88] Creswell, *Research Design*, 94.
[89] Creswell, *Research Design*, 21.

I will use Yin's first type of analytical strategy, which begins with a theoretical proposition.[90] In this regard, I will be using the pattern theories derived from Phase One as the propositions that will be tested out in this phase.

I interviewed thirty people selected in such a way as to include various age groups and both sexes from the following denominations: the Methodist Church, the Church of England, the Roman Catholic Church and the Pentecostal Church. The interviews also provided me with the opportunity to check "theories" which have arisen from the case study of Mount Zion. This stage of the research was thence mainly deductive.

Even though the approach at this stage was mainly deductive, it was not entirely so. I still left room for new ideas and understandings to emerge from this group. Such room would allow a denominational emphasis to emerge and enable me to compare the effect of denomination on Pneumatology. In order to attain this deductive/inductive balance, the method I used was a semi-structured interview. A semi-structured interview is, as a concept, less formal than a structured interview but allows less flexibility than an unstructured interview. They give the interviewer more control than s/he would have in an unstructured interview, whilst leaving some room for the interviewee to develop the subject further.[91] I conducted the interviews using a list of open questions derived from stage 1 of this research.

Interpretation of findings

Anthropologists rightly point out that a separation between description and interpretation is difficult because the way a person describes the world is highly influenced by how they interpret the world.[92] However, insights from ethnography might help in this respect because ethnographers speak of two kinds of interpretation.[93] The first is called "emic" interpretation. This is the "local" interpretation the ethnographer weaves through his description of what is taking place. The second is the "etic" interpretation which is when the ethnographer moves to interpret his or her findings with theories and models to those unfamiliar with the group studied.[94] My interpretation will have these two elements to it.

Even so, having used investigative approaches commonly found in the social sciences, I am careful in the "etic" interpretation so as to avoid the limitation that social scientists often encounter when conducting research in a religious environment or issue. This is illustrated by the following statement by Cameron et al while discussing the difference between emic and etic interpretation: "an emic explanation of spirit possession might be grounded in belief in

90 Yin, *Case Study Research*, 103.
91 Denscombe, *The Good Research Guide*, (1998), 113.
92 H. Cameron et al, *Studying Local Churches* (London: SCM, 2005), 29.
93 Cameron et al, *Studying Local Churches*, 29.
94 Cameron et al, *Studying Local Churches*, 29.

supernatural powers".[95] The anthropologist's etic theory might explain it as a means of attracting attention or expressing powerlessness on the part of the possessed. It would appear that in their "etic" interpretation, the theories available to social scientists limit their interpretation of supernatural occurrences to psychological or sociological phenomena. They are, usually, not able to take part in discourse taking place at the supernatural dimension.

This is a situation which anthropologists and sociologist themselves recognise. For example, in *Sociology and Liturgy*, Kieran Flanagan (1991) argued that anthropologists/ sociologists can never fully know what Christians experience in worship.[96] Another anthropologist, Martin Stringer, makes a similar point stating, among others, that "this highly subjective response is beyond the scope of the anthropological investigator".[97] For this reason, anthropologists investigating religious phenomena often find themselves restricted to such areas as ritual analysis, which discusses religious experiences in such terms as performance, symbolism, play or, as pointed out by David Martin, "anomie" and "alienation" which in his view "explain too much too soon".[98]

Central to this limitation is what the anthropologists themselves regard as "theological neutrality". Simon Coleman explains, "As social scientists, no matter what our personal convictions may be, we must remain as theologically neutral as possible: our discipline is concerned to understand the social functions and effects, rather than the truth-value, of any given religion."[99] Coleman develops his point further:

> Religion is shown to be about practice as well as belief, actions as well as ideas. And we see how religion is said to function to create social integration: it is defined not in terms of specific dogmas, but in terms of what it does. The effect of the definition is not to deny the existence of God, but simply to deny the relevance of the question to the social sciences.[100]

Coleman admittedly works in the functionalist approach to religion with which Emil Durkheim is associated. But neither the Marxist nor the Weberian approaches, which are the other sociological approaches, is concerned with the truth value of religion for its own sake. Curiously, this discipline, which at the very best sees the existence of God as irrelevant and at times operates on the

[95] Cameron et al, *Studying Local Churches*, 29.
[96] Cameron et al, *Studying Local Churches*, 94, quoting Kieren Flanagan, *Sociology and Liturgy: Re-presentation of the Holy* (London: Macmillan, 1991).
[97] M. Stringer, "The Worship and Action of the Local Church; Anthropological Strand" in H. Cameron et al (eds.), *Studying Local Churches* (London: SCM, 2005), 95.
[98] D. Martin, "Undermining the Old Paradigms: Rescripting Pentecostal Accounts," *Pentecostudies*, 5.1 (2006), 19.
[99] S. Coleman, "Anthropological Strand" in Cameron et al (eds), *Studying Local Churches* (London: SCM, 2005), 45.
[100] Coleman, "Anthropological Strand", 45.

basis that God does not exist, is what many theologians (who by definition are concerned with discourse about God) rely on for an interpretative framework. This leads to the absurd situation where Christian theologians give up their "inside knowledge" about Christianity and subject themselves to the same limitations that sociologists encounter when addressing theological questions.

The question arising from the foregoing is this: how does one conduct research on a theological question using social science methodology and yet avoid the limitations inherent in the social sciences. A number of writers have given answers to this question. A notable contribution has been made by John Milbank who initiated a movement now called Radical Orthodoxy.[101] Milbank's answer has been to denounce the adoption of social science approaches by Christians for their analysis in the first place.[102] He rejects the idea that the knowledge of social processes or the socio-historical aspects of Christianity should necessarily come from the social sciences. He points out that secular social theorists are themselves in disarray because thinkers influenced by Nietzsche are dismantling the claim by secular theorists that they have uncovered "the governing factors of human association".[103] Milbank urges theologians to acknowledge this development and rather than looking elsewhere for answers, "It is theology itself that will have to provide its own account of the final causes at work in human history, on the basis of its own particular, and historically specific faith."[104] He provides this account himself by arguing that there is no "pure nature" in the sense of created things standing apart from God. Instead, all life is already infused with divine grace. Having rejected the notion of a sharp line between the "secular" and the "spiritual" or between "nature" and "super nature", he provides an explanation of human association (i.e. social theory) from a theological point of view.

A more accommodating approach to the social sciences than that of Milbank has been advocated by Robin Gill. Gill's position is best understood in the context of his view on the wider subject of the place of theology within society. He believes that there is a complex web of interaction between theology and society. Unlike the Marxist understanding of theology which sees it as something totally determined by social forces (a product of the bourgeoisie) or the Weberian approach which sees social phenomena as having theological root, Gill sees the picture as much more complex with theology and social structures being both cause and effect at different points.

---

[101] J. Milbank, *The World Made Strange* (Oxford: Blackwell, 1997).

[102] Milbank, *The World Made Strange*, 2.

[103] Milbank, *The World Made Strange*, 2.

[104] Milbank, *The World Made Strange*, 380.

The full range of complexities would only be uncovered by the sociologist of knowledge studying theology as a multilayered activity, determined and determining a multilayered society through a series of varied interactions.[105]

This rules out simplistic, "mono-causal explanations" that might either suggest that theology is without qualification the product of a particular class or particular mode of behaviour or that it is totally autonomous, owing nothing to social phenomena.[106]

From this background Gill, who is professionally trained as both a sociologist and a theologian, approaches the two disciplines with much sympathy. He suggests that sociological and theological methodologies can work side by side. Hence, sociologists can work as if there are social determinants of all religious phenomena, and theologians can also work as if there is a "transcendent causality" behind such phenomena.[107] The two methodologies, in his view, are best seen as complementary rather than contradictory.[108] There is also no need to try to conflate one into the other to produce a single model.[109] It is only a model based on the principle of complementarity and not a linear, uniform model that can properly take account of the complexity and ambiguity of the situation. He gives the example of Maurice Wiles who suggests that theologians should approach the doctrine of creation by employing "two stories" – one which is scientific-historical and the other mythological.[110] Hence, in Gill's approach the theologian can work from his or her perspective, and be free to adopt a sociological perspective if it helps him to understand his social context, to complement his theological one.[111]

In considering what interpretive approach to adopt for this research project, I can see strengths and weaknesses in both of the above approaches. Many theologians would value the way Milbank's work, in general, is allowing theology to reclaim some ground from the secular approach of the social sciences.[112] A single theological framework would place the work securely within the discipline of theology. However, when he uses this theological framework not just for the "faith dimension" (or "divine dimension") but for the "social dimension" of a situation, Milbank's approach would mean losing all the benefits that might come from using social science methods and concepts. For its part, Gill's "two stories" or two methodologies approach resonates with a post Enlightenment mood that encourages multiplicity,

[105] R. Gill, *Theology and Social Structure* (Oxford: Mowbray, 1977), 133.
[106] Gill, *Theology and Social Structure*, 133.
[107] Gill, *The Social Context of Theology*, 132, 133.
[108] Gill, *The Social Context of Theology*, 132.
[109] Gill, *The Social Context of Theology*, 135.
[110] R. Gill, *The Social Context of Theology* (Oxford: Mowbray, 1975), 133-34.
[111] Gill, *The Social Context of Theology*, 135.
[112] See, for example, L. Malcolm, "Recovering Theology's Voice: Radical, orthodoxy," *Christian Century* 29 (Oct. 2000), 1074-1079.

diversity and complementarity. But in practice, in the context of a research project, a single researcher may not have the expertise to do both sides justice. The result might be that more weight is given to one side, either the theological or the sociological, creating a feeling of lopsidedness or incompleteness.

A third answer, which I considered, overcomes some of these difficulties. It comes from the field of empirical theology, specifically from the work of J.A. van der Ven. Empiricism, that is, "the view that the source of all knowledge is sense-experience" rose to prominence in the Enlightenment with the work of John Locke, Bishop Berkeley and David Hume.[113] After that, the tendency to emphasize the empirical qualities in different academic subjects, that is, focussing on observation and experimentation, flourished. In the twentieth century, the term "empirical theology" came into use in the European context to refer to the use of the methods of the empirical sciences in pastoral theology.[114] With the rise of post-Enlightenment thinking, leading to the demise of positivist approaches in epistemology, empirical theologians are leaving behind the strict understanding of empiricism in terms of the five senses and are becoming open to areas of reality where religion operates.[115] This has given rise to what is termed "radical empiricism" which refuses to identify experience with sensory data[116]. Van der Ven, who works in this post-Enlightenment understanding of empiricism finds that the idea of social progress no longer rings true:

> Our knowledge of the trenches and gas ovens of two world wars, the threat of nuclear and ecological holocaust, worldwide discrimination against women, homosexuals and people of colour and the unemployed, and the poverty of the great metropolises of the so-called Third World — all have forced us to become more reflexive, more modest and less arrogant.[117]

From this point of view, van der Ven considers the relationship between sociology and theology in the context of a research project. He looks at a number of approaches and finds them wanting. For example, he considers what he termed a "multidisciplinary" approach whereby the research findings are subjected to a social scientific analysis and the result of this analysis would form the basis of theological reflection. In van de Ven's view, this would make theology too dependent on sociological analysis. It might also cause a "sequencing" problem, such as deciding how to move from the sociological discourse of the first phase to the theological discourse of the second phase.[118] He also does not recommend an inter-disciplinary approach whereby the sequential relationship of the multidisciplinary approach is replaced by

---

[113] Cook "Epistemology," 222.
[114] Van der Ven, *Practical Theology*, 2-3.
[115] Van der Ven, *Practical Theology*, 9.
[116] Van der Ven, *Practical Theology*, 9.
[117] Van der Ven, *Practical Theology*, 22.
[118] Van der Ven, *Practical Theology*, 96.

cooperative approach which stresses interaction and reciprocity.[119] He prefers an "intra-disciplinary" approach whereby theology would borrow and integrate within itself the concepts, methods and techniques of the social sciences:

The intradisciplinary model requires that theology itself becomes empirical, that is, that it expands its traditional range of instruments, consisting of literary-historical and systematic methods and techniques, in the direction of an empirical methodology."[120]

Hence, van der Ven advocates retaining a theological goal and worldview whilst using analytical approaches from the sciences. This juxtaposition of the theological with the scientific has its opponents. But van der Ven defends it by pointing to similar practices in other fields, such as the intertwining of biology and chemistry in biochemistry and sociology and linguistics in sociolinguistics.[121] Another challenge is that as the retention of sociological insights is "intra" to the discipline of theology the researcher could lose the rigour and integrity of such insights.

This empirical-theological approach comes closest to what I intend to do in my interpretation in this study. I intend to work within a theological discourse, yet incorporate social scientific methods and concepts. In that way, theology and religion do not end up being treated as "derivative" and "inconsequential" or subordinate to the social sciences, which is a major concern of the Radical Orthodoxy Movement.[122] My main goal is to interpret the findings of the study to the discipline of theology, much like an ethnographer after living with and studying a social group would relate his or her findings to the academic discipline. This would lead me to discuss my findings in relation to broader Christian traditions on the person of the Holy Spirit, which would include existing literature on African Christianity and on Pentecostalism.

Research Ethics

Important ethical issues raised by the research were properly considered. Such consideration is not treated as an "add on" to the course of research but integral to it.[123] The seriousness of ethical consideration in research is highlighted by the comment of Payne and Payne that physical and social scientists work on the assumption that other scientists are behaving honestly:

They are not inventing data, lying about the success of their methods, suppressing findings or selectively reporting only those parts that support their particular theoretical position. Unless this state of affair prevails, we cannot rely on our

[119] Van der Ven, *Practical Theology*, 97.
[120] Van der Ven, *Practical Theology*, 101.
[121] Van der Ven, *Practical Theology*, 101.
[122] Martin, "Understanding the Old Paradigm," 19.
[123] Payne and Payne, *Key Concepts in Social Research*, 66.

discipline's stock of knowledge – in which case, the collective enterprise of research collapse.[124]

In other words, the unethical practice of one researcher can undermine the whole discipline.

Ethical issues may arise as early as upon choosing what issue to research, (such as deciding whether it is worth spending resources on, especially if it is funded from public funds or whether the research might exacerbate an already explosive social situation), it would definitely arise during fieldwork as the researcher deals with participants, and during the analysis and reporting of the findings as the researcher decides what should be in the report.[125]

In conducting this research work, I followed the ethical principles recommended in the Research Ethics Framework produced by the Economic and Social Research Council (ESRC) in Britain. These are as follows:

1) Research should be designed, reviewed and undertaken to ensure integrity and quality.

2) Research staff and subjects must be fully informed about the purpose, methods and intended possible uses of the research, what their participation in the research entails, and what risks, if any, are involved. Some variation is allowed for this provision.

3) The confidentiality of information supplied by research subjects and the anonymity of respondents must be respected.

4) Research participants must participate in a voluntary way, free from any coercion.

5) Harm to research participants must be avoided.

6) The independence of research must be clear, and any conflict of interest or partiality must be explicit (ESRC 2005).

These six principles are, broadly, endorsed by writers in the field of social research. Robson, for example, has written about many of the above principles and problems.[126] Creswell writes about the rigour required in social research and the need for triangulation of data.[127] Payne and Payne have written about the pressures from funding organisations and sponsors and the need for the independence of the researcher.[128]

These principles are self-explanatory and many of them need no further elaboration. However, since four out of six of the above principles are to do with the "right, dignity and safety of research subjects", I spell out below some of the dangers and the precautions I took (ESRC: 23).

---

[124] Payne and Payne, *Key Concepts in Social Research*, 67.
[125] Payne and Payne, *Key Concepts in Social Research*, 66; Robson, *Real World Research*, 31.
[126] Robson, *Real World Research*, 31.
[127] Creswell, *Qualitative Enquiry and Research Design*, 45.
[128] Payne and Payne, *Key Concepts in Social Research*, 68.

I ensured appropriate risk management from the outset. "Risk is often defined by reference to the potential physical or psychological harm, discomfort or stress to the human participant that a research project might generate" (ESRC: 21). Although risk can be more obvious in health related research, social research raises "a wider range of risk" which might include: "risk to a subject's personal standing, privacy, personal values and beliefs, their link to family and the wider community, and their position within occupational settings, as well as the adverse effects of revealing information that show illegal, sexual or deviant behaviour" (ESRC: 21).

My assessment was that even though there is very low risk to the participants' physical health, there is the risk that through describing their beliefs, participants in this project might open themselves up to ridicule, criticism, or even victimization after the interview. There might also be risk to the church because it might feel vulnerable to outside criticism based on the discussion of its beliefs. These risks were discussed with participants in order to receive their informed consent (See Consent Form, Appendix 1). "Informed consent entails giving as much information as possible about the research so that prospective participants can make an informed decision on their possible involvement. Typically, this information should be provided in writing and signed off by the research subjects" (ESRC: 24). This will enable me to conduct the research openly and without deception.

To minimise the risk, no value judgement was made on participants' beliefs. For participants, there was confidentiality and anonymity. All participants were given a pseudonym and personal information was kept to a minimum. Because of the risk to the church of outside criticism, the churches have been given a pseudonym in the final report and that report was discussed with the churches. I also kept the church updated on the progress of the research. Denscombe emphasizes the importance of regular, ongoing discussion with the gate keeper as the research progresses.[129] It is also possible that sharing their beliefs and personal stories might make participants in this project feel vulnerable. I, as the interviewer, was sensitive to this. Because, as the investigator, I was in a powerful position in relation to the participants, participants were given control over their participation. They could withdraw at any time and their consent and validation would be needed for the use of the final outcome. Creswell highlighted this need to consider power issues. He suggested reciprocity in the relationship, withdrawing gradually upon completion of research to reduce the feeling of abandonment by participants, sensitivity when dealing with marginalised groups due to their vulnerability.[130]

The research was conducted in compliance with relevant legislation, particularly, the Data Protection Act. The Research Ethics Framework states regarding the Data Protection Act:

---

[129] Denscombe, *The Good Research Guide*, (1998), 77.
[130] Creswell, *Qualitative Enquiry and Research Design*, 44.

It is important that those undertaking research are aware that most of the Data Protection Principles embodied in the DPA apply to their work. Social science research often involves the processing of sensitive personal data. Researchers should be aware that the processing of any information relating to an identifiable living individual constitutes "personal data processing" and is subject to the provision of the Data Protection Act...(ESRC: 18)

In compliance with this, I ensured that data are:

- obtained, specifically, for the purpose of this research
- not processed in a manner incompatible with that purpose
- adequate, relevant and not excessive for the purpose of this research
- kept up to date
- kept for no longer than is necessary for this project
- processed in accordance with the data subject's right
- kept safe from unauthorised access, accidental loss or destruction
- not transferred to any country outside the European Union unless that country has equivalent levels of protection of personal data.

All these measures enabled me to conduct this research at the ethical standard expected of social researchers at the University of Birmingham.

Conclusion

Methodology can be understood as the scheme of ideas that govern a work of research, deciding what specific tools are used and how they are applied. A choice of methodology often involves the consideration of a number of philosophical issues. In my own case, I considered the ontological, epistemological, axiological, and rhetorical issues raised by this project. In my consideration of the knowability of social reality my awareness of the complexity of human beings in comparison to chemical or physical elements moved me away from a positivist attitude to knowledge and towards adopting critical realism as the ontological and epistemological assumption underlying this project. I adopted the idea of reflexivity which involves owning up to my social location and values because of the effect these can have on the process and findings of the research. I declared my sympathy for the postmodern suspicion for metanarratives and the naive realist metaphysics that underpinned modernity.

The fieldwork of this project was done in two stages. The first stage is a case study of an African Pentecostal Church, that I have called Mount Zion in order to protect their identity. This church is based in East London. The second stage involved the interview of thirty two African Christians mainly from "historic" churches. Stage 1 was inductive, thus giving me the opportunity to develop new ideas about the doctrine of the Holy Spirit among African Christians, and Stage 2 was be mostly deductive, thus giving me the opportunity to check out the findings from Stage 1 on the interviewees. Even so, I used open-ended questions at this second stage to ensure that interviewees feel at ease while expressing their denominational peculiarities.

The fact that my research is on a religious question brings its own complexity to the normal course of social research. The question then was how to integrate social science approaches and insights with theology. This issue is particularly pertinent to the area of interpreting my findings. After considering three responses to this question, my position is to retain the theological world view and convey my findings to the discipline in a way that relates it to broader Christian tradition. I made it clear that my guiding concern would be to interpret my findings to the discipline of theology.

The research was conducted in an ethical manner, following the framework for social science research provided by the Economic and Social Research Council.

CHAPTER 3

Inductive Empirical Study: A Congregation

Induction has been described as a necessary, indispensable phase in empirical-theological research without which research would degenerate into an "empty, barren affair divorced from reality".[1] Van der Ven notes that without induction research would be an academic exercise with no application to real life. This chapter is an inductive study. It is the case study of a church based in London, which I have given the pseudonym Mount Zion in order to protect its identity. The leaders and members of the church will also be referred to by pseudonyms. My descriptive framework is made up of two parts: a) a description of the church, its context and what happened during the period I was visiting and observing. Here I will adopt the "funnelling approach" which narrows the setting from a wider environment before focusing on the specific church.[2] I will also include a vignette to help the reader enter into the case,[3] b) a description of patterns of relationship that I identified existing between theological themes. I have identified twelve such patterns between other themes and the theme of the Holy Spirit.

A description of Mount Zion and its context

East London

East London, where Mount Zion is situated, is comprised of seven communities (or boroughs), namely, Newham, Hackney, Barking and Dagenham, Tower Hamlets, Redbridge, Waltham Forest and Havering. Although it is a changing area, it has been described as having "a uniqueness of character which transcends period and generation".[4] For example, it has always been poor in comparison to the affluent Western parts of London. One record shows that in the late 18th century, whilst 18% of children born in West London died before the age of five, in East London, the figure was a staggering 55%.[5] Today, several indices show that East London communities are among the most

---

[1] J.A. Van der Ven, *Practical Theology: An Empirical Approach,* (Kampen: Kok Pharos, 1993), 115.

[2] J. Creswell, *Qualitative Enquiry and Research Design: Choosing Among the Five Approaches,* (London: Sage, 2007), 197.

[3] R.E. Stake, *The Art of Case Study Research* (London: Sage, 1995).

[4] W. Fishman, *The Streets of east London* (Nottingham: Five Leaves, 2006), 7.

[5] Fishman, *The Streets of east London*, 30.

deprived in the country. For example, the 2001 Census figures show most East London communities have a higher percentage of people unemployed and smaller percentage of people owning their homes than both the London and England averages. (http://neighbourhood.statistics.gov.uk).

Immigration has also played a part in giving East London its character. In the 1800s and 1900s ships docking in the East London ports "brought settlers and immigrants to swell London's population" as people of many different religions and ethnic origins made their home there.[6] Among these were Jews from Russia and Poland. Other waves have seen the Irish, Muslims from Asia, black people from the Caribbean and from Africa arriving to live there. Today, East London communities are among the most diverse in the country.

This social mix brings with it an amazing colour and diversity in food, clothing and cultural practices. It also brings social problems, such as racial tension. Some East London communities have been home to far-right racist organisations. At the time of the study, the British National Party, which is Britain's best known racist political party, had eleven elected members in the local government council of an East London community, Barking and Dagenham. This was far more than it had in any part of the country and made the British National Party the official opposition in that borough. Crime is yet another significant social problem. Some of the best known London gangsters were from East London. There is also the common perception that crimes such as burglary and knife crime among young people are higher in East London.

Three stories from one edition of the local newspaper, *The Newham Recorder* (18th March 2009), give us a flavour of what life is like for the residents of one East London community. The first story, "Free Checks on ticker", describes how mobile blood-pressure screening vans were being located in places around the borough. This has become necessary because "The borough is known to have London's highest incidence of premature death from heart disease." The second story is entitled, "Car Theft Gang Are Behind Bars" and explains, "A gang of car thieves – including two from Newham – who stole 30 luxury vehicles worth £1.5 million have been jailed for a total of more than 12 years." The story proceeds to describe how three men aged between 21 and 28, "pretended to be genuine owners and duped car dealerships into handing over replacement keys". The third story is entitled, "Oxbridge Trip for Talented" and runs, "a group of 30 children from Newham spent two days in Cambridge as part of a creative programme for gifted and talented pupils". The paper quotes an official who says, "We wanted to show these young children, from a disadvantaged East End background, what they can aspire to and achieve if they are prepared to work hard and aim high." Records show Newham residents to be among the poorest and least healthy in the country.[7]

---

[6] B, Girling, *East End Neighbourhoods: Images of London* (Stroud: Tempus, 1940).

[7] http://neighbourhood.statistics.gov.uk.

The actual neighbourhood where Mount Zion is based shares many of these characteristics. Beyond the negative attributes, however, it also has a colourful outdoor market, which takes place once a week. The market, which stretches the length of the main street, features scores of shops. Mount Zion is located near one of the busy streets. Along the street there are all types of shops that collectively give it an East London character. There is a big Ladbrokes betting shop, where many go to place bets on the day's sporting activities; a fruit shop, with produce displayed on big tables that extend well into the street; a restaurant advertising tea, coffee, cakes and other foods; a barber shop; a kebab shop and a number of hardware shops, selling various household items. There is also a hair salon, a small pub, a shop selling ready-made Asian clothes next to an abandoned shop with piles of rubbish in its front court. The street is often busy with black, Asian and white people in more or less equal numbers. The road itself is often busy with traffic, including the well-known red buses of London stopping to let off and pick up commuters. Not far from the church there is a big Sainsbury's super store and a MacDonald's restaurant.

Mount Zion

Mount Zion's church building does not significantly stand out against this background. The one-storey structure, in spite of being brightly painted, rather resembles a cinema, bingo hall or any other large building that one usually finds on a London street. In other words, it is not a traditional church building. On its front is written "Mount Zion". Inside, there is a big square hall, with a raised stage at one end. The seats are of the single, moveable type, not benches. They are usually arranged in straight lines, facing the stage, with aisles running from the back towards the stage. TV monitors have been installed at key locations, for those whose view of the stage was being blocked off by pillars. The church can accommodate about two hundred people. The stage, elevated above the ground level, is where the choir and the musicians perform. Whichever minister is leading the service also stands there. There are no windows, but the inside is well ventilated by an air-conditioning system. It is also sound-proof, so people out on the street do not hear the loud music and singing. There are good toilet facilities in the building, which is useful considering the numbers and the fact that many of the leaders and helpers spend their whole Sunday at the church, beginning with the first service and staying until the last one.

At the time of study, beginning in October 2007, Mount Zion had a membership of about three hundred. Many of its members did not live in the neighbourhood, but travelled to it from different parts of London and from the suburbs around London. A majority of these churchgoers were in their 30s and 40s. There were some in their 50s and very few in their 60s. There is a Youth Service which teenagers and those in their early 20s attend, so that age group was hardly present in the morning and evening services. There were about as many or slightly more women as men in the congregation, and about the same proportion among those performing different functions during the service, such as ushering. The church did not appear to keep figures of the ethnic origin of its members. However, from my observation, the congregation was comprised of mainly black people. Only a very small number of white people attended the services — I never saw more than five at any service. People of other ethnic origin or of mixed parentage probably made up about 10% of the total population. Among the black attendees, Nigerians predominated. But there were also other West and East Africans. Many within these groups were first generation immigrants who came to Britain in the 1990s. Apart from the Africans, there were also many of African-Caribbean background, of both the first and second generation. With regards to dressing, many people were dressed in suits or other Western-type attire. Very few wore traditional African clothes. People conversed in English. Given that the leadership and membership were mostly African, some of the members identified it as an "African church".

The church has both morning and evening services on Sundays and these have often full attendance. On a typical Sunday, there will be two morning services, one youth service and an evening service. At the time of study, the first morning service starts at 10.00 a.m. and the second at 12.00 a.m. The expectation is that the 10.00 a.m. service would end at 11.30 a.m. and the congregation would have thirty minutes to leave the hall. This changeover time also enabled the choir and the preacher to have a break and also gave time for any required physical changes to the stage to be made. Both morning services were identical and the sermons were often on the same theme. The premise behind two morning services was that those who could not attend at one time slot could attend the other. The evening service was different from the morning ones — different sermon and worship songs. In fact, many who came to one of the morning services also came back in the evening. The Youth service was completely different from the adult ones. It took place in the afternoon, that is, between the morning services and the evening service. This congregation had a separate minister, the Youth Minister.

The adult services usually began with a period of praise and worship when several songs were sung consecutively; some songs were repeated a number of times. The singing was led by a choir of about twenty men and women, usually smartly dressed in suits. They were backed by a band of three or four musicians. Praise and worship lasted about forty minutes. The second segment of the service was the sermon. Pastor Joe, the most senior minister of the church, often did the preaching. Sometimes, such as when Pastor Joe was away, one of the other pastors would preach. This segment would normally last another forty minutes. During my visit, I had the feeling that the sermon was the peak of the service for the congregation. It was as if all that happened before was actually leading up to the sermon, or as the church called it "the Word".

I observed Mount Zion over a fourteen-month period, from October 2007 to December 2008. I attended church services twelve times in the first six months and another six times in the remaining months. I also attended the church's other activities, such as their mid-week Bible study. This study took place in the same building as the services. Churchgoers were divided into groups depending on how long they had been coming and the progress they had made. I learnt about the church's Baptismal classes and read the manual that had been produced for that purpose. I also learnt about the church's provision of counselling for its members. During the fourteen months I was involved with the church, I participated in worship, listened to several sermons and took part in Bible study.

A service at Mount Zion

The following description of one of the services helps convey a part of what I experienced. It was a Sunday evening service and, as usual, some time had been spent on praise and worship. Pastor Joe came up to the stage and, instead of starting his sermon, he joined the singing and even started to lead it. The choir and the congregation sang along. This was unusual. In the past, Pastor Joe would come forward after the worship and begin to preach. There was much waving of hands and shaking of heads. He said some unintelligible words followed by the "God of heaven, you can do all things". The first part, as far as I can tell, is not in any known language. And he repeated this over and over while the congregation waved their hands, clapped or bounced up and down. Many of them appeared to be deeply caught up in the moment. This went on for more than ten minutes. "Come on, worship him tonight," said Pastor Joe. Then he spoke again "in tongues" followed by "God of heaven, you can do all things." All the time this was going on, Pastor Joe was walking back and forth on the stage. Most of the congregation had their eyes closed as they said their own prayers. Many of them appeared to be "speaking in tongues" as well – that is, speaking in a language which the speaker does not know and cannot identify.[8] At least one person could be seen shedding tears as she offered her own prayers in tongues. Even Pastor Joe's voice showed much emotion as he spoke again "in tongues".

When Pastor Joe paused and remained silent for some time the voice of the congregation could be heard. In the background, low, soft music was being played. This went on for several minutes. Then Pastor Joe started to speak in tongues again followed by the words "God of heaven, you can do all things." This seemed to give the congregation even more energy and they reacted with more hand waving and head-shaking. Some started to bounce up and down. "Hey!" exclaimed Pastor Joe, continuing to speak in tongues followed by "God of heaven, you can do all things." "Come on, sing it" the music leader said to

---

[8]   V.S. Poythress, "Linguistic and Sociological Analyses of Modern Tongue Speaking," *Westminster Theological Journal* 42 (1979), 367-88.

the congregation. And the congregation responded, by singing the line over and over. This went on for a long while.

Then, Pastor Joe stopped at the pulpit. This signalled that he was about to start preaching, and the place started to quieten down. But instead of preaching, he started to repeat the same words and the congregation again responded. Some people were, at this point rolling on the floor, caught up in a kind of trance. "Praise God's name, praise God's name," Pastor Joe encouraged the congregation. He made more utterances in tongues, and then followed with the same words he had repeated earlier. "Praise the Lord, Praise the Lord," Pastor Joe shouted, his eyes firmly closed. He encouraged, "Come on, somebody magnify his name. God of heaven, you can do all things. [Speaks in tongues] God of heaven, you can do all things. God of heaven, you can do all things." Then he started a prayer, proclaiming blessing and glorification to God's name. At a point, he asked the congregation to clap for God, which they did. He continued to pray, asking God to bless the congregation, to fulfill his purposes in their life. Occasionally, he shouted and muttered in tongues.

After this time of prayer, Pastor Joe looked around the hall, adjusting his papers which were on the pulpit. This was his signal that he was about to start preaching. Then he told the members of the congregation to greet each other and then take their seats. He reminded them that God is always bigger than any problem they might have. Then he announced the Bible passage he would be preaching from and started to preach. The sermon lasted about forty-five minutes. After the sermon, it was time for collection. Several buckets were passed around hall which people put envelopes of money into. While this was going on, the band played more gentle songs and the congregation sang along. At the end of the collection, some announcements were made. After that, another minister stepped forward and led the congregation in the saying of the Grace (a well-known Christian prayer based on 2 Corinthians 13:13). That was the end of the service and the people dispersed.

The interviews

Toward the end of my participant-observation period, I started to interview the church members and leaders. Conducting the interviews after having observed the church for a long period enabled me to ask questions based on my observations. In selecting those to be interviewed, I worked with "a gate-keeper" who had been assigned by the church management to assist me. I used the maximum variation sampling approach to select participants. In that approach, participants are chosen for a sample to reflect a wider population. The emphasis is to represent as many sub-groups as possible within the larger population. Irving Seidman, for whom maximum variation sampling "provides the most effective basic strategy for selecting participants for interviewing studies," points out that in this approach "The range of people and sites from which the sample is selected should be fair to the larger population for readers of the study to connect to what they are reading".[9] Even though generalisations might not be made from the study as a whole, as this is often not possible from a qualitative study, a fairer reflection of the larger population would make it more difficult for the result of the exercise to be dismissed as idiosyncratic.[10]

In my sample, I made sure I had both men and women, representatives of different age groups, ministers of the church and lay members, people of different nationalities, first generation immigrants, those born in this country and so on. I interviewed twelve people the list of whom are shown in Appendix 1. Based on my knowledge of this group, I avoided asking them their specific ages as such a question could make them uncomfortable. Instead, I gave them an age range to choose from. In the rest of this chapter I have used this range to describe their age. The fact that there were four pastors among the interviewees, who were in their forties, accounts for why this age group predominates. In reality, there were probably as many people in their forties as in their thirties at the Sunday services, based on my observations. (There was no official record of the age of the church members. Even if there had been one, the church would probably not have made this available to me.) As the table indicates, two out of the twelve were born in the United Kingdom and had lived in the UK all their life. I have indicated these as "British-Caribbean" and "British-Nigerian". The other ten were first generation immigrants from either the Caribbean or Africa. This reflects the predominance of first generation immigrants in the church. All the people I interviewed had been members of the church for over five years.

By interviewing both the members and the leaders of this church I tried to ensure that the doctrine of the Holy Spirit which comes through in the interviews is one that is shaped from both sides of the pulpit, that is, a combination of the professed theology of the church and the ordinary theology existing within its members. The interview protocol, which includes the questions I asked the participants, is shown in Appendix 2. The pseudonyms and personal characteristics, including the countries of origin of the interviewees are shown in Appendix 3.

The Identified Patterns

From my observations, interviews and study of church documents, I identified the following patterns:

a)   A paucity of verbal references to the Holy Spirit during worship and sermons

b)   A strong link between the Holy Spirit and the daily life of individual church members

---

[9]   I. Seidman, *Interviewing as Qualitative Research* (New York: Teacher College Press, 2006), 52.

[10] Seidman, *Interviewing as Qualitative Research*, 52.

c) **A relationship between the Holy Spirit and the church's** worship

d) A relationship between the Holy Spirit and Biblical interpretation (hermeneutics)

e) The Bible as the source of the in-filling of the Holy Spirit and tool for the verification of inspired word

f) **A belief that the church's ministers were inspired by the Holy** Spirit

g) A belief that the Holy Spirit is a real person and related to the Father and the Son

h) A cosmology that is spiritual in essence and forms the background to concepts of the Holy Spirit

i) An anthropology that is spiritual in essence and related to concepts of the Holy Spirit.

j) A link between the Holy Spirit and the empowerment of individual members

k) Some difference in the emphasis between men and women in how they understood the Holy Spirit

l) A coherence between how young and the older participants in the study understood the Holy Spirit

Each of these "pattern theories" has been identified because the theme within them interacted in a significant way with the theme of the Holy Spirit. The "pattern theories" are discussed more fully below.[11] As already stated, pattern theories do not have the kind of causal links one finds in quantitative studies, but instead contain a relationship.[12] In other words, what I have looked for are relationships that are identifiable and not relationships where one element causes the other.[13]

The paucity of verbal references to the Holy Spirit
during worship and preaching

The first thing I noticed at Mount Zion, to my surprise, was that there were few actual references to the Holy Spirit during church services. There was a sermon preached by Pastor Joe soon after I started visiting the church which dealt with how the Holy Spirit relates to a Christian. Apart from that, however, other sermons, the church songs, and the prayers said during services rarely mentioned the Holy Spirit. I asked the members and church leaders the reason behind this and received a number of different answers. Christy, aged 41-50,

---

[11] J. Creswell, *Research Design: Qualitative and Quantitative Approaches* (London: Sage, 1994), 94.

[12] Creswell, *Research Design*, 94.

[13] Creswell, *Research Design*, 94.

who came to Britain from the Caribbean twenty-five years ago, and has been with Mount Zion from the very beginning, told me that every church service begins with prayer to welcome the Holy Spirit and most close with "the Grace", which refers to "the fellowship of the Holy Spirit":

> If you come at the beginning of the service, one of the things you will notice is that they will always welcome the presence of the Holy Spirit. In all that we do, that is why we pray. It's because as believers we know that we rely totally upon the Holy Spirit. Everything, in terms of the teaching, the time of worship, or even breaking people up into different groups, all those things it's the Holy Spirit. The minister must prepare himself when it comes to talking to a group of people or even to a person, and the way he prepares himself is through prayer and relying on the Holy Spirit. . . . The Holy Spirit will never leave us nor forsake us. The Holy Spirit is always there with us.

A similar explanation was given by Liz, who was also of black-Caribbean descent, but was born in this country. Liz, who joined Mount Zion fifteen years ago, told me she was very surprised to hear my observation that the Holy Spirit was rarely mentioned during the church services. She told me about some of the songs that actually mentioned the Holy Spirit by name. She said that in addition to the Sunday services the departments within the church organisation begin their business by praying that the Holy Spirit comes in.

A different explanation was given with regards to the nature of Sunday services. Pastor Lara, a Nigerian, who, like Pastor Christy, had been with Pastor Joe from the very beginning, reminded me that Pastor Joe had preached on the Holy Spirit about a year ago. Then she offered an explanation for my observation:

> It may be from the basis that at least with the older established people they have been taught and it's become like a principle. And then in terms of our true membership, not attendees, before you can become a member of Mount Zion, you would have done Baptismal Class; it would have been taught there. You would also do membership class; it would be taught there. You also do Workers Class and elements would be taught there. . . . So in terms of the main service, Pastor Joe's main style is seeker sensitive. It is trying to draw all the people and teach them basic principles, and then we deal with the deeper stuff at these other settings.

Michael, who was originally from Ghana, and worked in the field of education, gave me a similar answer:

> Things are structured in Mount Zion in such a way that our Sunday services tend to focus on maybe teaching and preaching. On Sundays they take things as given; they assume that people are at a level. . . . The worship leader may also invite the presence of the Holy Spirit through a song. But typically where it gets taught is, we have the Worker's Class where we are taught about the Holy Spirit.

He went on to name classes where old and new members were taught about the Holy Spirit.

Only a small minority, two out of the twelve I interviewed, told me that much as they understood the reason behind it, it was an issue that might be worth revisiting. One of them was Momo, a Nigerian. He said it was an important issue and illustrated his point by saying that a person would have no credibility if he never brought up the name of another person they claim to be a very close friend. He also said the issue was of particular importance to new members:

> It makes us realise that we could have easily forgotten that somebody is sitting down there that needs to hear about the Holy Spirit — a new born-again Christian. What if they don't come on Thursdays to the classes? Do they have to go to Thursday classes to hear about the Holy Spirit? And do they not have to hear it also apart from the classes as a way of confirming and buttressing, because in the classes they may be limited by time. Outside the class there is possibly more time.

The people I spoke to were generally surprised to hear this observation and much of what they said pointed to many references to the Holy Spirit in a behind-the-scenes way. Even after taking into account the two that thought the issue needed revisiting, it is fair to say that the response that most accurately captured the feelings of the church members I spoke to on this issue was that given by one of the pastors. Pastor Kenneth, who came originally from Ghana in the early 1990s, stated simply that what mattered was that the church worked in the full knowledge that all it did was in the power of the Holy Spirit and not the number of times they mentioned the name of the Holy Spirit. They mentioned the Holy Spirit when it was necessary:

> The Holy Spirit works in us; He is with us. So we know that it is He who is at work in us. Therefore I don't know whether the person has to mention it…He is working in us, He is living in us, He is directing. It is an ongoing thing…As and when it is necessary to mention the Holy Spirit, you mention it.

A strong link between the Holy Spirit and the daily life of individual church members

My interviews showed that they understood every aspect of their life, both as a church and as individuals, as lived in the company and guidance of the Holy Spirit. They spoke with confidence about how the Holy Spirit guided them even through the most mundane aspects of daily life. Regarding this, Pastor Kenneth said:

> You can't go wrong when the Holy Spirit is leading you. Supposing you were going home. . . . He can show you and guide you as to what route to take, where you won't have much traffic. He can be as specific as that.

He also said:

43

We need to depend on the Holy Spirit. . . . When you are going into business He can tell you don't go into business with this person. You will not understand why He is saying that but he knows why. . . . You will be sitting with someone and he will begin to show you exactly what that person is. I believe he is so real. The more we depend on him the more we win.

Momo, who had been a member of the church for fourteen years, said:

The Holy Spirit is a personality that we relate with so it cannot be boxed into some mechanical timing. He is somebody we need to relate with every time. Anywhere we are there is an opportunity to speak to the Holy Spirit. . . . I believe we need the Holy Spirit every time. If I go down that corridor, [and] somebody says something to me, if I don't depend on the Holy Spirit I might say the wrong thing. So I need the Holy Spirit every second of every minute of every hour of every day.

Liz described how she would call on the Holy Spirit before and during conversations:

When I am talking with people, normally I am praying inside, "Lord, guide me; help me say the right things." My phone rings, I look at the number and even if I have to do a "missed call", I'll miss the call so that I pray and I ask God, "Let me say the right thing to this person," especially if I know it is a counselling need or just know that I need to correct somebody or something and I feel that I haven't totally heard from the Holy Spirit and I am still working in my flesh. I'll miss the call and then I'll call back and say, "Sorry I missed your call".

She went on to say that even at that very moment that I was interviewing her, she was calling on and relying on the Holy Spirit. However, not all members/leaders went that far. In fact one person, Pastor Lara, went out of her way to say to me that she was not one of those people who say "that the Holy Spirit told me to sit on the chair". Even so, she went on to describe how the Holy Spirit guided her through her day-to-day work.

They also saw the Spirit guiding them by changing their nature when they become born again. Evelyn, who used to go to a Church of England church in the past but joined Mount Zion five years ago said:

As we are studying the word of God and the Holy Spirit is teaching us the word of God that we are studying, he begins to make the word we have studied to become live in us. So that on a daily basis, whatever it is that we are doing . . . we are doing as the word is saying.

That is, apart from the nudges or hunch-like direction which one can get from time to time, the Holy Spirit can direct a person on daily life issues by changing his nature and thus making him think and act as the Spirit would like that person to.

44

The church's training manual also describes the involvement of the Holy Spirit in the life of believers: It describes how the old self, "flesh" is in constant conflict with the new nature. But the Holy Spirit helps the Christian to not live according to the flesh. The manual quotes Romans 8:2, 4 and 23.

From my observations, what the church members/leaders said about the involvement of the Holy Spirit in their daily lives was consistent with their actions and also with what they said regarding other issues. They did not appear to make a distinction between worship and daily life in this regard. Rather, they appeared to see the two as a continuum. One person said to me that a person cannot have church life and ordinary life as two separate things. "That is contradictory," she said. A similar comment was made by another member who said, "Worship is whole life dedicated to giving glory to God."

A relationship between the Holy Spirit and the church's worship

Worship was very important to the church. A typical service lasted for about an hour and a half and sometimes about half of that time was spent on singing praises to God. This often involved much dancing, clapping, and loud cheering. This was also an important time in their relationship with the Holy Spirit. For example, when I asked Pastor Lara whether the Holy Spirit was involved with Mount Zion, she simply described to me what had happened during the previous night's service:

> When you come and you are present at some of our services, you will see that for yourself. A case in point is last night. It was obvious. It was so obvious that something happened . . . it was so much that the worship just went to another level.

So much was the Spirit's presence, she said, that the lead pastor found it difficult to stop singing and start preaching. Even the congregation's reaction was different, she said:

> If you are also sensitive in the Spirit, it's not a time to be frivolous, because you just knew. And the way the reaction was happening in the congregation. Oh no, it was tangible that something had happened.

The church members had a number of different understandings of why they spent so much time worshipping during the church services. The commonest was the view that this was the expected way of coming into God's presence, in line with Psalm 100:1: "Worship the Lord with gladness; come before him with joyful songs." But in addition to this was also the view that this was a way of welcoming the Holy Spirit. Evelyn said:

> We want to create an environment where the Spirit of God will come. So we worship and we praise God and we celebrate his glory, his presence, and we lift him up so that he can come and take precedence over our gathering. So that even if people are getting on stage to sing or they are getting on stage to preach, because we have created that atmosphere, God is already in control.

Similarly, Eva, who came from the Caribbean many years ago and had been a member of Mount Zion for eleven years, said:

> Praise and worship is a fundamental way of worshipping God. This is one way of ushering the Spirit of God into the place, into the church . . . singing and worship time is a time for people to loosen up and relax and let the Spirit of God come in and take control.

There was much speaking in tongue during the Sunday worship services. Sometimes the preacher of the day would suddenly start speaking in a strange language. Quite often the congregation would follow his or her example. This speaking in tongues was sometimes accompanied by hand gestures, swaying or other physical movement.

One member told me how the authenticity of speaking in tongues was validated by a miracle that happened in her life. Liz had been brought up in an Evangelical church which she had attended fervently for many years.

> We came to Mount Zion from the church I grew up and was later converted in, which was an Evangelical church. My husband was the one who discovered Mount Zion on TV. At first I wasn't very keen because of the religious background I came from — the only church that I ever knew, grew up in and had been saved by — I didn't know about the Holy Spirit, speaking in tongues.

She gave this description of how she started speaking in tongues:

> Before coming to this ministry, I suffered acutely from arthritis, which would put me in bed for three or four days. I used to joke and say that I can tell the weather by the pains in my joints. I'd be like, "It's going to start raining" because the pains would start in my joints. I would be constantly on pain killers. . . . When we first started coming here, because I didn't understand speaking in tongues, I would enjoy the whole service, but as soon as they started speaking in tongues, I would be holding my head down, saying O Lord, just let this part be over, and one day I just said Lord, if this is true and this is right, cure me of this arthritis. And that's all I said.

And she was healed. Some weeks later it started to rain and she did not feel the usual pains. She did not even know it was raining until a friend called her saying, "I'm just trying to see if you need anything":

> I said, "No. Why would you think that?" She said, "It's raining outside." And I am like "Oh yes, it is, isn't it" and I was walking about the house shouting, "It works, it works" and I was screaming "It works, it works!" I did not notice that it was coming up to rain or that it was raining. And I was like "I'm cured, I'm cured."

For Liz, through receiving this healing, the Holy Spirit removed her inhibitions towards speaking in tongues.

I observed and experienced great joy and electricity in their services. Worship was, evidently, a part of church life that the members really enjoyed. Momo put it this way:

> That is a church that I am a member of. That is the church I believe Pastor Joe is leading as well. A church of the Holy Spirit. A church where we pray, we sing, we dance, because these are weapons of the Holy Spirit. They are weapons of warfare, weapons of righteousness.

A relationship between the Holy Spirit and Biblical interpretation (Hermeneutics)

The church thought of the Holy Spirit and the Bible as intertwined. Participants were all keen to stress that the Bible was worthless without the interpretation offered by the Holy Spirit. Michael asserted that it was "foolishness" to those who do not read it with the help of the Holy Spirit:

> The Holy Spirit desires to be involved in the way that people read the Bible. In Mount Zion, we are taught to invite the Holy Spirit to be involved in it. . . . the extent to which we allow him will determine the extent to which he will be involved in the study of the Bible.

He explained further:

> The Bible says that the word of God is foolishness to those who are outside. So before we became born again, when we read the Bible, we could not understand it. We could not understand how somebody was crucified on the cross two thousand years ago and today we say that his blood will wash away our sins. So when we invite the Holy Spirit into our Bible reading he highlights what God wants to say to us. So he gives us revelation. He shows us how God wants to be a blessing to us.

Liz, who described how she was cured of arthritis, said something similar:

> Before you read, you ask the Holy Spirit to teach you because without that, you are just reading and you are just retaining intellectual information. To me you are gaining history… unless you ask the Holy Spirit to guide you to bring a revelation as you are reading. Sometimes you can read the same passage six times, the seventh time you be like "Wow, I never looked at it that way before." . . . In my previous ministry, I knew most of the Bible back to front, every story every parable. But now, I am like, "Wow, I didn't see it that way before." Because I believe the Holy Spirit is now illuminating and I have learnt how to study the word with the help of the Holy Spirit.

Pastor Abasi, who came originally from Nigeria and worked as an architect in London, put it this way:

> The main thrust or principle that guides me is the Bible. That is the reference point of everything that I do. And over and beyond that is the role of the Holy

Spirit. . . . The Bible is great and is the final authority of God's word as you know, but at the same time it is the written word. But also there is the Spirit of God that makes the written word relevant and gives it life, makes it relevant and applicable to our very situation.

John, who came to Britain from Kenya four years before and at the time of the study had been a member of Mount Zion for three years, had a similar point. When I asked him what guides him through life he said, "Personally, I am guided a lot by the Bible and, obviously, the teachings of the church, and by reading books."

Another dimension to this for the church was that the Holy Spirit could use the Bible to alert Christians of something important by "giving them a word" at the particular time they were reading the Bible. This point was made by Pastor Abasi:

When you begin to read and study, he gives you a word. He makes something in the word of God come. And he gives you witness. He touches situations around you and you will know that this is God speaking to you.

He also described how sometimes, when you are in the middle of a situation and don't know what to do, the Holy Spirit would remind you of what you read some time ago:

When you study the word of God, you pray and move on. When you are in the midst of the test, and everything is chaotic, then he brings what you have studied in privacy and says this is the answer. He puts that word in your spirit, in your tongue, as you say it, faith comes and boldness comes.

This was also echoed by John: "The Holy Spirit reminds us of the scriptures when we are going through troubled times. Let's say, for instance, you come face to face with adversity and you don't have the Bible there with you, the Holy Spirit brings the word into remembrance. The Holy Spirit is our best friend."

The Bible viewed as source of the in-filling of the Holy Spirit ### and as a tool for the verification of "inspired" word

I found that while, on the one hand, they believed that one needs the Holy Spirit to interpret the Bible to a reader, they also stressed that a Christian needs the Bible to understand who the Holy Spirit is and to be filled by him. Pastor Abasi said:

Our thinking of the Holy Spirit is informed by our understanding of the word of God. In John 14 Jesus Christ refers to the Holy Spirit as a person. Our understanding of the scriptures is the basis, it's not the end, but it's the basis. We must read the word of God, study it, and when we begin to study it, then we begin to pray. Because truly God is real, the Holy Spirit is real. . . . As you read through and as you meditate on the word, you find that your thinking begins to change, and therefore your actions begin to change.

Evelyn made a similar point, giving the example of Joshua in the Old Testament:

> Take for example when God said to Joshua "I am taking you as the one who are going to be leading the people of Israel". Bible says in Joshua 1:8, he didn't say to him "Go here, go here, go here." God said to him "study the Bible, study the laws of Moses. Study that one, that's all I want you to do". In the same way, to us as believers, the Bible says, "The word of God is Spirit." So every time we are studying the Bible, we're filling ourselves with the Spirit of God.

As Pastor Abasi asserted, the Bible also helps discern what is really of the Spirit among the feelings and "hunches" that one gets from time to time:

> If you don't read the word of God and something is speaking to you, you don't know who it is because there are so many voices around the world that we live in. There is the voice of the devil, also demons. How do we distinguish these from the voice of the Holy Spirit? It is when we read the word of God. So whatever that voice is saying to you, if it is in line with the word of God and the timing is right, then you know that this is the Spirit of God speaking to you.

Pastor Abasi was so convinced of the need to always have the Bible and the Holy Spirit together that he sounded this warning:

> We need both. The Holy Spirit works with the word. . . . If we ignore the Bible and just want to say "Holy Spirit this, Holy Spirit that", before you know it, the Devil is so subtle that he would want to get his voice in. The way to keep that out is to make reference. So that whatever you hear, even from the Holy Spirit, he wants you to check with the word because he will never contradict himself.

Obviously, this is a church that regards the Bible very highly. The pastors and members often quote Bible verses to support their point. Michael, told me that what he liked most about the church was that in their preaching, "If it is not in the Bible they don't preach it." He also said that as one of those delegated to pray for people who brought in prayer request, "If prayer point is not in [the] Bible we don't pray it."

For Evelyn the words of the Bible could create a new reality which would take precedence over their actual surroundings:

> Personally, when I'm studying the Bible, I can sit down for two hours or I can sit down for thirty minutes. But whatever I get from it is the revelation the Holy Spirit gives to me . . . like an opening of the word in my own spirit . . . so I understand this word on a much personal level. And it also becomes reality to me. It becomes reality to me, so that when I go out in the street, then that word is my reality. It's not a matter of what I am seeing around me. It is a must that the word

I have received at home is what I must do. The Bible says the word of God is the Spirit.

The church's belief that its appropriation of the Bible was directed by the Holy Spirit might be behind a practice I have observed in this and other churches in which preachers use biblical texts to speak directly to the congregation. For example, in the same sermon of 2007, Pastor Joe described how the Holy Spirit led Philip to the Ethiopian in Act 8:29. He pointed out that when Philip called out to the Ethiopian, the Ethiopian let him into his chariot, because Philip was led by the Spirit of God. Pastor Joe then told the congregation that in the same way God will open doors for them. There was not, as one often sees in the established denominations, an attempt to interpret the Biblical event in the context of Biblical times before applying it to the present day.

This was a common practice in the church. In another sermon preached at the church, the preacher (not Pastor Joe) read out from Genesis a part of the story of Joseph , who was sold into slavery by his brothers but later became a great man in Egypt, then the preacher told the congregation that God will in the same way disgrace their enemies. As in the previous example, the preacher was proclaiming Joseph's blessing to the congregation without going through the process of comparing the Biblical context with the contemporary one.

A belief that the church's ministers are inspired by the Holy Spirit

Many saw the ministry of Pastor Joe as an indication of the presence of the Holy Spirit in their church. Momo pointed to the Pastor's vision of Mount Zion as a "church without wall", not limited by geography or skin colour.

> It means the Holy Spirit is the one leading this church. It is not a church that is bound by the limits that man tends to put in place.

They attributed the spontaneity that I observed in their church services to the presence and leadership of the Holy Spirit. Momo explained that the ministers depend on the Spirit always, so even though they would have prepared beforehand, God can still change the message:

> [God] drops something in their spirit again to say delve on that a bit more, delve on this one a little bit more, skip that one. . . . I believe that is what they are doing-just obeying the Holy Spirit.

A similar point was made by Pastor Kenneth:

> Sometimes you prepare a message and you get to church and he tells you this is not what I want you to preach. And you have to change it. He gives you enough information for you to be able to preach on it.

Evelyn also attributed the flexibility to the leading of the Holy Spirit. "I think it is God himself, the Holy Spirit leading them to do it." She described sometimes noticing Pastor Joe when he is preaching stop to pray "in his spirit" then carrying on with the sermon. She said she herself, sometimes, at home or on the bus finds that "somebody just comes into her spirit" and she would start speaking in tongues:

> I know when the Spirit of God is at work anything is possible. Some ministries, I've heard the Spirit of God might just lead them to not teach, and just worship and praise God for the whole time of the service. And that is God ministering.

There were also several stories of times when the lead pastor had stopped during his sermon to call out a church member and give him or her a message or perform an act of healing. Michael, the Ghanaian, said this is why people keep coming back. He found that when he is going through a challenging time, when he comes to church "word will just come" for him. "You can see the role of the Holy Spirit in the whole thing," he said.

Behind this attitude was the recognition of the sovereignty of the Holy Spirit. Changes can happen at any point in time because they cannot say "no" to the Spirit. One member captured this well when I asked him why the ministers often repeat themselves when preaching, like when Pastor Joe said, "Speak, Jesus speak; Jesus, speak; speak, Jesus, speak." The member answered, "Sometimes we also can't explain. He may be led of the Holy Spirit to say something seven times or three times or once or twice. We don't always understand it."

I also found that the church members were very conscious of the power of the Holy Spirit and they often saw this in the context of the work of their ministers. Some of this power they saw in the healing acts which many of them said they had witnessed. Pastor Christy made this point:

> There are so many testimonies of people who even had cancer and because the Holy Spirit had revealed it to Pastor Joe, he called those people forward. They went back to the hospital, and it was cleared. And this is not of man. This is of the Holy Spirit.

Pastor Kenneth described his own healing from stroke and said:

> That is a typical example of what the Holy Spirit can do. People go through situations where through prayer in the Holy Spirit they are able to receive their deliverance.

Many saw the power of the Holy Spirit most commonly in the effectiveness of their ministry, such as their sermons, prayers and evangelism. Pastor Kenneth described how the Holy Spirit would give you what to say to a person so they would be saved:

> You can go and talk, talk, talk; but if he's told you what to say, you can say one thing and the person would say, "How did you know this?" And you say it is the Holy Spirit that has told you to say it. You just say one thing and you just strike a chord in the person's heart . . .

He also said the Holy Spirit gives you the right message when you teach, helps you remember what you had forgotten so you can present them:

> You can preach any message and the message will not have effect. But when the Holy Spirit is involved in what you are doing, oh, you can be sure it will have effect.

For Pastor Christy, who was involved in the counselling of the church members, this power was evident in the revelations that the Holy Spirit gave in pastoral situations:

> If there is something that is going on in a person's life. . . . The Lord shows me what's going on in the person's life. Not all the time do people want to talk about different things that they go through. But the Holy Spirit will reveal that this person is going through a difficult time because such and such has happened to him.

The power of the Spirit was also seen to be behind the very words of the sermon, whether it was heard in the church or on TV in people's homes. Evelyn made that point:

> Yes the word is gone; now the Spirit goes and activates the word in that person's life. That whole family is touched; a whole generation has been saved.

Another church member put it simply: "The Spirit of God is alive in the word of God."

Finally, there was also the belief that the Spirit directed the church's ministries by changing the nature and character of those who minister. Evelyn made that point:

> The Holy Spirit in us perfects our character to the nature of Christ. As Christ is we also become. And when we become that we begin to think like God. So the work that God wants us to do, we begin to do them anyway, because now we are in the image of Christ.

A belief that the Holy Spirit is a real person and related to the Father and the Son

Where the church sounded most familiar to me as an Anglican Christian was in their understanding of the nature of the Holy Spirit. From every indication, the church saw the Holy Spirit as a member of the Trinity, co-equal with the Father and the Son. Pastor Christy gave this description:

> The Holy Spirit is the third person of the Trinity. He is God. He is real. He is the person I rely on. He is my counsellor, he is the one that stands by me, he is the one that counsels me, he is the one that cares for me, and he is the one that gives me the wisdom that I need. So he is a real person that we speak to.

This was supported by the view expressed in the church's training material. It described the Holy Spirit as God, equal to the Father and the Son. The material referred to Matthew 28:19: "Therefore go and make disciples of all nations, baptizing them in the name of the Father and of the Son and of the Holy Spirit" and argued that by saying this Jesus showed that for him the Holy Spirit is equal to himself and the Father.

The church's view that the Holy Spirit was God, co-equal with the Father and the Son, was also supported by a sermon preached by Pastor Joe before I started my research. The text of this and other sermons were made available to me. In one of his prayers during the sermon, he said: "Father, help them . . . Spirit, help them . . . Jesus, help them." By referring directly to the Father, the Holy Spirit and Jesus, he showed the Trinitarian background to his thinking. And by addressing them directly, he showed that he thought of each of them as a person.

Equally important were the comments on the subject by the young Kenyan man, John, particularly because it was unprompted. When I asked whether the Holy Spirit was involved in miracles, he answered:

Yes, I think. I believe the Holy Spirit is involved in miracles because he is powerful. The Holy Spirit is as powerful as God the Father, God the Son and God the Holy Spirit. We believe that they are co-equal. We believe that because the Bible says that God spoke, he said, "Now let us create man in our own image," we believe that he was addressing God the Son and the Holy Spirit when he said, "let us." So in the same way that God worked together with him to accomplish things, we believe that he still works together with him to bring about miracles.

The commonest words used by the church to describe the Holy Spirit were also very familiar to me. Most of those I spoke to described the Holy Spirit as a Comforter and a Counsellor. Eva, the oldest of the interviewees, explained regarding this:

Jesus said, when he left earth he would send the Holy Spirit. He is a comforter. He is the Counsellor. He is the one that dwells in us. He is the candle, in a way, the light that is in us, in the depth of us. And he wakes me up, he feeds me, he guides me, he leads me, he is life. The Spirit of God is life.

Another person described him as a Counsellor, Comforter and Advocate who was "Here to enforce the agenda of God."

The church members also saw the Holy Spirit in another familiar role, which was as a Revealer/Interpreter. Michael, in fact, used this to support the view that the Holy Spirit was working in Mount Zion:

Several times people have approached me after service and said, "Ah, that message really spoke to me," hundreds of people in the service at a time. The Pastor doesn't see people every day of the week. He spends most of the time running the church, praying, studying the word and spending time with God. How does he communicate to specific areas of people's needs? It can only be the Holy Spirit. That is one major role of the Holy Spirit.

In other words, the Holy Spirit revealed to the pastor what the people were going through week after week. Pastor Kenneth made a similar point:

> Before Pastor Joe comes to preach on a Sunday he would wait on the Lord, to hear from the Holy Spirit. . . . Many times somebody will be in the house, you might be battling with something and you would want to know a way out and all that. And you come into the service and he ministers and you go back and you realise that it was you he is talking to. So real. And there would be instances where the Holy Spirit can make Pastor Joe know who is in the service, and the circumstances someone is going through. . . . He preaches the word and you know what you need to do.

Pastor Joe spoke at length about this in the sermon referred to above. He said that the Holy Spirit was able and willing to lead and guide Christians to where God wants them to be. He promised the church members that the Holy Spirit was going to guide them in the forthcoming year in different aspects of their life because the Holy Spirit knows the future.

A cosmology that is spiritual in essence and forms the background to concepts of the Holy Spirit

I found that there was within the church a strong sense of what they often called "the spirit realm". Once in a sermon, Pastor Joe told the congregation that there is a spiritual realm and that if they let the Holy Spirit reveal that realm to them, they will do well in life. This sense of a spirit realm was also behind much of what the church members said about the Holy Spirit. Evelyn gave this explanation for why Pastor Joe sometimes repeated himself when he was preaching, such as saying the words "speak, Jesus, speak" three times:

> I would again think that the Spirit of the Lord might have shown Pastor Joe something and to that end he is not speaking to the human mind, Pastor Joe is speaking to the spiritual atmosphere. Because when the Pastor gets on, yes they preach to us too, speak to our spirit and to our mind, but don't forget the Bible says the word of God is Spirit. And Spirit meeting spirit. Even in church there are demonic forces still at work. So he is preaching to us but he is also preaching to the demonic forces.

She continued:

> Yes he is speaking, but, at the same time he is addressing things in the spirit realm. From him stopping to speak things you may not understand or we may not understand; he is actually addressing systems or the spiritual atmosphere that he is acknowledging in his spirit.

To the church members, Pastor Joe was often doing two things at the same time when he spoke in church. Evelyn gave this example:

I would have a situation in the week and I would come into the service and Pastor Joe would be preaching and he would just stop and say "You that lady etc, etc. God says so and so" and you would just know that it is God addressing your situation. So whereas we are a hundred people coming on Sunday, every one of us, the Bible says we are engraved in the palm of God's hands, and he knows our individual situations. So, when we come in and the Pastor is ministering, he is addressing those individual situations and also addressing the spiritual realm — we just know it is God at work. So we're edified and also demonic forces are also destroyed and rebuked and so God's will be done on earth.

The spirit realm was employed as an explanation by Michael to the same questions, namely, why the Pastor repeats himself:

There are two counsels in this world. There is the Counsel of God and the Counsel of the Enemy — two different kingdoms. At each point in time, either the Counsel of God or the Counsel of Satan is manifested. The Bible says that the kingdom of God suffered violence, and the violent take it by force. So sometimes what happens is that the more you speak the Counsel of God, the more you enforce it over the Counsel of the Enemy.

The statement about taking the kingdom by force was a reference to Mat 11:12. John, the young Kenyan man, also deployed this idea of a spiritual cosmology in his explanation of another practice among the pastors. I asked him why the pastors, when they were preaching, often switch to praying. He gave this answer:

I would say it is a lot about being in the Spirit. Because we as Christians believe that we are not just two dimensional. We believe in the fourth dimension, which is the spiritual world. And we believe that there is God, we believe there is Jesus, the Son of God, and we believe in the power of the Holy Spirit. So it depends on how the preacher is being led by God. Normally, if you were in the spirit world, the whole church would know, will be in tune with whatever is happening on the stage.

"Spirit-man" Anthropology

Related to this concept of the spirit realm was the concept of "the spirit-man". Pastor Joe also spoke about this once. He said people were first spirit before they were physical beings. He told them that sometimes people do not hear God because they are not born again, so their spirit is not active. This concept of spirit-man was very much in the mind of many church members when they thought about the Holy Spirit. Evelyn described the Holy Spirit in this way:

He is God himself in us living in our spirit and working those things that God wants to do. So he is the person of God in our spirit-man so he leads us according to the wisdom and the knowledge and the fullness of God to do those things that God has already ordained to be done on the earth today.

55

Over the course of the interviews, it also became clear that the church members thought about the "spirit-man" as something in opposition to the "flesh". Pastor Lara described how her "flesh" once got in the way so she could not see the miracles God was doing during a big public event. Many people who came to the event were visibly ill. Some came in crutches:

> You could genuinely feel the expectation level. And I just said, "God, you've got to show up." And it wasn't long when the ministration started that I knew that the Holy Spirit was now showing me something else that I hadn't seen in my flesh, because my flesh at the time was taking over. And it was like fear. Seeing these people in their various situations, I couldn't kick into that higher level. . . . But when the Holy Spirit started to minister to me, I had to repent of my unbelief. And that's when I was then able to see the miracles take place. I did. And I was just weeping before the Lord. It was just amazing to see the simplicity of people's faith . . . but it took my eyes being opened for me to be able to see.

The concept of "flesh" and "spirit-man" gave rise to the two expressions: "in the flesh" and "in the spirit". In the above account, Pastor Lara could not see the miracles because she was operating in the flesh – "I hadn't seen in my flesh." At other times, church members spoke of operating "in the spirit". Evelyn, speaking about how the Holy Spirit relates with the human spirit, said:

> When we are in the spirit and the Spirit has advocated Christ in us we are now in the nature of Christ. Our spirit becomes very sweet and a good atmosphere for the Spirit to dwell in. So when he takes us out [i.e. outside the church], we become sensitive to the needs of people.

There were examples of the spirit-man being the source of good decision. In a previous section, I described how a miracle convinced a member of the church of the authenticity of speaking in tongues. For another member, Eva, it was "her spirit" that did the same for her. Eva gave this description of what she saw of the church members the first time she visited:

> They were dancing and clapping. I was still not sure, so I was not really dancing or clapping. I was looking on. They were speaking in tongues. I did not know what it was so I'm thinking, Oh, they are speaking their own language. Because it is predominantly an African church and I was not used to the language. I was like I don't know why they are speaking in their language and I don't understand. So I'm not sure if I belong here. That's what I was saying to myself.

At the time, she was not sure she would go back, but as she put it, "My spirit kept going back to the message." At her next visit, there was an altar call and she responded. After that, she became a fully committed member.

This membership, she said, brought many benefits to her at a deep level. She had been brought up Roman Catholic, but in the church service at Mount Zion she felt very different. "It was very real. I was very clear. My life had to change," she said. She had been in a crisis because she had lost two family members within a short period of time.

> That was very traumatic for me. Somehow I felt knowing Jesus as Lord and personal saviour is going to make me understand truly what life is about. And the question for me was: would I ever see my mother again? Would I see my brothers again? And what is life all about? That was the questioning. When I gave my life, I knew I was totally serious. I knew this is where I was going. But the confirmation of that was that every time I came to church there is something happening to me. The message is speaking to me, speaking to me deep in my heart. It's unravelling, you know, what is life about? You can't do anything; you can't trust a man, as it were. But you could only trust in God. He is truly the answer.

She ended the testimony by restating the realness of the Holy Spirit. "The Spirit of God is real and that I didn't feel I knew before. Although I knew I believe in God, there was nothing real for me," she said. It is noteworthy that this all happened because at a critical point, "her spirit" helped her make the right decision.

A link between the Holy Spirit and the empowerment of individual members
From my observation and the church's literature, it was quite clear that the promise of God's blessings in all aspects of life was a major feature of the church's teaching. For example, in one sermon, the preacher, one of the senior ministers of the church, told the congregation that God wanted them to rise above the level they had been operating at in their lives. He told them that the new year will be better than the past one "in the name of Jesus". He told them that their life, career, home, finances will all be better "in the name of Jesus". The church members, for their part, were not shy of declaring either their desire to be blessed materially or God's desire to do so. One of them said,

> We are joyful that he is our provider. He is good to us . . . we are happy that our king takes care of us. Our king gives us victory. And when we do that, he does more things for us.

For them the concept of blessing was linked to that of empowerment. God's blessings of good health, material provisions and spiritual strength empower them to face day-to-day challenges and achieve greater heights as individuals. God also empowers them to carry out their own particular ministry. This emphasis on blessing/empowerment was reflected in their understanding of the work of the Holy Spirit. For example, in a sermon, Pastor Joe told the congregation that when God gives them the understanding of the Holy Spirit, they will exceed the people around them. That understanding of the Holy Spirit will make them succeed in business or their chosen field. He told them about Daniel who went from being a mere foreigner to become a Prime Minister and said something similar will happen to them. He also gave them the example of one of their church members who recently emigrated to Canada to start a business and within a short time, his business was worth millions of dollars.

This view that the Holy Spirit empowers the believer to make a success of their life was common among the church members and showed itself in different forms. Michael said that Mount Zion taught the church members to be "achievers":

> Mount Zion teaches us to be achievers, to get to know God for ourselves. The systems in Mount Zion are not designed to get people to keep running to pastors all the time. Systems are designed for people to stand on their own so that in the middle of the night if there is something happening in your family, something wrong with your child, if you have travelled abroad, you are somewhere, and there is nobody to help you, you can stand on your own and rebuke the enemy.

With this boldness, he said, "The church does not belong to Pastor Joe. The church is part of the kingdom of God. And the kingdom of God has its way of doing things like any other kingdom." When he spoke about worship, he saw it in terms of empowerment:

> Worship takes us into intimacy as children of God and brings the glory of God to our services. And the residue of that rests upon us for the rest of the week. It helps make us victorious and empowers us when things get difficult.

Mount Zion's goal of empowering was not just for the ministers, he explained:

> Not just as preachers, but both in the market place, even in setting up charities, you know, in whatever we do, to become, I'll say, Obamas. To be an example, to remove shame, especially from black people. The Holy Spirit empowers us and helps us to fulfill that role. And when all of that comes together, the agenda of God gets fulfilled.

He even described Jesus Christ in those terms:

> Jesus Christ is the word of God. He is the Son of God. He is the embodiment of, let me say, achievement. He is the embodiment of success . . . when the Holy Spirit revealed Jesus Christ to me that he is the embodiment of success, I began to desire that more than anything else. That is key, really.

Pastor Abasi, the architect, told me how his career had turned around as a result of encountering the Holy Spirit at Mount Zion. He had left the church he belonged to because, as he put it, he "could not marry [his] experience with the word of God". And his career "was not going anywhere". He described how he felt the first day coming to Mount Zion, and listening to the sermon: "I felt like going through desert and coming to sea and waves. The word of God was coming in wave after wave and each wave was setting me free." Many years on, looking back, everything had changed:

Personally, everything, where I am today and what I have achieved both in my circle of work and in my home, I would never have been able to achieve it without the Holy Spirit.

He continued:

I say to a lot of people when we have time to talk, when you see a black man come over to England to study a career and you see them successful, they are achievers. Because you come here, you have to double-prove yourself . . . but God gives you the grace to be able to achieve it. Because without the Holy Spirit you just can't.

Some difference in the emphasis between men and women in how they understand the Holy Spirit

I detected a difference in the emphasis between men and women. Even though this was a small number of people, it is noteworthy that the emphasis on empowerment discussed above came from men. For Pastor Abasi, the power of the Holy Spirit enabled him to "double prove" himself as black people often have to do in a foreign land. For Michael, the goal of Mount Zion is to turn people into high achievers, like Obama. I found this same emphasis on empowerment among the younger male members of the church. John, the Kenyan man, said this about why he came to Mount Zion:

The reason why I like Mount Zion is because the word is strong. It's balanced. I also like Mount Zion because they are forward looking. They are people with a vision that are going somewhere. And I would like to get involved with that kind of group of people that are heading somewhere. Because I also have a dream and in getting involved with people that have been there, I also get to figure out how I can launch out my dream.

Some comments from the women could also be interpreted as indicating empowerment by the Spirit, but these, rather than suggesting the socio-economic or political empowerment I encountered among men, appeared more like empowerment to be better pastors, to give a better quality of pastoral care. Liz, for example, said the church was encouraging every member to be a pastor to others. By this, she meant that they should be prepared to be sensitive to the problems of others, and pray for and advise them as necessary. Pastor Christy, as seen earlier, talked about the Spirit enabling her to have discernment in the counselling context. Pastor Lara was empowered by the Holy Spirit in her relationship with colleagues in the church. This enabled her to deal with both junior and senior colleagues fairly, without fear or favour. She talked about how the Holy Spirit helped her always to remember that all were saved by the grace of God, and nobody saves themselves. It did not matter to her whether she is dealing with a child or an archbishop:

I will always respect you, but you will never ever replace God in my life, and neither will you replace my own level [of spiritual maturity]. I am not intimidated. I may not say things the same way as you, but I always take my leading from how I am led by the Lord. And that has helped me in so many situations.

This attitude comes from her knowledge that "God has given me that ability to be confident in who I am in him and be able to relate and often discern where people are at."

Even when one of the women I interviewed, Eva, made a socio-political point, there was a different tone to it compared to what I heard from men. She said, Mount Zion motivated one to do better, but "doing better" was not for your personal progress, but for society as a whole. She also said any personal growth was so other people would see Christ in one.

The second difference in emphasis was related to the Bible and the Holy Spirit. Although taken as a whole, the church members I interviewed held the work of the Holy Spirit and the Bible together, I noticed that the women tended to emphasise the Holy Spirit more while the men were more likely to emphasis the role of the Bible. For example, Pastor Lara, in discussing the principles that guided her in her work talked about how she relied on the Holy Spirit to guide her:

I have to be careful that it is not my human understanding that I am using in a particular situation or about a particular person. . . . I try my best to always ask the Holy Spirit to help me, that I will not say the wrong thing.

However, Pastor Abasi gave this response to the same question: "The main thrust or principle that guides me is the Bible. It is the reference point of everything that I do." He added, however, that "over and beyond that is the role of the Holy Spirit". He would later warn against the dangers of not using the Bible to check out what people might think they were hearing from the Holy Spirit. John also began his answer to the same question in a similar way: "Personally, I am guided a lot by the Bible and, obviously, through the teachings of the church, and by reading books." Michael made more or less the same point when I asked him what he liked about the church. He said it was the fact that the preaching is biblically based: "If it is not in the Bible, they don't preach it." As one of the church's "intercessors", he also emphasised intercessions. But much as he was keen to pray for people, "If prayer point is not in the Bible we don't pray it", that is, if the request for prayer that was being made could not be justified Biblically, he would not pray on that request.

One could say that there was a kind of "masculinity" about the responses I got from most of the men, both in terms of their desire to be empowered to take on the socio-economic demands of their environment and in their emphasis of the Bible as providing a counter-balance to the uncertainty that could result from total reliance on the Holy Spirit. The women I interviewed did not appear to have any such concerns about the Holy Spirit. They were on the whole more likely to bring in the Holy Spirit in their comments without being prompted. Evelyn, far from using the Bible as a check against a possible excessive appeal to the Holy Spirit, in effect wrapped up the Bible with the Holy Spirit by constantly referring to this statement in the Bible, "the word of God is Spirit." (Jn 6:63) On one occasion, she used this to make the point that when people read the Bible, they were in fact filling themselves with the Holy Spirit. It suggested to me that she was so comfortable with the reign of the Spirit that she did not see the need to emphasise Biblical truth that stood independently.

A coherence between the understandings of the Holy Spirit shown by the young participants in this study with the rest of the church

I found that the young members' understanding cohered with the response of the rest of the church. Out of the twelve people I interviewed, three were much younger than the others. These included a young man, Geoff, eighteen, whose parents came from Nigeria but who was born in UK; a young woman, Daya, twenty, who came originally from Zimbabwe and has been a member of Mount Zion for over eight years; and, John, twenty-five, originally from Kenya, whom we have already come across earlier in this chapter. Daya, the twenty year old, female student, described the Holy Spirit as a teacher:

The Holy Spirit reveals a lot of things to me. For me, personally, I get dreams and I find that it's in those dreams that the Holy Spirit is trying to teach me and show me something.

The Spirit was also her comforter.

Sometimes I can be really, really sad and when I cry, I know that the Holy Spirit is there and he is the one teaching me and he is the one speaking to me.

"I can truly say that the Holy Spirit is my best friend," she said. Her stress of the teaching element and the sense of an intimate and concrete relationship resonate with the responses I got from Pastor Christy, Eva and others described earlier.

Geoff, the eighteen year old man, who has been a member of Mount Zion since he was a toddler, when I asked him why the pastors at Mount Zion switched from preaching mode to praying mode when they were giving their sermon, said it was because the Pastor is sensitive to the Spirit:

It may be things that he senses in his spirit, that there is a spirit that is not of God, so he has to pray in tongues to bind it. Most of the time if you see a pastor that's preaching and starts praying, it is something that he senses in his spirit.

By way of example, he told me he himself prayed at the start of the interview, saying, "Lord, take away my flesh let this not be of me but of you, so your name could be glorified."

Geoff's point about sensitivity to the Holy Spirit was the same point made by Pastor Kenneth and many other interviewees. Also, his prayer for the right responses to my questions is similar to what I got from Liz and others. Even the content of the prayer, in particular, the reference to the "flesh" that should be taken away resonates with Pastor Lara's story about how "being in the flesh" once prevented her from seeing miracles.

The answers given by these three young members when asked (bear in mind they were interviewed individually) whether they thought the Holy Spirit was present in Mount Zion or in the work of the church's ministers, were not only similar to each other, but also echoed what I heard from older members. They pointed, among other things, to the ministry of Pastor Joe. Geoff said:

> The Holy Spirit is definitely hundred percent within Mount Zion because by their fruits you shall know them . . . it hurts me so much to see that a lot of people do not have the same relationship that our spiritual father, Pastor Joe, has with the Holy Spirit. Look what the Holy Spirit is doing for Mount Zion.

Daya said the Holy Spirit was involved in the church because the Pastor's words match her thoughts and his prayers match her concerns:

> It's like, wow! That's exactly what I was thinking on my way to church. How did Pastor Joe know that? Or you'll be like, wow! He is praying on that point, that's exactly what I am going through. What is going on?

She also said she senses the presence of God during praise and worship, "And I believe that the presence of God is the Holy Spirit."

And John said the Holy Spirit was involved because the church was run in an orderly way. He also made the point about "word of knowledge", that is when a Pastor tells you what you are going through:

> He ministers to people in a way that people can relate to. That is the reason why people keep coming over and over again, because he says things that help the people to go through whatever they are going through and to bring a solution to the problem. Those are reasons why we know that Holy Spirit is involved in the church.

Perhaps most striking was how the responses from these three fell neatly along the gender lines already described. Much like the men we have seen, John and Geoff, strongly emphasised the place of the Bible in shaping their faith. John put the Bible first in his list of guiding principles and Geoff had a Bible open on his lap throughout his interview. Sometimes he would flip through the pages to quote parts of it in answer to my question. Like the other men I interviewed, both also emphasised the Spirit's work of empowering people to face life and be successful. As shown earlier, John liked Mount Zion because it was for people who were "going somewhere" and would help him to "launch his own dream". For Geoff the "new life" meant getting the professional basketball contract that he was hoping for.

Daya's response, on the other hand, resembled what I had heard from the women. For example, when I asked her what she liked about Mount Zion she pointed not to external things or what she might achieve in the future but to the loving relationship between church members and how the church has helped her grow spiritually:

And also, this is the church where I got born again. Where God saved my life. That is one of the reasons that I am here. It is my home.

I also noticed when I attended the youth service and a young woman was giving a testimony, references to the Holy Spirit came naturally to her, much like I noticed with the older women I interviewed. Some of these similarities might be explained by the fact that many of the young people attended the main services, in addition to their youth service, and so had fed on the same diet of worship songs and sermons as the older members. Even so, the level of coherence across the ages was noteworthy.

Conclusion

In reporting this case study, my main descriptive framework has been the pattern of relationship between the theme of the Holy Spirit and other theological themes. This placed all the analytical categories at the same conceptual level. It also meant that there was a consistent criterion by which themes are included, namely, that there was a significant interaction between that theme and the theme of the Holy Spirit.

My research revealed to me that this was a church for which the Holy Spirit was very important. Curiously, they did not use the words "Holy Spirit" very often in their Sunday services. However, as I found, they felt it was present with them always and that it was a presence they needed very much. One phrase I heard time and again was that "The Holy Spirit is real" or a "real person". There was a strong sense among the members and ministers that this was a person who was actively involved in their life and not merely a concept in people's imagination or a mere theoretical idea for academic study. I found that key aspects of their beliefs about the Holy Spirit were such as one would find among Christians from many other denominations. For example, all the members and leaders I spoke to stated clearly that the Holy Spirit was part of the Trinity. They constantly referred to the Holy Spirit as "he" and not as "it" to emphasize that this was a person, and they saw his work in terms of comfort and guidance.

I was struck by the extent to which their thinking about the Holy Spirit and their use of the Bible were woven together. I found that there was a very strong emphasis in this church on how one needs the Holy Spirit in order to read the Bible effectively as a Christian. Otherwise, one would be reading the Bible as a mere book of history or for other academic purposes. The Holy Spirit, for them, brought the Bible to life and made it relevant to the particular reader at the particular point in time. The Holy Spirit could also act at specific moments in one's life, such as when one was facing complex circumstances, to remind one of key Biblical texts to solve the problem they were facing. Just as the Holy Spirit helped out with Bible reading, the Bible helped out in the knowledge of the Holy Spirit. The Bible also acted as a yardstick for checking that revelations they receive are really from the Holy Spirit.

The ministers talked about how they were guided in their ministry by the Holy Spirit. One spoke about being guided in counselling situations by the Holy Spirit revealing to her what was happening in the life of the people she was talking to. There were also several examples of the Holy Spirit being involved in the process of preparing and delivering sermons. All these I did not find unusual. What was more striking was how involved they felt the Holy Spirit was in their daily life. For many in the church, the Holy Spirit was guiding them even in the most mundane of things. Some of the members understood the work of the Holy Spirit not only in terms of guidance but in terms of sustaining physical life itself. However, this latter aspect was not widespread.

Clearly, the empowerment of its members was an important goal in this church. Several sermons given in the time I visited had that theme. This could be clearly seen in their understanding of what the Holy Spirit does. Among the men, in particular, there was the sense that the Holy Spirit was empowering them to face the socio-economic challenges resulting from being immigrants in this country. There was also a tone of empowerment among women, although it often had a different emphasis. One of the pastors talked about being empowered in her personal and professional relationship in a way that enabled her to resist intimidation. This was one of two areas where I detected a gender difference. Another gender difference showed in the way the women appeared to be "all in" in their relationship with the Holy Spirit, whereas some of the men I spoke to could be seen as using the Bible to hedge their bet on what might be attributed to the Holy Spirit.

The thought pattern of the members of this church had a strong spiritual aspect to it. They were very aware of the spiritual dimension of life and the world and, in terms of the human person, they were very aware of the spiritual aspects. This formed the background to how they thought about the Holy Spirit. In a sense, the Holy Spirit was the Spirit of God engaging evil forces in the realm of spirits on their behalf. For, example, the practice whereby the pastors repeat themselves several times was often understood not simply in terms of oratory emphasis but as a way of delivering spiritual blows to any demonic entities present. Also, praise and worship at the beginning of the service was often seen as a spiritual activity to sweep away any evil forces present that might hamper the people's communion with God. Since for them what happens in the spirit realm manifests in the physical, the victories which the Holy Spirit won for them in that dimension could lead to prosperity and good health.

CHAPTER 4

Literature Survey

Before the pattern theories that were derived from the inductive study in Chapter 3 are tested in the next stage of fieldwork, they have to be linked to established theories and knowledge. Van der Ven has noted that placing the inductively obtained pattern-theories "into a broader more generally recognised framework" in this way ensures that unrelated data are included in the investigation. By so doing one avoids "empirical-theological ventriloquy", which is where an investigator simply reinforces their own presupposition.[1] So, at this stage, I will review what has already been written on each of the areas covered by the pattern theories.

Carrying out a literature review at this point also coheres with the normal process of inductive research. Creswell has noted that in theoretically oriented qualitative studies such as ethnographies, researchers introduce literature early "as an orientating framework".[2] However, in grounded theory studies, case studies and phenomenological studies, "literature will serve less to set the stage for the study".[3] Hence, for the latter group, Creswell recommends that "the literature is presented at the end" so that "it becomes a basis for comparing and contrasting findings of the qualitative study".[4]

I will begin by describing how the review was carried out and the criteria used for including and excluding materials. Then, I will present the result of the review. In the final section, I will describe the conclusion reached from the review.

Rationale

The fact that this literature review was carried out after the inductive fieldwork is critical for the form that it takes. Creswell points out that when the review is carried out after fieldwork, "the literature does not guide and direct the study but becomes an aid once patterns or categories have been identified".[5] Hence,

---

[1] J.A. Van der Ven, *Practical Theology: An Empirical Approach* (Kampen: Kok Pharos, 1993). 116.

[2] J. Creswell, *Qualitative Enquiry and Research Design: Choosing Among the Five Approaches* (London: Sage, 2007), 30.

[3] Creswell, *Qualitative Enquiry and Research Design*, 30.

[4] Creswell, *Qualitative Enquiry and Research Design*, 30.

[5] Creswell, *Qualitative Enquiry and Research Design*, 30.

rather than trawling through literature on African Pneumatology to arrive at "orientating framework" to "guide and direct the study" this review focuses on the theories already identified. The main criterion for including or excluding the material would be whether or not it elucidates the theory under consideration.

Since Mount Zion is characterised by its African origin and a Pentecostal inclination, principal consideration is given to academic work on African Christianity and Pentecostalism in this review. I attempt to include literature from different parts of Africa and the major writings on the subject. Customarily, a literature review concentrates on peer-reviewed, academically published work. This review gives priority to that very category of literature. However, my literature search shows that scholarly work on the subject of African Pneumatology is not extensive. This is ironic, considering the fact that African Christianity is widely known to be Charismatic-oriented. But this lack of an extensive scholarly work was not a surprise to me. It was what attracted me to the area in the first place, and was the very reason I chose an inductive approach to the study.

The scarcity of published academic work on African Pneumatology, however, necessitated the inclusion in this review of the huge literature which has been published by African Pentecostal ministers in recent decades. This body of literature directly from the practitioners has much to add to our understanding of African Christianity. I have also borne in mind a point made by the African scholar, Justin Ukpong. Ukpong notes that continuing to disregard the ordinary African readers of the Bible by scholars "will lead to sterile scholarship".[6] Although Ukpong made this point with regards to Biblical scholarship, I believe it applies to theology in Africa in general. So, I believe the inclusion of the work of these ministers helps me avoid this study becoming "sterile scholarship" and makes it more widely relevant.

In effect, I have mainly reviewed three kinds of literature: 1) studies of African Christianity, 2) studies of Pentecostal Christianity, and 3) the emerging literature from African Pentecostal ministers in both Britain and the African continent. The material I reviewed includes books, journal articles and unpublished theses. I made use of the ATLA religion data base for tracking down relevant journal articles I identified.

Finally, a point made by Yin is pertinent here. Yin argues that "case studies, like experiments, are generalizable to theoretical proposition and not to populations or universes".[7] The goal of the investigator "is to expand and generalize theories (analytic generalization) and not to enumerate frequencies

---

6 J. Ukpong, "Developments in Biblical Interpretation in Africa: Historical and hermeneutical Directions" in *The Bible in Africa: Transactions, Trajectories and Trends* (Leiden: Brill, 2000), 26.
7 R. Yin, *Case Study Research — Design and Methods* (London: Sage, 1984), 34.

(statistical generalization)"[8] For this reason, this literature review focuses on how the pattern theories I identified might be expanded and not on how Mount Zion could be regarded as a sample of African churches in Britain. With regards to wider application, the interest is on the theories and not on Mount Zion per se.

To facilitate the understanding of the twelve theories, I have grouped them into five headings based on the five dominant themes I identified in them. The five themes are 1) the deity of the Holy Spirit, 2) the personhood of the Holy Spirit, 3) the background worldview of the church, 4) the empowering role of the Holy Spirit and 5) the interaction between the Bible and the Holy Spirit.

The Deity of the Holy Spirit.

Under this theme, two out of the twelve theories are discussed. These are: 1) the relationship between the Holy Spirit and worship and 2) the paucity of explicit reference to the Holy Spirit during worship.

Holy Spirit with worship

I had found at Mount Zion a strong association of the Holy Spirit with the worship service. A similar association has also been found in the African Initiated Churches. Afe Adogame showed that the Celestial Church of Christ believed that the hymns and songs which they used in their worship services were revealed under the influence of the Holy Spirit:

> All hymns used for devotional services are expected to be only those that are given to the church through the mouth of prophets/prophetesses while possessed by the Holy Spirit and are usually songs which no one is believed to have ever offered before.[9]

The church's founder assured the church members that many more songs "will the Holy Spirit give unto the church" if they did not borrow songs from other churches. Adogame also found that some of the church's hymns contained words or phrases in "spiritual" language, unintelligible to non-members, "perhaps an apparent form of *glossolalia*".[10] Hence, the church members believed the Holy Spirit was always working hard to make their worship possible.

Similarly, J. Kwabena Asamoah-Gyadu highlights regarding the Sunsum Sore how their view of "God's Spirit as real and communicating with his people in worship" has made the difference between them and other churches

---

[8] Yin, *Case Study Research*, 34.
[9] A. Adogame *Celestial Church of Christ* (Frankfurt: Peter Lang, 1999), 134.
[10] Adogame *Celestial Church of Christ*, 137.

in the country.[11] Sunsum Sore is the collective name for the first wave of African Initiated Churches that arose in Ghana from the early twentieth century, equivalent to the Aladura group of churches in Nigeria and the Zionist churches in the southern African countries.[12] Their view of God allows them to take the "irrational aspect of religion" seriously and to be spontaneous:

> Such spontaneity is a marked feature of Pentecostal spirituality that enriches the nature of worship. In place of reliance on a fixed programme, the Spirit can be manifested in tongues, songs and prophesies, giving worshippers a sense of the presence of God.[13]

Asamoah-Gyadu further notes that in this spontaneous worship style of the Sunsum Sore, "the Spirit is expected to guide worship and lead it in unpredictable directions".[14] Their songs, which are simple, biblically based choruses often originating from personal religious experiences, are seen as "evidence of the Spirit's presence".[15]

The United Church of the Cherubim and Seraphim (Cherubim and Seraphim for short), one of African Initiated Churches that started from Nigeria, is yet another example of where similar connections have been made. J.A. Omoyajowo, in his study of the church, states that practically every meeting service begins with the leaders directing church members to pray for the Holy Spirit to descend.[16] Hermione Harris's study of the same church in London shows that their association of the Holy Spirit with their worship services continues in the Diaspora.[17] She points out that the church's watch night services "provide an opportunity for a spiritualist (*elemi*) to experience possession by the Holy Spirit".[18] During a particular service, she observes how the hymns "encourage the insipient sweep of the Spirit through the congregation".[19] She describes how the Spirit manifests in the visible actions of the congregation:

> Around me, women are becoming possessed. Aladura Sister Opayinka's broad body twists violently. Shrieking, she shunts backward over to the men's side of the hall, a sister on either side to support her. She proves too much for them;

---

[11] Asamoah-Gyadu, *African Charismatics: Current Developments within Independent Indigenous Pentecostalism in Ghana*, (Leiden: Brill NV, 2005), 54.

[12] Asamoah-Gyadu, *African Charismatics*, 21

[13] Asamoah-Gyadu, *African Charismatics*, 54.

[14] Asamoah-Gyadu, *African Charismatics*, 54.

[15] Asamoah-Gyadu, *African Charismatics*, 54.

[16] J.A. Omoyajowo, *Cherubim and Seraphim – The History of an African Independent Church* (New York: Nok, 1982), 98.

[17] H. Harris, *Yoruba in Diaspora: An African Church in London* (New York: Palgrave Macmillan, 2006).

[18] Harris, *Yoruba in Diaspora*, 111.

[19] Harris, *Yoruba in Diaspora*, 113.

falling flat on her back, she brings them toppling down with her in a heap on the flour.[20]

So much was the Spirit moving that at a point, the noise was "deafening" as the "cacophony of entranced voices" continued even after the singing had stopped.[21] Somebody who is "shouting in the Spirit" is attended to.[22] Even those not possessed are swaying and dancing, confident in "the vitality of the Spirit".[23]

The association of the Holy Spirit with worship services is also present in the African Pentecostal Churches. It is captured in Asonze Ukah's description of the services of the Redeemed Christian Church of God (RCCG).[24] Although he does not explore in detail the theological content of the services, the names the services have been given by the church are themselves revealing. One of the services is called the "Holy Ghost Service". Ukah describes this as "the most popular single ritual of the RCCG".[25] This is in fact more than an act of worship. Rather, it is a "programme of prayers and vigils that attracts close to 300,000 people" to the camp. Part of the two-day programme of the Holy Ghost Service is a particular night called Holy Ghost Night. This Holy Ghost Night is "advertised as a miracle event" with people urged to "be available for a miracle".[26] There is also the Holy Ghost Congress, which is a three-day event aimed at a worldwide audience.[27]

The review of the writings of African Pentecostal ministers does not show much writing on worship. However, Stella Adekunle, who is the founder of the UK-based Sword of the Spirit Evangelical Outreach Ministries, describes prayer sessions to be followed by Christians looking for answers to specific problems.[28] She makes it clear that each session should begin with praise and worship. The implication is that worship brings the Christian close to God, (Father, Son and Holy Spirit), who the prayers are offered to. For example, in the section entitled "Fire of Restoration Possess My Life" she recommends that the session begins with a reading of Exodus 3. This should be followed by praise and worship made up of two songs that she wrote out in full and then prayer points which include the plea "Holy Spirit fire, melt away every stony

---

[20] Harris, *Yoruba in Diaspora*, 115.
[21] Harris, *Yoruba in Diaspora*, 115.
[22] Harris, *Yoruba in Diaspora*, 113.
[23] Harris, *Yoruba in Diaspora*, 113.
[24] A. Ukah, *A New Paradigm of Pentecostal Power: A Study of the Redeemed Christian Church of God in Nigeria* (Trenton: Africa World Press, 2008).
[25] Ukah, *A New Paradigm of Pentecostal Power*, 240.
[26] Ukah, *A New Paradigm of Pentecostal Power*, 242.
[27] Ukah, *A New Paradigm of Pentecostal Power*, 240.
[28] S. Adekunle, *Crossing your Jordan* (London: Sword of the Spirit Evangelical Outreach, 2007).

ground in my heart, in the name of Jesus" and "Holy Ghost, arise in your power and destroy the root of sin in my life, in the name of Jesus."[29]

The belief that the Holy Spirit enables Christian worship and is present when it is taking place is common among Pentecostals. W. Shepperd after comparing worship in different Christian denominations notes that Pentecostal worship is "characterized by an attitude of allowing the Holy Spirit to lead, an attitude that means Pentecostal worship tends to be less structured than that of other groups."[30] Within this central characteristic, there are variations depending on the denominational origins of the particular group.[31] Pentecostal churches which began in the early twentieth century emphasised the work of the Holy Spirit in worship:

> The central focus of the service is not the sermon or the music, but the moving of the Holy Spirit. There is the expectation that God will minister in love to the worship through the agency of the Holy Spirit.[32]

Neil Hudson, a minister in the Pentecostal church, describes how at the first time he encountered a Pentecostal service, he was attracted by the "vibrancy and immediacy of the worship".[33] He observes that "worship was no longer simply a rational, cognitive assent to certain articles of the creedal statements of the church". Rather, it was a time when worshippers were "encouraged to experience the presence of God" in their midst.[34] Much of this was attributed to the presence of the Holy Spirit during the service. For example, church members engaged in something called "dancing in the Spirit".[35] Just as in Mount Zion, in this Pentecostal church the service moved from "praise" to "more reflective and intimate worship" after some time:

> The songs become simpler in lyrical content and more intimate in emotional intensity. The words are easily remembered and many of the songs are sung without the need for books or overhead projectors. It is accepted that during this period, the gift of tongues or prophecy may be exercised.[36]

Hudson's description of worship is remarkably similar to the worship service which took place at Mount Zion, as described in the previous chapter. However, a notable difference I observed between Mount Zion and the

[29] Adekunle, *Crossing your Jordan*, 117.
[30] J.W. Shepperd, "Worship" in Stanley M. Burgess and Edward M. van der Maas (eds), *The New International Dictionary of Pentecostal and Charismatic Movements* (Grand Rapids: Zondervan, 2003), 1219.
[31] Shepperd, "Worship," 1219.
[32] Shepperd, "Worship," 1219.
[33] D.N. Hudson, "Singing a New Song in a Strange Land" in Keith Warrington (ed.), *Pentecostal Perspectives* (Carlisle: Paternoster, 1998), 177.
[34] Hudson, *Pentecostal Perspectives*, 177.
[35] Hudson, *Pentecostal Perspectives*, 189.
[36] Hudson, *Pentecostal Perspectives*, 190.

Pentecostal services described above is that at Mount Zion it is the sermon, not the worship, which is the "main event" of the service.

The review thus shows that the strong association of the Holy Spirit with worship is a common phenomenon for the African Initiated Churches, the African Pentecostals Churches and the wider Pentecostal movement.

Verbal References

I had also noticed at Mount Zion that, in spite of the strong association of the Holy Spirit with worship, there were hardly any verbal references to the Holy Spirit during worship. When the Spirit was mentioned it was in the role of an enabler of worship rather than as an object of worship.

A similar phenomenon has been shown by studies of African Initiated Churches, such as Adogame's study of the Celestial Church of Christ of Nigeria. To be sure, Adogame's study shows that the church believes strongly in the Holy Spirit.[37] Their constitution states categorically that the name, organisation, doctrines, beliefs and rituals of the church were primarily derived by the inspiration of the Holy Spirit.[38] One of their tenets reads: "It is ordained by the Holy Spirit that members are forbidden to engage or participate in any form of idolatry . . . ."[39] Yet, according to Adogame, the church offers their prayers to Jehovah, Jesus Christ and Holy Michael.[40] Although Adogame himself does not draw this conclusion, the implication of this is that the Holy Spirit is left out when it comes to naming who is the focus of prayer.

H.W. Turner notes that for the Church of the Lord, Aladura of Nigeria, reference to Holy Spirit "was not as universal as you would expect in a revelatory prophet healing church."[41] He highlights, specifically, that some of the early, foundational documents contain no reference to the Holy Spirit, contrary to what one would expect of a church "where pneumatological beliefs receive the chief emphasis"[42]:

> There is no reference to the Holy Spirit in the articles on doctrine or membership, but in the historical preamble to the constitution, his work is referred to as the means by which God called, empowered, and directed Oshitelu for the foundation of the church. It is as though belief in the Spirit, like belief in God, is so basic that it is assumed rather than declared.[43]

---

[37] Adogame *Celestial Church of Christ*, 130.
[38] Adogame *Celestial Church of Christ*, 130.
[39] Adogame *Celestial Church of Christ*, 131.
[40] Adogame *Celestial Church of Christ*, 141.
[41] H.W. Turner, *African Independent Church II – The life and faith of the Church of the Lord (Aladura)* (Oxford: Clarendon, 1967), 334.
[42] Turner, *African Independent Church*, 334.
[43] Turner, *African Independent Church*, 336.

Turner noticed that pneumatological interest tended to be revealed in more informal ways in incidental publications and the practical life of the church. Even though this is not specifically to do with a worship setting, it is another case where the obvious relationship a church has with the Holy Spirit is not explicated.

As I have already stated, this study's review of the writings of African Pentecostal ministers found that they have not written much about worship. This is not surprising. Pentecostals tend to be more interested in worshipping than in reflecting on worship! What little reflection there was fitted the pattern of the Holy Spirit as an enabler of worship rather than one to be worshipped. For example, Enoch Adeboye in his book, *God the Holy Spirit*, gave this description of how the Spirit enables him to plan the worship service:

> When I first received the Holy Spirit, anytime I was leaving my home to the church, the Holy Spirit will tell me the person who would preach, the person who will pray and the songs we would sing in the church. God is no respecter of persons.[44]

This treatment of the Spirit can be seen in the work of UK based African ministers. For example, Albert Odulele of Glory House, London, who is of Nigerian descent, in the chapter of his book, *Understanding God's Voice*, on the subject of praise refers to "God" about fifty times, Jesus Christ about three times and the Holy Spirit only once.[45] The single reference to the Holy Spirit was, in fact, a quotation of Act 13:2, "the Holy Spirit said, 'set apart for me Barnabas and Saul...'" Odulele, no doubt, believes that the Holy Spirit is included in his reference to "God". Nonetheless, it is noteworthy that in his discussion of worship, the object of worship was "God." He explains that "Praise, worship and thanksgiving moves God" and worship "ministers" to God and emphasizes "the Person and Ability of God" and declares God to be "Sovereign and Supreme".[46]

A review of wider Pentecostal literature shows that this lack of interest in referring explicitly to the Holy Spirit is not peculiar to Africans. M. Cartledge found, after observing the Assemblies of God in Birmingham, that, "The Holy Spirit does not appear to be explicitly addressed as a person in worship."[47] At a wider level, Veli-Matti Kärkkäinen notes that within Pentecostalism there is the phenomenon of not specifically worshipping the Holy Spirit.[48] Kärkkäinen points out that for Pentecostals, "The Holy Spirit is not the centre of the

---

[44] E. Adeboye, *God the Holy Spirit* (Lagos: Christ the Redeemer's Ministries, 1997), 6.

[45] A. Odulele, *Understanding God's Voice* (London: OVMC, 2003), 55.

[46] Odulele, *Understanding God's Voice*, 58, 61

[47] M. Cartledge, *Testimony in the Spirit: Rescripting Ordinary Theology* (Farnham: Ashgate, 2010), 48.

[48] V. Karkkainen, *Pneumatology – The Holy Spirit in Ecumenical, International, and Contextual Perspective* (Grand Rapids: Baker Academic, 2002).

worship. Rather, in the power of the Spirit, the focus is on Jesus Christ and God."[49] This fits the pattern I observed at Mount Zion, whereby there was a short prayer at the beginning of the service to ask the Holy Spirit to come and "take control" of the proceedings and a prayer of Grace at the end, which includes the words: "the fellowship of the Holy Spirit". But during the service what was verbalised as the focus of worship was "God".

In conclusion, the paradox I observed at Mount Zion whereby they strongly believed the Holy Spirit was present in their worship but hardly ever mentioned him, has been shown by the literature review to not only be common among other African Initiated Churches and African Pentecostals, but also in line with the beliefs and practices within the wider Pentecostal movement. However, the Pentecostal practice of treating the Spirit as an enabler of worship and not the object of it must raise questions about the extent to which all Pentecostals see the Holy Spirit as God.

Personhood of the Holy Spirit

Related to the issue of the deity of the Holy Spirit is the Spirit's personhood. Under this section, two theories are discussed, 1) the view that the Holy Spirit is a "real" person and 2) the belief that the Holy Spirit is involved in the daily life of individual members.

Holy Spirit as a "real" person

At Mount Zion the members of the church I spoke to and the church's documents had been at pains to describe the Holy Spirit as a real person, and not a theoretical concept or an entity which existed in the past. I also found that some of my sources brought up the Trinity in the course of answering other questions, that is, without my prompting.

This is an area where the literature suggests some differences between the African Initiated Churches and African Pentecostal Church like Mount Zion. Studies of African Initiated Churches have shown that even though their members see the Holy Spirit as both a person and a force from God, the sense of the Spirit as a force is more prevalent. M.L. Daneel writing about the ministries of Johane Maranke of the African Apostolic Church and Bishop Mutendi of the Zionist Christian Church of Zimbabwe, narrated how on the first day when Bishop Mutendi stood up and preached, "Many believers were possessed by the Holy Spirit. The people present got frightened and some of them ran away." [50] He pointed out that the Holy Spirit was "the main agent" directing the judgement pronouncements against sinners, the healing ministries and the building of new communities. From the 1940s and 1950s:

---

[49] Karkkainen, *Pneumatology*, 91.
[50] M.L. Daneel, "African Independent Church Pneumatology and the Salvation of all Creation," *International Review of Mission* 82.326 (April, 1993), 146.

Healing and protection against evil forces now manifested more than anything else than the pervasive presence of the powerful Spirit of God. Speaking in tongues became the prelude to all prophetic diagnostic sessions, during which the Holy Spirit would reveal to the prophet the cause of the patient's illness.[51]

There is the clear sense that the whole church, both ministers and members, were experiencing the Holy Spirit in a tangible way.

Both Omoyajowo and Harris convey in their study of the Cherubim and Seraphim how the members experience the Holy Spirit as power in their life. Omoyajowo observes that the church teaches that the Holy Spirit is Christ's "personal representative" sent to the world by the Father.[52] He makes communion with God possible, bestows life, equips for service and so the true believer can do anything. "The Holy Spirit, it has been said by the U.C.C.&S, enters into the soul of every sanctified believer and dwells therein, giving the believer power to lead a holy life and to conquer sin."[53] Similarly, Harris describes how the members of the Cherubim and Seraphim church in London often experience the power of the Holy Spirit within them and among them. The following prayer gives an indication of their thinking in this area:

> The power which you have given to the ocean is different from other seas; the power with which you have consecrated the lagoon is different from the rivers; the power which you have given to the Cherubim and Seraphim is different from all other churches. This type of Holy Spirit, come and endow us with it.[54]

In Turner's study of the Church of the Lord, he points out that there was an emphasis of the teaching and empowering work of the Holy Spirit "through inner inspiration rather than visible possession."[55] He described the case of a young member who told him how it was through the Church of the Lord, that he was able to experience God as a Spirit inside him. "Only through the Church of the Lord I got it. It's through fasting and prayer I came to realize that particular kind of power. God is with us, a Spirit," the young man said.[56] Turner also refers to a lecture by one of the ministers of the Church of the Lord which states that the Holy Spirit is "within you every day; you feel her presence by burning desire to watch and pray...".[57] Turner, however, observes that the Holy Spirit is often presented as the power of God and relationship between the Holy Spirit and Jesus Christ is neglected. This prompted him to ask "whether this may not be an African modalism" in its inner tendency.[58] In other words, they

---

[51] Daneel, "African Independent Church Pneumatology," 149.
[52] Omoyajowo, J. A. *Cherubim and Seraphim*, 98.
[53] Omoyajowo, J. A. *Cherubim and Seraphim*, 98.
[54] Harris, *Yoruba in Diaspora*, 87.
[55] Turner, *African Independent Church*, 340.
[56] Turner, *African Independent Church*, 340.
[57] Turner, *African Independent Church*, 340.
[58] Turner, *African Independent Church*, 342.

were presenting Father, Son and the Holy Spirit as different modes that God chooses to operate in (or appear) at different times, rather than as three distinct persons.

Omoyajowo's statement that the Cherubim and Seraphim teaches that the Holy Spirit is a "personal representative" of Christ and Turner's observation that the Church of Lord emphasis inner inspiration rather than visible possession all fit the pattern of the New Testament and so add to the sense that for these churches the Holy Spirit is a person. Indeed, Anderson argues that since Africans do not tend to divide up a person's essential being into parts and do not think of the "spirit" as an invisible, incorporeal entity that can exist alone, but in fact the whole person, the Holy Spirit cannot be thought of as "some sort of mysterious, intangible, manipulable force that can exist somehow outside of oneself".[59] But this sense of personhood of the Holy Spirit is not always obvious in the theology and practice of the AICs.

By contrast, Israel Olofinjana in the book *Reverse in Mission and Ministry* states clearly that in the doctrine of the Holy Spirit of the KICC, an African Pentecostal Church, "the Holy Spirit is understood as a person and not as a wind or force".[60] Similarly, the present study's review of the writings of African Pentecostal Church ministers suggests that they are more emphatic than their AIC counterparts about the personhood of the Holy Spirit. This gulf between the two groups is addressed directly by Evangelist Kenneth Onyeme in *The Holy Spirit Exposed.*[61] He laments that "some Christian denominations claim that the Holy Spirit is not a person but rather the force of God" and states that "the Holy Spirit is a person…He is the third person in the Godhead. The Holy Spirit should be worshipped just as the Father and the Son. There is the need to know the Holy Spirit as a person and more intimately."[62] Onyeme also claims that "the Holy Spirit is not human person but a spirit (Divine person). He is God Almighty equal to the Father and the Son John 10:30; the difference is their responsibility".[63] A similar point is made by Pastor Chris Oyakhilome who observes how people wrongly perceive the Holy Spirit as a cloud from heaven, a bottle of anointed oil or their prayer handkerchief.[64] Oyakhilome dismisses these notions and affirms: "The Holy Spirit is the third person of the Godhead."

The review also showed that, compared to the AICs, the African Pentecostal Churches give less emphasis to visible possession and more emphasis to encountering the Holy Spirit as an inner inspiration. The fact that they expect

---

[59] A. Anderson, *Moya* (Pretoria: University of South Africa, 1991), 19.

[60] I. Olofinjana, *Reverse in Ministry and Mission: Africans in the Dark Continent of Europe* (London: Author House, 2010).

[61] K. Onyeme, *The Holy Spirit exposed* (publishing details not stated, undated).

[62] Onyeme, *The Holy Spirit exposed*, 3.

[63] Onyeme, *The Holy Spirit exposed*, 5.

[64] C. Oyakhilome, *Seven things the Holy Spirit will do in you* (Lagos: Love World, 2004), 12.

the Holy Spirit to act in their daily life is also a sign of how real he is to them. For example, when Gilbert Deya tells those in financial difficulties to pray: "I call upon the Holy Ghost to **bring finance to me.**"[65] This can only be because he thinks of the Holy Spirit (or Holy Ghost) as working at the present time and being interested in day-to-day issues. The ministers also often describe intimate encounters with the Holy Spirit. For example, Lawrence Tetteh in *Benefits of Anointing* describes how the Holy Spirit directed him during church events by putting thoughts in his mind. On occasions the Spirit asked him to kick, slap or anoint sick people with oil and in each case the person concerned was healed.[66]

The literature shows that among the African Pentecostals, even though prayers were often directed to "God" or "Jesus Christ", there are examples of prayers directed to the Holy Spirit. In *Goliath Killing Prayers*, Leke Sanusi recommends many prayer points that address the Holy Spirit directly.[67] One prayer point read, "Holy Ghost, show me clearly the weapons in my hand for slaying my Goliath in the name of Jesus."[68] Another said, "Holy Spirit, expose every power using the covering of darkness to work against me in the name of Jesus."[69] Such direct reference to the Holy Spirit can also be seen in the writing of Stella Adekunle. In one of her prayer recommendations she writes: "Holy Ghost, arise in your power and destroy the root of sin in my life, in the name of Jesus."[70] The clear sense from this is that these African Pentecostals see the Holy Spirit as a person in his own right and not simply as the power of God.

One exception to this pattern of difference between the AICs and the African Pentecostal Churches is the work of Edmund Anyahamiwe of the London-based Church Worldwide Incorporated, entitled the *Flesh of God*.[71] Anyahamiwe analyses the Holy Spirit (or Holy Ghost) in terms of the holiness of God and the "Ghost" of God. He notes that God's name is Holy and then writes:

> Besides His name being basically Holy, all attributes of His qualifying adjective are holy. His word, law, character, His heaven, arm, hill, works, seed, city and all things of His are holy.[72]

Turning to the word "Ghost", he explains that "God, whose name is Holy, is also a Ghost. This is his spiritual being. He is a Spirit with immortal body"[73] Anyahamiwe thus appears to understand the Holy Spirit (or Holy Ghost) not as

---

[65] G. Deya, *Dangerous Prayers to Break Satan's Force* (Eastbourne: Stock, 2003), 107.

[66] L. Tetteh, *Benefits of the Anointing* (London: LT Media Ministries, 2002).

[67] L. Sanusi, *Goliath Killing Prayers – How to Overcome Every Giant of your Life* (No publisher address: Oraworld, 2003).

[68] Sanusi, *Goliath Killing Prayers*, 8.

[69] Sanusi, *Goliath Killing Prayers*, 22.

[70] Adekunle, *Crossing your Jordan*, 117.

[71] E. Anyahamiwe, *The Flesh of God* (Voice of the Church, 2003).

[72] Anyahamiwe, *The Flesh of God*, 118.

[73] Anyahamiwe, *The Flesh of God*, 118.

a person distinct from the Father and the Son, but simply as a description of the nature of God, that is, as God's attributes of holiness and "ghostness". He further indicates the modalistic nature of his Trinitarian understanding when he states that the manifestation of God in the flesh is what is called Jesus.

Anyahamiwe's modalistic understanding of the Trinity resembles what one sometimes detects in the Trinitarian theology of some African Initiated Churches. This study's review of the new generation of African Pentecostal Churches, however, shows that the view articulated by Anyahamiwe in *The Flesh of God* is an exception. As I have already stated, these new Pentecostal churches have a stronger recognition of the Holy Spirit as a person of the Trinity and not just an attribute of God.

Personal Involvement of Holy Spirit in daily life

One indication of the sense that the Holy Spirit is a real person is the strong belief among the members of Mount Zion that the Spirit was closely involved in the daily life of Christians, even directing them in what might be seen as quite mundane matters. The tendency to involve God in all aspects of life is a well-documented aspect of African Christianity in Africa and it is often traced to the influence of African traditional religion. Mbiti mentions that the content of prayer of Christians in Africa is often an "almost complete duplication" of pre-Christian African prayer:

> In traditional African prayer, the main items of public prayer are: life, health and healing; prosperity and men's work (in the fields, hunting, fishing, travelling, etc); salvation and delivery from war, adversity and danger; one's life's journey from conception, through birth, initiation, puberty, marriage, procreation, death and the hereafter; for rain and end of famine; dealing with spirits.[74]

Mbiti's list goes on and shows how African traditional prayers and, in that sense, their religious concerns cover the needs of the whole of life. As Mbiti indicates, it is this spectrum that African Christians take over, adding to it a "new life situation arising out of Biblical revelation and out of changing life in modern Africa."[75]

Anderson, in his study of African Initiated Churches in southern Africa, highlights the emphasis these churches give to daily life and how this is often linked to the work of the Holy Spirit.[76] He explains that in what he calls the "spirit-type" churches "the all-embracing Spirit is involved in the individual and community life". For a people who have always had a need to be identified with the spirit, Africans in these churches meet this need in the Holy Spirit:

---

[74] J. Mbiti, *Bible and Theology in African Christianity* (Oxford: Oxford University Press, 1986), 84.

[75] Mbiti, *Bible and Theology*, 84.

[76] Anderson, *Moya*, 8.

In the Spirit-type churches it was discovered that the biblical doctrine of the Holy Spirit was not as detached and uninvolved as Western missionaries often made it out to be! The African need for divine involvement was met in the doctrine and especially in the enacting of pneumatology, which becomes in Africa both contextualised and a manifestation of Biblical reality.[77]

Other scholars of African Christianity show that the inclusion of daily life issues within Christianity was so important to African Christians that the tendency to do so has been the main attraction of the African Initiated Churches to Africans. S. Maimela writes that many African Christians believed the missionary churches were not interested in their daily misfortunes, illness, barrenness, poverty etc., while on the other hand, the African Initiated Churches had an "open invitation to the Africans to bring their fears and anxieties" to their gathering.[78] H.W. Turner notes that a study of the place of the Holy Spirit and the hymns used by the Church of the Lord showed that its members were not interested in "religious experience" as understood in the West, but with "vital concerns of life and security, with calamities avoided, rescues from evil and practical success."[79] Similarly, Omoyajowo remarks that the Cherubim and Seraphim believe that the actions of the Holy Spirit cover "the entire life of the believer".[80]

In Ogbu Kalu's study of Pentecostal churches he is clear that for many Africans in the Diaspora, membership of these churches is part of their efforts to survive in a difficult environment.[81] He stresses "the high level of marginality and racism" these Africans suffer in Europe, alongside Caribbean immigrants.[82] Hence, religious affiliation is used by some of these immigrants to "reinforce ethnic identity, solidarity, and to develop survival skills".[83] Much like their forebears in Africa, these immigrants hold to the spiritual worldview of the primal cultures and find Charismatic churches attentive to their deeply felt needs.[84] In particular, Kalu points out that "the moral system among the born-again Christians helps the new immigrant to be frugal, hardworking, focused, able to internalize the Western value system, and willing to eschew wasteful lifestyles".[85]

This study's review of the writings of African ministers shows similar ideas. In the African continent, Enoch Adeboye writes, "When the Holy Spirit comes

---

[77] Anderson, *Moya*, 9.
[78] Maimela, 1985, 71; quoted in Anderson, *Moya*, 30.
[79] Turner, *African Independent Church*, 358.
[80] Omoyajowo, J.A. *Cherubim and Seraphim*, 98.
[81] O. Kalu, *African Pentecostalism: An Introduction* (New York: Oxford University Press, 2008).
[82] Kalu, *African Pentecostalism*, 284.
[83] Kalu, *African Pentecostalism*, 284.
[84] Kalu, *African Pentecostalism*, 288.
[85] Kalu, *African Pentecostalism*, 287.

into your business, the unknown business will become known. . . . If you are selling ordinary water and the Holy Spirit comes into it, your water will be the only one everybody wants to drink."[86] He points out that nothing is impossible for God. The Holy Spirit can step into the life of a "messenger", that is, the lowest ranking job in an organisation, and they will become a Managing Director.[87] Chris Oyakhilome makes a similar point. He notes that the Spirit that raised Jesus from the dead will destroy cancer, get rid of tumours, HIV and diabetes:

> That's why I am telling you your suffering is unnecessary. Your poverty is unnecessary. Your struggling is unnecessary. You don't need to struggle or suffer anymore. You don't need to be poor anymore. If that same Spirit lives in you, He will make you a success.[88]

Similar ideas have been expressed in the British context. Gilbert Deya describes how one should seek the help of the Holy Spirit to deal with many of life's problems. In a section of the book entitled, "Personal prayers to specific problems in your life," Deya writes out prayers for "those who are homeless", prayers "against high blood pressure and diabetes", prayers for "when you are going to a job interview" and prayers "for when you are about to be sacked".[89] There were also prayers for "when you are attending a family funeral" and for "when you are in financial difficulty".[90] The clear impression was that prayers could be written for any life circumstance but the writer was only limited by space. Many of these prayers contain references to the Holy Spirit. For example, the prayer to be said by the homeless says, "I come to you, God the Father, God the Son and God the Holy Spirit. Touch me and bless me with accommodation."[91] The prayer to be said by those in financial difficulties include the words, "I speak to you money, come to me. I call upon you the Holy Ghost to bring finances to me."[92]

Hence the strong link I found at Mount Zion between the Holy Spirit and the life of individual members can be found among the AICs and can also so be found among the African Pentecostals in both Britain and Africa. It is an aspect of the sense the churches have of the Holy Spirit as a real person. However, in the case of the African Initiated Churches (that is, the older group of African churches), their tendency to speak of the Holy Spirit as the power of God can obscure their sense of the Holy Spirit as a real person.

---

[86] E. Adeboye, *Holy Spirit in the Life of Elijah* (Lagos: Christ the Redeemer's Ministries, 1997), 2.
[87] Adeboye, *Holy Spirit in the Life of Elijah*, 1.
[88] Oyakhilome, *Seven things the Holy Spirit will do in you*, 68-69.
[89] Deya, *Dangerous Prayers to Break Satan's Force*, 79, 81, 93, 85
[90] Deya, *Dangerous Prayers to Break Satan's Force*, 104, 106
[91] Deya, *Dangerous Prayers to Break Satan's Force*, 79.
[92] Deya, *Dangerous Prayers to Break Satan's Force*, 107.

Existing literature also shows that Pentecostals have the sense that the Holy Spirit is involved in their daily life. The general belief among them is that the encounter with the Spirit during worship does not end there but, rather continues in daily life. Hudson, for example, comments on how Pentecostals in England would end their Sunday services with a rousing hymn or chorus "designed to encourage the believers to re-enter the sceptical world with renewed faith in a God who is at work in their lives".[93] Similarly, Daniel Albrecht, who writes about Pentecostal practices from the perspective of ritual analysis points out that "It is believed and stated continually in Pentecostal services that God desires to minister to people's needs, even the ordinary, daily personal needs."[94] He also identified within Pentecostal services openness to the work of the Spirit which they adopt as "an ideal for all of life".[95]

In spite of these examples, the sense of the involvement of the Holy Spirit in daily life I found in the literature of the wider Pentecostal movement was weaker than what I had observed at Mount Zion and gleaned from literature on African Christians.

The Holy Spirit and worldview

Three pattern-theories will be discussed under this heading: 1) the existence within the church of a cosmology that is spiritual in essence and forms the background to concepts of the Holy Spirit, 2) the existence of an anthropology that is spiritual in essence and related to concepts of the Holy Spirit, 3) a coherence between the understandings of the Holy Spirit shown by the young participants in this study with the rest of the church, implying that they are bucking the trend of Western secularism and postmodernity.

A spiritual cosmology

I noticed that the church has a way of seeing the world which was spiritual in essence. So, for example, Pastor Joe's words were often understood as not only conveying a meaning to those present but, in fact, having more significant impact in the spirit realm on both good and evil forces.

A similar assessment has been made about the African worldview of the African Initiated Churches. Anderson found that the doctrine of the Holy Spirit was given prominence in these churches because unlike the mainline churches which had no answer to man's physical needs the AICs worked from the traditional African worldview that sees all things as forming a material-spiritual unity:

The African spirit world is a "personal", inter-related universe in which an individual as a living force is dependent upon all other forces for existence. The

[93] Hudson, *Pentecostal Perspectives*, 188.
[94] D.E. Albrecht, "Pentecostal Spirituality: Looking Through the Lens of Ritual," *Pneuma* 14.2 (Fall, 1992), 118.
[95] Albrecht, "Pentecostal Spirituality," 119.

emphasis on receiving the power of the Spirit, a power greater than any power that threatens this existence is really good news.[96]

Hence Anderson notes that the demonstration of God's power through the all-pervading Holy Spirit would often convince people that God is really more powerful than the evil forces they feel surrounding them.[97] Their need "for divine involvement was met in the doctrine of the Holy Spirit".[98]

Githieya's study of the Church of the Holy Spirit (Arathi) of Kenya shows that it is an example of where a highly spiritualised cosmology is in operation. The world was a place where good and bad spirits were engaged in battle and the result of that fight impinged on human life. Githieya writes:

> Arathi ideas about spirits were dualistic, divided between the Holy Spirit (a good spirit) and the spirit of error (a bad spirit). The spirit of error manifested itself in false teachings, such as the paternalistic teachings of mission churches or colonial views of oppression. It also manifested itself in Gikuyu religious teachings and practices, which Arathi regarded as ritually impure.[99]

They also believe the "bad spirit" causes evil to happen, and is manifested in such things as social division and pride.[100] The Holy Spirit, on the other hand, "brought power and renewal to the life of believers".[101]

These observations resonate with what has been found among Pentecostal churches in Africa. Kalu has noted that African Pentecostals, unlike the mainline churches, have an emphasis on the African primal worldview and try to "root their message into the African maps of the universe".[102] In an article entitled "Preserving a worldview: Pentecostalism in the African Maps of the Universe", Kalu describes this African worldview in greater detail. He points out that Africans perceive space in three dimensions: the sky, the earth and the ancestral or spirit world. Each of these dimensions of space is "peopled" with four kinds of spiritual beings. There are deities such as the Supreme Being in the sky and the Earth deity who is on earth; there are ancestral spirits that live underneath the earth; and there are spiritual forces "imbuing the whole of the world of the living".[103] This is, therefore, a universe in which all realms of life

---

[96] A. Anderson, *African Reformation: African initiated Christianity in the 20th century* (Trenton, New Jersey: Africa World Press, 2001), 255.

[97] Anderson, *African Reformation*, 229.

[98] Anderson, *Moya*, 9.

[99] F.K. Githieya, "The Church of the Holy Spirit – Biblical Beliefs and Practices of the Arathi of Kenya, 1926-50" in Thomas Spear and Isaria N. Kimambo (eds), *East African Expression of Christianity* (Oxford: James Currey, 1999), 237.

[100] Githieya, "The Church of the Holy Spirit," 237.

[101] Githieya, "The Church of the Holy Spirit," 237. See also, Adogame, "Engaging the Rhetoric of Spiritual Warfare," 502.

[102] O. Kalu "Preserving a Worldview" in *Pneuma* 24.2 (Fall, 2002), 122. 116-17.

[103] Kalu "Preserving a Worldview," 120.

are sacralised, the three dimensions of space are bound together and the visible and the invisible interweave.[104]

It is also a world in which people's sense of their existence is an unstable one, given all the other forces at work. In this worldview, if a family fails to provide a decent burial for a dead relative, the dead person will visit them "making demands and causing trouble for them"; marine spirits can control people, making them morally unstable and wayward; spiritual forces abound with "mysterious, ubiquitous power that permeates all area of life" and which can be used to diminish another person's health and resources; and the Earth deity supervises the moral order and can afflict those who offend by stealing, adultery, incest, and other offences unless they propitiate her.[105] Hence Kalu writes, "The vision of existence is a precarious one as evil forces, which besiege the human world, endeavour to ruin the capacity of individuals, families, and communities to live a prosperous life."[106] It is a very religious worldview, as people seek higher spiritual powers for their protection. As Kalu puts it, "going through life is like a spiritual warfare".[107]

Kalu saw the Pentecostal churches that have "exploded" into existence in many parts of Africa since 1970 as a continuation of the religiosity emerging from the African worldview. An important goal of life for Pentecostals is victorious living. For that, the search is for power to succeed in the difficult socio-economic and political environment.[108] "Victorious living" is pursued by defending oneself against the work of demons and principalities.[109] In both African Pentecostalism and the African primal worldview, social, economic and political problems are regarded as diseases requiring spiritual cures. Both also see physical illness as possibly having religious, social or natural causes. Hence, Kalu writes that "Pentecostalism in Africa derived her coloring from the texture of the African soil . . . and her fruits serve the challenges and problems of the African ecosystem more adequately than did the earlier missionaries."[110]

The same cosmology is also in operation among African Pentecostals in Britain. The prayers of Gilbert Deya convey a sense of a very active spirit realm — and one from which much evil emanates.[111] In one prayer he writes: "I destroy the powers of the spirit sent to bring heart attacks which affect people at night, when they are sleeping."[112] In another prayer, he writes: "I destroy all the influencing spirits that control people even at night . . . Let those spirits die!

---

[104] Kalu "Preserving a Worldview," 122.
[105] Kalu "Preserving a Worldview," 119, 120.
[106] Kalu "Preserving a Worldview," 120.
[107] Kalu "Preserving a Worldview," 122.
[108] Kalu "Preserving a Worldview," 129.
[109] Kalu "Preserving a Worldview," 139.
[110] Kalu "Preserving a Worldview," 122.
[111] Deya, *Dangerous Prayers to Break Satan's Force*.
[112] Deya, *Dangerous Prayers to Break Satan's Force*, 66.

die! die! Let them perish before they reach me."[113] He also prayed to destroy "the spirit of hatred sent by witches to make people hate me".[114] Similarly, the prayers of Stella Adekunle convey a sense of warfare in the spirit realm.[115] In one prayer she writes, "Blood of Jesus, disengage every demonic activity and engagement over my business." In another she prays, "Any power, spirit or personality that has fired arrows of evil label or mark into my life, receive double disgrace."[116] Another prayer says, "Holy Ghost fire, search through the second heaven, the earth and under the earth and release every caged star and destiny in my family, in the name of Jesus."[117] These and other prayers make it clear that for these Africans, health, business, relationships, and other aspects of life are all to do with events in the spiritual realm.

From this follows the idea of the Holy Spirit as an actor in that realm. In the prayers of Stella Adekunle, there is the image of Holy Spirit as a fire-bearing figure ready to throw "consuming fire" at villains in the spirit world. For example, she recommends this prayer to those having problems: "You mountain of problems from evil pronouncements by witch doctors and white garment herbalists melt now, by the fire of Holy Ghost."[118] In another she writes: "Every local power or demonic forces contending with the power and anointing of God in my life, dry up and die by Holy Ghost fire." The same sense of the Holy Spirit as an active agent in the spirit realm comes through in the prayers of Sanusi, such as when he prays: "Holy Spirit, expose every power using the covering of darkness to work against me in the name of Jesus," and Gilbert Deya, when he says, "I destroy every assignment of the witches from East to West and from South to North, by the blood of Jesus.[119] Let all their evil assignments planned against me be confused and terminated by the Holy Spirit."

Hence, available literature shows that the essentially spiritual cosmology I found at Mount Zion which is foundational to their concept of the Holy Spirit is shared by other African Pentecostals in both Africa and Britain and also by the African Initiated Churches. The likelihood is that this has its origin in their African traditional worldview but has been continuously reinforced by the Bible, which has a similar cosmology.[120]

Pentecostal literature suggests that something similar to the cosmology I found among the members of Mount Zion which sees the world as a spiritual theatre can be found in the wider Pentecostal movement. It has been noted, for example, that Pentecostals interpret their experience in the context of the

---

[113] Deya, *Dangerous Prayers to Break Satan's Force*, 66.
[114] Deya, *Dangerous Prayers to Break Satan's Force*, 67.
[115] Adekunle, *Crossing your Jordan*, 130.
[116] Adekunle, *Crossing your Jordan*, 130.
[117] Adekunle, *Crossing your Jordan*, 118.
[118] Adekunle, *Crossing your Jordan*, 127.
[119] Sanusi, *Goliath Killing Prayers*, 22; Deya, *Dangerous Prayers*, 56.
[120] See for example, Anderson, *Moya*, 120-21.

"strange new world of the Bible".[121] As C.H. Kraft remarks: "Scripture clearly portrays human life as lived in a context of continual warfare between the kingdom of God and the kingdom of Satan."[122] Kraft's examples include Paul's statement that the Christian struggle is not against flesh and blood, but "against the spiritual forces of evil in the heavenly realms", the temptation in the Garden of Eden (Gen. 3) and Yahweh's conflicts with the gods of Israel's neighbours, such as Baal, Ashteroth and Chemosh. Kraft goes on to describe the categories of spirits and warfare constantly raging in the world. There are "ground-level warfare" and "cosmic-level warfare". The cosmic level warfare involves dealing with territorial spirits, institutional spirits, special-function spirits overseeing prostitution, abortion, etc., object-spirits assigned to buildings and ancestral spirits.[123]

The literature thus shows that the well-developed cosmology found at Mount Zion is a common feature among African Pentecostals and the African Initiated Churches. A comparable cosmology can also be discerned from the literature of the wider Pentecostal movement. This coherence between the African and Pentecostal cosmology means that in a church like Mount Zion, the two sources will be mutually reinforcing each other.

A spirit-leaning anthropology

At Mount Zion the concept of a person had both a physical and a spiritual dimension, but tended to give priority to the latter. This is, however, different in a number respects, according to available literature, from how Africans traditionally understand a human being. Mbiti gives the assessment that Africans traditionally think of a human being as integral to his or her community.[124] "In traditional life, the individual does not and cannot exist alone except corporately. He owes his existence to other people, including those of past generations and his contemporaries. He is simply part of the whole."[125] But this is not simply a practical issue for Mbiti has pointed out that the very awareness of the individual of his or her existence is mediated through the community:

Only in terms of other people does the individual become conscious of his own being, his duties, his privileges and responsibilities towards himself and towards

[121] F.D. Macchia, "Theology, Pentecostal" in Stanley M. Burgess and Edward M. van der Maas (eds), *The New International Dictionary of Pentecostal and Charismatic Movements* (Grand Rapids: Zondervan, 2003), 1204.

[122] C.H. Kraft, "Spiritual Warfare" in Stanley M. Burgess and Edward M. van der Maas, (eds), *The New International Dictionary of Pentecostal and Charismatic Movements*. (Grand Rapids: Zondervan, 2003), 1091.

[123] Kraft, "Spiritual Warfare," 1095.

[124] J. Mbiti, *African Religions and Philosophy* (Oxford: Heinemann, 1990).

[125] Mbiti, *African Religions and Philosophy*, 106.

other people. . . . The individual can only say: "I am, because we are; and since we are, therefore I am."[126]

Mbiti describes this relationship between the individual and his or her community as "a cardinal point in the understanding of the African view of man" and as a relationship that is "very religious" because of the sense in which the individual is created by his community.[127] Because, as Mbiti also notes, the community in Africa includes recently dead relatives, this bond between the person and their community is spiritual in essence.

A related point is made by Turner who explores the Church of the Lord's understanding of what a human being is from the perspective of their pursuit for personal spiritual development.[128] He notes that there is, on one hand, the "recognition of the dignity and splendid potential of man" and, on the other hand, "many frustrations to human development" which can be found in the man himself and in the world around him.[129] He also comments that these forces acting against the realisation of man's potential were seen to be more external than internal to the human being, even though both aspects are present. For example, the church's hymns often present man as a sinner and one of their leaders spoke of "the inner evil spirit in man" and of a "spiritual conscience" that is in line with God's will.[130] However, Turner finds the development of their thoughts in this "intensive" direction (that is, inward to human beings) rather restricted.[131] This might be traced to the African view of the universe which Turner describes as "an integrated view of life, in which nature, man, and the spiritual world form a total community".

Rufus Burrow's study shows that even when Africans think along this "intensive" direction, the emphasis remains on the unity of the parts. In the article "Personalism and Afrikan Traditional Thought",[132] Burrow observes that in the West African cultural tradition "the human person is a physico-spiritual being. The person is not *either* body *or* spirit in human form, but both at once: an embodied self, a body in which God has implanted the life force."[133] The person's physical side links them to their ancestry, whereas the spiritual side "is thought to be most like God."[134] He notes that the soul (or spirit) and the body "are not one and the same, although they are integrally connected".[135] In that

---

[126] Mbiti, *African Religions and Philosophy*, 106
[127] Mbiti, *African Religions and Philosophy*, 106
[128] Turner, *African Independent Church*.
[129] Turner, *African Independent Church*, 359.
[130] Turner, *African Independent Church*, 359.
[131] Turner, *African Independent Church*, 357.
[132] R. Burrow, "Personalism and Afrikan Traditional Thought," *Encounter* 61.3 (Summer, 2000), 321-48.
[133] Burrow, "Personalism," 328.
[134] Burrow, "Personalism," 328.
[135] Burrow, "Personalism," 329.

sense, African traditional thought recognises a "body-mind" dualism.[136] But the emphasis is on the unity: "The whole person — body and mind — is sacred. It is not just the mental or spiritual aspect of the person that is worthy of this designation. . . . African traditional culture was always clear about this."[137]

Similarly, J. Kwabena Asamoah-Gyadu has noted that the Sunsum Sore, the collective name for Ghanaian African Initiated Churches, has retained this Akan anthropology in which the components that make up a person are seen as interrelated.[138] They avoided the fragmentation of body, mind and spirit associated with Western thought. This interrelationship means that "Africans view life in holistic terms with 'body and spirit', the 'sacred and secular' and the 'psychological and theological' being held together as one whole".[139] For the Sunsum Sore it yields dividends for their ministry. It means that they can "unite body, mind and spirit in intense Spirit-led congregational prayers, prophecy, healing and communication with and from the divine".[140] Asamoah-Gyadu points out that it is from this unity of body, soul and spirit that Sunsum Sore gets its name, because for them the manifestation of the Spirit of God through bodily movement was not abnormal.[141] Rather, "they are visible signs of God's presence among his people".[142]

The present study's review of the work of African Pentecostal ministers shows a movement away from key aspects of these African ideas. Among Pentecostals in the African continent the Kenyan Pentecostal minister, Paul Nyamu writes that human beings have been made in the image of God to have a triune nature, which consists of spirit, soul and body.[143] He illustrates this with three concentric circles which have the "Spirit" as the innermost circle, the "soul" as the middle circle and the "physical body" as the outermost circle.[144] Nyamu also describes the "spirit of man" as made of three components, namely, intuition, worship and conscience:

> These three components are revived to activity when one is born again. It is through these three faculties that the Holy Spirit works in the life of a believer. Before one is born again, the spirit is dead, and therefore he cannot discern the will of God (he cannot receive inspiration), he cannot worship God, and his conscience is insensitive to his sinful way of living and thinking.[145]

---

[136] Burrow, "Personalism," 329.
[137] Burrow, "Personalism," 328.
[138] Asamoah-Gyadu, *African Charismatics*, 2005.
[139] Asamoah-Gyadu, *African Charismatics*, 47. See also, Anderson, *Moya*, 15
[140] Asamoah-Gyadu, *African Charismatics*, 47.
[141] Asamoah-Gyadu, *African Charismatics*, 48.
[142] Asamoah-Gyadu, *African Charismatics*, 48.
[143] P.K. Nyamu, *The Holy Spirit: His Baptism* (Nairobi: International Bible Society, 1984).
[144] Nyamu, *The Holy Spirit*, 79.
[145] Nyamu, *The Holy Spirit*, 80.

During that time the "flesh" which is wicked and depraved is in control. But once one is born again "a struggle for dominance starts" between the spirit "now made alive by the Holy Spirit" and the flesh.[146] Hence, one finds in the writings of Paul Nyamu the same kind of prioritising of the spiritual aspects of a human being I found at Mount Zion and the relating of those spiritual aspects to the work of the Holy Spirit.

Similar ideas can be found among Pentecostals in Britain. Matthew Ashimolowo in *Divine Understanding*[147] gave this description of what happens when a person becomes born again:

When you were not born again, you are body first, then soul, then spirit. The day you got born again, it was reversed. You are now spirit, soul and body. So God the Spirit wants to talk to the spirit called Matthew Ashimolowo. I'm a spirit living in a body. This body is my vehicle. That is why if I spend more money on this body and less on my spirit then my economy is misplaced. If my spirit listens to God the Spirit then we are together. We are in connection. We are connecting. Praise God! Then I am being led by him.

He went on to describe how this connection between the Holy Spirit and the human spirit could produce good results through "sanctified imagination":

You can receive positive images in your spirit by the Holy Spirit. A sanctified imagination leads to invention. Somebody saw this microphone in their spirit. Somebody saw this speaker in their spirit. The shoe on your feet was somebody's imagination. If the man who is not born again can imagine good things how much more you . . . so good images in your spirit is one of the signals of the Holy Spirit.[148]

He also asserted that the human spirit becomes more sensitive to the Holy Spirit when a Christian learns to speak in tongues. He encouraged them, therefore, to learn to speak in tongues because in so doing, they would be "sharpening" their spirit to know how to hear God and how to recognize the voice of God.[149]

Ebianga Frank-Briggs gives this description of hearing the Holy Spirit:

Man is a spirit, living in a body and having a soul. This is explicitly clear in 1 Thessalonians 5: 23. As a new creature, the Holy Spirit dwells in us (Jn 14: 16, 17), and bears witness with our spirit that we are Sons of God.[150]

[146] Nyamu, *The Holy Spirit*, 80.
[147] Ashimolowo, *Divine Understanding*, 2007, tape 2, side 1.
[148] Ashimolowo, 2007, tape 2, side 1.
[149] Ashimolowo, 2007, tape 2, side 1
[150] E. Frank-Briggs, *Unbreakable Laws of Father* (London: Emmanuel House, 2001), 119.

Albert Odulele, a London-based minister, writes along similar lines. He explains that humankind is spirit, soul and body.[151] He also reflects the priority which the spirit has:

> Unlike the body, the spirit man is not created from the ground, gravel or gaseous things, it comes directly from GOD...The spirit-man is the real you, it is eternal in nature and without "him" the body remains lifeless just like Adam was before the breath of life.[152]

Human spirit, he points out, lives for all eternity:

> Life and death apply to the spirit-man in terms of separation from or re-union with God and not cessation of existence. When the physical body dies, the spirit-man continues to exist in a wholly different state.[153]

According to Odulele, when a person is "saved", it is the spirit-man that becomes "born again" not the body or the soul.[154] It is also the spirit-man that "enables a real perception of the spirit realm" and "allows a proper relationship with God".[155]

The prayers of Adekunle, Sanusi and Deya show how this anthropology opens the door for Pneumatology to develop in a particular direction. For example, the conception of a human being as having spiritual aspects means he or she becomes a being the Holy Spirit can reside in and transform, even fighting from within to remove sin and sinful tendencies. In her prayers, Adekunle writes, "I purge the Adamic nature in me with the blood of Jesus and by the Holy Ghost fire . . ." and, "Holy Ghost thunder, strike down every stronghold of sin in my life and lift up the pillar of righteousness . . ." and, also, "Sword of the Spirit, cut off every root of worldly pleasure in me and fill me with your spirit . . ."[156] Sanusi prays: "Holy Spirit, keep my heart and mind at perfect peace . . ." and "Father, let the Holy Spirit be permanently resident in me . . ."[157] Similarly, Deya prays: "I destroy the power of the spirit of the devil that influences me to do bad things . . . let the Holy Spirit confuse them."[158]

Something similar can be seen in wider Pentecostalism, such as in the writing of the well-known white-American Pentecostal, Kenneth Hagin. Hagin writes, "you *are* a spirit; you *have* a soul; you *live in* a body . . . Remember, your body is *not* the real you; your *spirit* is the real you."[159] He observes the danger the body, the "outward man", poses to the Christian as it "always want

---

[151] A. Odulele, *Prosperity of the Soul* (London: OVMC, 2007), 23.

[152] Odulele, *Prosperity of the Soul*, 27.

[153] Odulele, *Understanding God's Voice*, 28.

[154] Odulele, *Understanding God's Voice*, 29.

[155] Odulele, *Understanding God's Voice*, 29.

[156] Adekunle, *Crossing your Jordan*, 198, 210.

[157] Sanusi, *Goliath Killing Prayers*, 22.

[158] Deya, *Dangerous Prayers*, 67.

[159] K. Hagin, *Listen to your heart* (Tulsa: Rhema Bible Church, 1992), 21.

to fulfill the desires of the flesh".[160] So Hagin warns: "If you – the spirit man on the inside – don't control your body by presenting it as a sacrifice to God, your body will begin to control you.[161] And . . . you will reap corruption and cause great havoc in your life (Gal. 6:8)." Just as was seen with the African Pentecostals, Hagin also shows the Pneumatological concerns underlying this anthropology. "A Christian who lives only in the natural realm according to his physical sense will not be able to accurately listen to his heart and follow the Holy Spirit's leading."[162] Other Pentecostal preachers write in similar vein. Myles Munroe notes that "Human beings are essentially spiritual beings who live in physical bodies to carry out their governing responsibilities in the material world of the colony of earth."[163] And Benny Hinn points out that unlike human who value "outward appearance" God works to strengthen the "inner man" and to give "spiritual strength".[164]

The evidence thus shows that on this issue African Pentecostals have moved away from African traditional thinking in two important respects. Whereas African traditional thinking and some of the AICs see a human being in terms of his community and environment, the African Pentecostals are much more inward focused in their thinking. Secondly, whereas the traditional African thought and the theology of the AICs reviewed emphasised the unity of the components of a human being, contemporary African Pentecostal ministers appear to be emphasising the distinctiveness of these components and, particularly, the superiority of the spiritual dimension to the physical dimension. On this issue, the African Pentecostals are closer to some areas of the wider Pentecostal movement than to African thought.

Young people, secularism and postmodernity

It was observed at Mount Zion that the young people did not appear to have adopted a new understanding of the Holy Spirit. In other words, their more secular environment does not appear to have significantly changed their pneumatological ideas from those of the older generation. A number of factors could be responsible for this. The first is that studies of African Christianity have shown young people to be a very religious subset of society, often at the centre of new religious movements. Kalu observes the central part played by young people in different parts of Africa in spreading Charismatic Christianity in the continent. He writes:

> Most parts of Africa witnessed the sudden surge of young puritan preachers in the 1970s, who signified a new cycle of revivalism that swept through the continent in

---

[160] Hagin, *Listen to your heart*, 23.
[161] Hagin, *Listen to your heart*, 23.
[162] Hagin, *Listen to your heart*, 21.
[163] M. Munroe, *The Most Important Person on Earth: The Holy Spirit, Governor of the Kingdom* (Nassau: Bahamas Faith Ministries International, 2007), 51.
[164] B. Hinn, *Welcome Holy Spirit* (Lagos: Thomas Nelson, 1997), 191.

the post independence period, bringing with them a religious tradition whose face has changed drastically in every decade and whose full import is still in the making.[165]

In Malawi, young boys and girls called "aliliki" (i.e. preachers) started holding large revival meetings which attracted crowds of people. They advocated a very moral lifestyle and their meeting were characterised by excitement and emotionalism.[166]

In Nigeria similar phenomenon were taking place, first in the secondary schools and later in the universities, particularly through the work of the Scripture Union. As the university students were sent around the country as part of a national service programme, they spread this Charismatic Christianity to the country, beyond their campuses. These young people organised in several different groups but "cooperated under the fire of the Holy Spirit".[167] Hence Kalu notes that "a key aspect in the revival is the participation of university students".[168] In general, he points out that the youth in both secondary schools and universities "created a new culture of Pentecostalism in which the leadership was more highly educated than in earlier pneumatic challenges by the Aladura or the prophetic movement".[169] Despite their education, they retained the "fluid dynamism" of a "spirit-driven movement" and "deconstructed the Western model of the mission churches".[170]

Similarly, Asamoah-Gyadu has noted how youth gospel music manifested in Ghana as part of the pneumatic character of Ghanaian Christianity[171]. These groups, such as the Joyful Way Incorporated, themselves became vehicles for the spread of Charismatic Christianity.

There are testimonies of the spontaneous outbreak of Holy Spirit phenomena, that is, speaking in tongues, weeping, loud cries, and healing, in schools where groups like JWI ministered.[172]

Asamoah-Gyadu notes that the Joyful Way Incorporated also rejected the strict ethical ideas of the evangelical church, "particularly its aversion to fashion and association of modern musical instruments with profanity and worldliness".[173]

A second factor possibly lying behind our observation at Mount Zion is that many young people of African origin still retain the worldview, including the cosmology and the anthropology of their African parents. This is even more

---

[165] Kalu, *African Pentecostalism*, 88.

[166] Kalu, *African Pentecostalism*, 87.

[167] Kalu, *African Pentecostalism*, 89.

[168] Kalu, *African Pentecostalism*, 90.

[169] Kalu, *African Pentecostalism*, 93.

[170] Kalu, *African Pentecostalism*, 93.

[171] Asamoah-Gyadu, *African Charismatics*, 2005.

[172] Asamoah-Gyadu, *African Charismatics*, 107.

[173] Asamoah-Gyadu, *African Charismatics*, 107.

likely if they have not lived in this country for many years. It is noteworthy that out of the three young people I interviewed, two of them had only been in the country for less than ten years. Even if a more secular, more modern way of thinking takes over in their outlook, this is unlikely to happen within ten years. As I noted in 2007, based on a survey of fifty Africans living in London, it takes a period of about 20 years for a significant change to occur in the worldview of African immigrants from an African to a Western one. A change in worldview would produce a corresponding change in Pneumatology.[174]

Thirdly, even though there exists an age group ranging from late teens to late thirties who are largely missing in Western churches, many young people buck this trend.[175] W. Kay and L. Francis discuss how many young people in the United Kingdom live out the tenets of organised religion in the face of the pressures of work and adulthood.[176] They point out that much of the adult world in Western countries is characterised by the secular rather than the religious and the influence of the church has waned considerably. Yet many young people uphold that pattern. For example, Youth With A Mission (YWAM) is a well-known organization which uses young people to evangelize people around the world. Founded by a young college student living in California, it now has branches around the world and several thousand young enthusiastic volunteers.[177] The young people at Mount Zion may be part of this trend.

Fourthly, apart from the effect of secularism in reducing the influence of religion, Postmodernity also has an effect on Christianity in the Western world. On the one hand, Postmodernity demands that all religious accounts, including Christianity, relinquish their claim to transcendent, unique truth.[178] As a result, Postmodernity is characterised by much fragmentation. As Sampson writes, "Incredulity towards metanarratives and radical egalitarianism of representation in postmodernity have combined to prevent any one tradition or ideology from being granted priority in unifying all others."[179] As this is the world in which the young people are growing up, with the waning of the authority of traditional institutions, it is not surprising that many of them have drifted from the church. Yet, on the other hand, the postmodern mood is more open than modernity was to faith and religious experience. The result is that for many people,

[174] Chigor Chike, *African Christianity in Britain* (Milton Keynes: Author House, 2007), 66.
[175] R. Martinson, "Spiritual but not religious: Reaching an invisible generation," *Currents in Theology and Mission* 29.5 (2002), 328.
[176] W. Kay, and L. Francis, *Drift from the Churches* (Cardiff: University of Wales Press, 1996).
[177] E.B. Robinson, "Youth With A Mission" in Stanley M. Burgess and Edward M. van der Maas (eds), *The New International Dictionary of Pentecostal and Charismatic Movements* (Grand Rapids: Zondervan, 2003), 1223.
[178] P. Sampson, "The Rise of Postmodernity" in Philip Sampson, Vinay Samuel and Chris Sugden (eds), *Faith and Modernity* (Oxford: Regnum, 1994), 38.
[179] Sampson, "The Rise of Postmodernity," 41.

disenchantment with organised religion does not necessarily mean a lack of interest in the spiritual.

All this means that there is a complex web of factors underlying what was observed about the young people at Mount Zion. The fact that among the young people in that church are both first and second generation immigrants further complicates the picture. While the first generation immigrants would most likely be operating in the African worldview they were formed in, the second generation would include those who, like YWAM and other young Christians in the West, are bucking the trend of secularism and the antagonistic aspect of postmodernity. Further studies would be needed to disentangle these factors and weigh their relative effects.

Empowerment by the Holy Spirit

Under this theme of empowerment three pattern theories will be discussed: 1) The link between the Holy Spirit and the empowerment of individual members, 2) The belief that the church's ministers are inspired (or empowered) by the Holy Spirit and 3) The difference in the emphasis between men and women in the way they understand the Holy Spirit.

Empowerment of individuals

The awareness that evil spiritual forces abound all around them means that for many Africans religion is about searching for and aligning with more powerful forces to protect them. Anderson writes, "To the African, one's life, one's very existence – in other words, one's being – is inextricably tied up with one's power. To live is to have power; to be sick or to die is to have less of it."[180] Anderson remarks that in traditional African societies people who have problems take them to traditional diviners who not only have the power to discern the source of the problem but also the means to counteract it.[181] But in the African Initiated Churches people appeal to the Holy Spirit.[182] The African Initiated Churches, he notes, "are founded on the doctrine of the Holy Spirit," because, "the genuine power of the Holy Spirit can effectively meet existential needs in the African spirit world".[183]

Omoyajowo's study of the Cherubim and Seraphim is one example of an AIC where the Holy Spirit is seen in this way. Omoyajowo points out that the church believed that "through the activities of the Holy Spirit the true believer can do anything".[184] He gives the following quotation from the constitution of the Cherubim and Seraphim: "There is no limit to the usefulness of the one who makes room for the working of the Holy Spirit of God upon his heart and lives

---

[180] Anderson, *Moya,*, 64.
[181] Anderson, *Moya,*, 60.
[182] Anderson, *Moya,*, 69.
[183] Anderson, *Moya,*, 69.
[184] Omoyajowo, *Cherubim and Seraphim*, 98.

a life wholly consecrated to God."[185] Hence the Cherubim and Seraphim believe the Holy Spirit not only regenerates and sanctifies, but also, "illuminates, empowers, protects, works wonders and gives guidance" to the believer. He gives the believer "power to lead a holy life and to conquer sin".[186] The power of the Holy Spirit is therefore seen as the "fundamental principle of general efficacy".[187] Another example from an AIC is Turner's study of the Church of the Lord. Turner observes that to the church, "the main work of the Spirit is to guide and empower, and so to deliver individuals from all evils".[188]

Kalu's exploration of this power concept in African Christianity relates it to the continent's socio-politics. For example, he saw the African religious movements of the early twentieth century as part of the African response to European economic and political abuse and the wave of African churches formed after World War 2 as constituting "the second African challenge to colonial Christianity".[189] Regarding Pentecostalism, he connects its spread in Africa to political independence:

> I conclude that a charismatic wind blew through the African continent in the postindependence period that first hit the youth and women, and later overawed the resistance of the mainline churches. In each country, certain socio-economic and political factors determined the pattern of the early concerns. But the various strands connected across national boundaries.[190]

Hence, Kalu sees African Pentecostalism as "embodying Africans' quest for power and identity through religion."[191]

Regarding African immigrants in Europe, Kalu's analysis follows more or less the same line. He notes, for example, that these African immigrants "hold to the spiritual worldview of the primal cultures".[192] He also points out that many of the immigrants see the African churches they belong to as "cultural refuges where they can transmit their indigenous cultures and values to their children".[193] Apart from this functional dimension, Kalu is keen to point out the spiritual dimension. The religious implication of their retention of the African worldview is that these immigrants still give the concept of power a central place in their Christian faith. Kalu observes that many African ministers travel around the world to perform deliverance rites for African immigrants. "Such powerful prayers," he explains, "are supposed to open the gates of 'hard'

---

[185] Omoyajowo, *Cherubim and Seraphim*, 98.
[186] Omoyajowo, *Cherubim and Seraphim*, 98.
[187] Omoyajowo, *Cherubim and Seraphim*, 10.
[188] Turner, *African Independent Church*, 340.
[189] Kalu, *African Pentecostalism*, x.
[190] Kalu, *African Pentecostalism*, xi
[191] Kalu, *African Pentecostalism*, 4; Harris, *Yoruba in Diaspora*, 10. Githieya, "The Church of the Holy Spirit," 237; Asamoah-Gyadu, *African Charismatics*, 135.
[192] Kalu, *African Pentecostalism*, 288.
[193] Kalu, *African Pentecostalism*, 287.

nations for the benefit of the immigrants."[194] Hence, "Powerful healers and prayer warriors attract large numbers of votaries."[195]

This study's review of recent writings by African Pentecostal ministers shows that in both Africa and in Britain, these ministers are emphasising the role of the Holy Spirit to empower the believer. Enoch Adeboye notes that "the Holy Spirit is referred to as the power of the Highest.[196] He has all powers including the powers of the Most High." Through the Holy Spirit the believer can have power to construct or destroy.[197] "When We are filled with the Holy Spirit, whatever decree we make shall be established".[198] Adeboye recounts the episode in Luke 5:1-11, where Peter, following Jesus' instruction, caught much fish. He says that from that incident it took just one encounter between the Holy Spirit and Peter for Peter's life to be transformed. He makes the following inference:

> The moment the Holy Spirit wants to come into your life, He will come suddenly. The change that will transform you from a beggar to a millionaire will come suddenly. The change that will transform you from somebody that people have been praying for to somebody who will wave his hands and the lame will walk will come suddenly.[199]

Similar ideas can be seen among British based ministers. Gilbert Deya, a Kenyan-born minister based in the UK gave this description of an incident at one of his church gatherings:

> The devil worshippers sent a woman to disrupt our meeting. It was very unfortunate for her because there was too much anointing in the meeting. She was slain to the ground by the Holy Spirit. The Holy Spirit made her disclose all their secrets. She confessed that she came to create confusion in the meeting.[200]

He gave more details of the incident:

> When the Holy Ghost appeared, I raised my hand and she as well as the congregation fell to the ground and she could not get up. The demon in her spoke, saying they were going to kill her because she allowed herself to be thrown down by the anointing: the anointing had taken their powers and they could not carry out their mission. . . . I released more fire of the Holy Ghost on her and the demons kept manifesting.[201]

---

[194] Kalu, *African Pentecostalism*, 288.
[195] Kalu, *African Pentecostalism*, 288.
[196] Adeboye, *God the Holy Spirit*, 10.
[197] Adeboye, *God the Holy Spirit*, 25.
[198] Adeboye, *God the Holy Spirit*, 26.
[199] E. Adeboye, *Holy Spirit in the Life of Peter* (Lagos: Christ the Redeemer's Ministries, 1999), 105.
[200] G. Deya, *The Stronghold of Generational Curses* (Eastbourne: Stock, 2003), 73.
[201] Deya, *The Stronghold of Generational Curses*, 73-74.

Odulele explores another dimension of the power of the Holy Spirit. Using Biblical stories about great feats, such as David's slaying of Goliath (1 Sam. 17), Joshua's victories in the promised land (e.g. Josh. 5 and 8), and Elijah's triumph over the prophets of Baal (1 Kgs 18), he points out that hearing God comes from being sensitive to the leading of the Holy Spirit. It also has many benefits:

> The ability to constantly hear God is an unparalleled asset of life. It will transform your ministry and impact your marriage irrevocably. Your finances, business and career will receive a "turbo-injected" boost and zoom ahead unhindered and unrestrained. The present struggles become history, and your future aspirations will become realities.[202]

These are just a few examples of what is a common feature of African Christianity in Britain, namely, the emphasis of the powerful acts of God often carried out by the Holy Spirit.

Kärkkäinen shows that the emphasis on empowerment by the Holy Spirit that I found is not exclusive to African Christians but can be seen among Pentecostals in general. He points out that "Pentecostal/Charismatic approaches emphasize empowerment through the Spirit for witnessing and service."[203] This emphasis is integral to their belief that there has not been a cessation of spiritual gifts since the early church, as some denominations tend to argue; rather, the Holy Spirit continues to perform miraculous acts in the world today. He also points out that such emphasis on power goes back to the New Testament and the early church. Hence, he writes:

> The transforming power of the Spirit is evident at the beginning of the history of the Christian church. Actually, the birth of Christianity at Pentecost is a dramatic work of the Spirit: Three thousand repent, and Charismatic elements are visible.[204]

P.J. Grabe makes the same point:

> Contrary to classical Protestantism, which argues that the charismata and "supernatural gifts of the Spirit" ceased with the close of the apostolic era, Pentecostals believe that the Pentecostal "endowment with power" is available to all generations.[205]

He also takes a similar line on the Biblical root of this belief, stating that Pentecostals have been convinced that the focus on the power of God "uncovers a neglected theme in the Scriptures".[206] For him, "this biblical focus

---

[202] Odulele, *Understanding God's Voice*, 15.
[203] Kärkkäinen, *Pneumatology*, 92.
[204] Kärkkäinen, *Pneumatology*, 91.
[205] P.J. Grabe, "The Pentecostal Discovery of the New Testament Theme of God's Power and Its Relevance to the African Context," *Pneuma* 24.2 (Fall, 2002), 238.
[206] Grabe, "The Pentecostal Discovery," 225.

on the power of God" is one of the main attractive aspects of Pentecostalism."[207]

I can conclude from this that the belief at Mount Zion that the Holy Spirit empowers the church members is shared with African Pentecostals in Britain, the African Initiated Churches and the wider Pentecostal movement.

Empowerment of ministry

Within Mount Zion it was clearly important to the members that their ministers were working under the inspiration of the Holy Spirit. A similar phenomenon can be found in the African Initiated Churches in Africa. J.A. Omoyajowo describes how in the Cherubim and Seraphim the Holy Spirit calls and enables the leaders of the church by giving them special gifts.[208] He observes that many leaders of the Cherubim and Seraphim claim that they received their "call" in a dream.[209] One of the ministers, Peter Aluko, dreamt of a little man telling him, forcefully, "I have been sent to arrest you." He became very ill from that experience, and when he recovered, he joined the church.[210] It was customary for the church ministers to get a revelation through a vision or by falling into a trance.[211] Prophecy, whereby people predict what will happen in the future, was also a regular part of church life. Omoyajowo points out that as a church, they laid much emphasis on the gifts of the Spirit and they believed that "as the true worshippers of God, they have been endowed with all the spiritual blessings made manifest on the Day of Pentecost".[212] The church, however, believed that the Holy Spirit gave these gifts not to every member but to "spiritual workers", such as "visioners" and prophets:

> These offices are not among those to be filled by election or promotion. As spiritual offices, it is the Holy Spirit who calls people into them. Those who are called are then ordained and they are worthy of much reverence and honor.[213]

Asamoah-Gyadu's study also shows that within the Sunsum Sore a high priority is given to the idea that the churches ministers were inspired by the Holy Spirit[214]. Asamoah-Gyadu explains that what made the Sunsum Sore different when they appeared on the Ghanaian religious landscape dominated by Western founded mission churches "was the active expression given to religious experiences explained in terms of the activity of the Holy Spirit".[215] He points out that the religious transformation of one of the ministers, William

[207] Grabe, "The Pentecostal Discovery," 225.
[208] Omoyajowo, *Cherubim and Seraphim.*
[209] Omoyajowo, *Cherubim and Seraphim*, 132.
[210] Omoyajowo, *Cherubim and Seraphim*, 132.
[211] Omoyajowo, *Cherubim and Seraphim*, 128.
[212] Omoyajowo, *Cherubim and Seraphim*, 127.
[213] Omoyajowo, *Cherubim and Seraphim*, 128.
[214] Asamoah-Gyadu, *African Charismatics*, 2005.
[215] Asamoah-Gyadu, *African Charismatics*, 44.

Egyanka Appiah of the Musama Disco Christo Church, manifested itself in speaking in tongues, vigils of intense prayer, dreams and visions. The Sunsum Sore, in general, believe that "The Spirit among others reveal the will of God and fills men and women with new powers of prophecy, utterance, prayer and healing."[216]

Asamoah-Gyadu further observes the same belief of Holy Spirit inspired ministry in a later Charismatic movement, the Charismatic Ministries.[217] These are church organisations that emerged from the mid-1970s after the "Pentecostalisation" of existing conservative evangelical church and parachurch bodies.[218] Asamoah-Gyadu observes that these Charismatic Ministries posed a challenge to the traditional concept of ministry held by existing churches. They emphasized inspiration by the Holy Spirit against ordination. To them, "the people God has raised as his 'end-time militia' are not trained specialists like priests but ordinary men and women who through their experience of God's Spirit share in the work of ministry".[219] There was a "democratisation of ministry" and a "delegitimatisation" of sacred places, objects or person.[220]

Hermione Harris suggests that this way of understanding ministry has been carried to Europe by migrating members of the African Initiated Churches. Harris notes that the Cherubim and Seraphim's belief that spiritual and organisational authority was not the prerogative of ministers or priests, but could be achieved by members persists in Diaspora.[221] They had the mantra, "every member a priest" and congregational participation in worship was encouraged. The view in the older denominations that the minister or priest was privileged with regards to communicating with God as the person who conveys God's sacramental grace is jettisoned. Instead, they assert that every lay individual can communicate with God directly, bypassing any intermediaries. They believed that every member of their church has access to the power of the Holy Spirit.[222]

A similar relationship can also be found in the work of Pentecostals in Africa. Kwame and Beatrice Owusu-Ansah write: "The church today, above everything else needs to operate in the power and anointing of the Holy Spirit to bring tremendous success and increase in the kingdom of God."[223] They make this observation:

---

[216] Asamoah-Gyadu, *African Charismatics*, 46.
[217] Asamoah-Gyadu, *African Charismatics*, 2005.
[218] Asamoah-Gyadu, *African Charismatics*, 108.
[219] Asamoah-Gyadu, *African Charismatics*, 127.
[220] Asamoah-Gyadu, *African Charismatics*, 127.
[221] Harris, *Yoruba in Diaspora*, 50.
[222] Harris, *Yoruba in Diaspora*, 50.
[223] K. Owusu-Ansah and B. Owusu-Ansah, *The Secrets of the Anointing that Breaks Every Yoke* (Kumasi: Great Expectations Worship Centre, 2003), 29.

A leader's success in the ministry depends mainly on the anointing on his life. Without the anointing, a leader can't bring forth fruit that endures to eternity. Without it a minister will be dead, without any life at all.[224]

They warn that "attending theological seminaries and colleges, and obtaining many degrees does not automatically bring the anointing in the same way;" nor do having a great preaching style, gaining good ecclesiastical positions, such as becoming a bishop or an archbishop, good music and dancing, effective planning or having a strong, tall physique.[225] The anointing comes only from the Holy Spirit. It is "the overflowing of the power of the Holy Spirit in a person who is consecrated or set apart for God".[226]

A similar view is found among the British based African Pentecostal Church ministers. Lawrence Tetteh, the Ghana-born minister based in London, describes "anointing" as the power God bestows on Christians in order that they might do his work:

I have seen this power manifest at meetings and transform lives, with the sick receiving their healing and people being set free from bondage. Many receive their salvation, and other miraculous breakthroughs occur at these meetings. It is this source of power that I owe my life to, and I am grateful to the Lord for His Spirit upon me.[227]

For Tetteh, the anointing is a sign of the presence of the Holy Spirit. It means that "God is empowering us with His Spirit for his work."[228]

Tetteh argues that there are different levels and different types of anointing. He described once when a woman was miraculously healed at an event at which he was ministering. "As I was ministering, the Holy Spirit began to speak to me," he says.[229] The Spirit told him to sing the song "Great Is Thy Faithfulness, O God My Father".[230] When he did and laid hands on the woman, she was healed. Regarding this, Tetteh writes that God

released an appropriate level of anointing on His servant at the right place and at the right time to break a certain yoke and set individuals that are ready free. The Lord uses us through the Holy Spirit's anointing to accomplish His tasks. It is not by our natural ability or might that these great feats are happening.[231]

[224] Owusu-Ansah and Owusu-Ansah, *The Secrets*, 29.
[225] Owusu-Ansah and Owusu-Ansah, *The Secrets*, 29, 31.
[226] Owusu-Ansah and Owusu-Ansah, *The Secrets*, 10.
[227] Tetteh, *Benefits of the Anointing*, 9.
[228] Tetteh, *Benefits of the Anointing*, 14.
[229] Tetteh, *Benefits of the Anointing*, 32.
[230] Tetteh, *Benefits of the Anointing*, 9.
[231] Tetteh, *Benefits of the Anointing*, 33.

The level or type of anointing one receives depends "on the level of one's calling".[232] Each level has its "divine purpose" for one's life and the "uniqueness" of that calling. In general, anointing helps Christians to see the things of the Spirit; it destroys spiritual "yokes" in the lives of the individual; it backs up the word of God that a person speaks; and it brings "inner changes" to Christians, making them bear "fruits of the Spirit".[233] He also asserts that the anointing of the Holy Spirit is working in the world today.[234]

Pentecostals also, in general, believe in the empowerment of ministries. Anderson, writing about mission and evangelism among early Pentecostals, states that "these have always issued from their strong Pneumatology" because "their efforts were grounded in the conviction that the Holy Spirit was the motivating power behind all such activity".[235] Individuals believed the Spirit had called them into mission often through such spiritual forms of revelation as a dream or a vision. They also believed that their spirit baptism had given them the languages of the world. When to their surprise they discovered they could not really speak other people's languages in the field, they were not deterred because "they were not motivated by the tongue they had been given but by the Spirit who was in them".[236] Anderson points out that, until recently, Pentecostals did not have a formal training for their ministers or even a "ministers" class.[237] They believed, rather, that "the Spirit speaks equally to each believer regardless of gender, education or social status", making each Pentecostal believer "potentially a minister".

Hence, the importance attached to the Spirit-empowerment of ministers is common to African Pentecostals, the African Initiated Churches and the wider Pentecostal movement.

Empowerment of women

At Mount Zion I had noticed that the men were more likely to recommend checking out whatever is seen as the work of the Holy Spirit with what is recorded in the Bible. The women, on the other hand, appeared more able to trust what they perceive as the work of the Spirit. Studies of the spiritual life of African women throw light on the subject. Philomena Njeri Mwaura observes that African women have a particular attraction to churches which emphasise the work of the Holy Spirit because such a church "provides women with opportunities in worship, and leadership".[238] Women are finding involvement

---

[232] Tetteh, *Benefits of the Anointing*, 52.
[233] Tetteh, *Benefits of the Anointing*, 41, 46, 75, 12, 11.
[234] Tetteh, *Benefits of the Anointing*, 45.
[235] A. Anderson, *Introduction to Pentecostalism* (Cambridge: Cambridge University Press, 2004), 206.
[236] Anderson, *Introduction to Pentecostalism*, 206.
[237] Anderson, *Introduction to Pentecostalism*, 208.
[238] P.N. Mwaura, "Gender and Power in African Christianity" in Ogbu Kalu (ed.), *African Christianity: An African Story* (Trenton: African World Press, 2007), 367.

in these churches liberating and, in some cases, getting back the same kind of spiritual roles they had in traditional African religion, such as acting as mediums, diviners, prophetesses and priestesses.[239] attributes much of this to how the Holy Spirit operates:

> In the Pentecostal tradition, all Christians have the possibility of receiving the same experience and gifts of the Holy Spirit as described in the New Testament. Women, just like men, therefore experience the Holy Spirit and are endowed with the ability to dream, see visions, prophesy, preach, teach, exorcise and heal.[240]

She points out that by claiming that "God's Spirit empowers them to heal" the women in these churches "join God in a constant struggle against personal and communal oppression".[241]

These points are supported by Asamoah-Gyadu's study of the role of women in Ghanaian prophetic churches, the Sunsum Sore. Under the heading "innovative gender ideology" he claims that similar to what happens in African traditional religion where spirit-possession is rife among women and women dominate the priesthood, the church affirms the spiritual leadership of women.[242] This is even though the church still excludes women from its hierarchy and from decision-making positions. This affirmation of the spiritual role of women is due to the church believing that their prophetic and healing powers come from the Holy Spirit. Asamoah-Gyadu observes that in the Anglican, Presbyterian and Methodist churches women were still largely marginalized:

> In sharp contrast to the marginalisation of women in the miniseries of traditional Western mission and classical Pentecostal churches, the Sunsum Sore initiated a shift in the significant number of women who were possessed by the Holy Spirit eventually ending up as prophetesses in these new independent churches.[243]

Similar observation has been made by Nahashon Ndungu[244] about another African Initiated Church, the Akurinu churches of Kenya. He notes that while men dominate the leadership positions, most of the prophets (or "Anabii") were women. Ndungu points out that the dominance of the leadership positions by men is based on their reading of the Old Testament traditions and of St Paul's teaching on the role of women in 1 Corinthians 14:34-35 and 1 Timothy 2:8-15. But as regards prophecy, they believe this is one of the gifts of the Holy Spirit "which is given to a person irrespective of age or sex".[245] The prophets mediate

[239] Mwaura, "Gender and Power," 367.
[240] Mwaura, "Gender and Power," 367.
[241] Mwaura, "Gender and Power," 377.
[242] Asamoah-Gyadu, *African Charismatics*, 55.
[243] Asamoah-Gyadu, *African Charismatics*, 57
[244] Ndungu, "The role of the Bible" in *The Bible in Africa: Transactions, Trajectories and Trends* (Leiden: Brill, 2000).
[245] Ndungu, "The role of the Bible," 246.

between God and the people in the church and their duties include revealing baptismal names, identifying marriage partners, revealing evils in the church and praying for people.[246]

This picture of restriction by structures, on the one hand, and release through spiritual gift, on the other, coheres with Kalu's analysis. Kalu believes that women's participation in church leadership is being restricted by the patriarchal nature of African societies and churches.[247] Even the African Initiated Churches which appear to have given women some room:

on closer look, despite the fact that female prophetesses and founders exercised ritual and administrative powers, women were still restricted through the enforcement of Levitical prohibitions and gender ideology sourced from indigenous society.[248]

As regards Pentecostals, Kalu identifies four prominent ways African women are seen in Pentecostal church circles. First is the group of the "founders" like Margaret Wangare of Kenya, Dorcas Olayinka in Nigeria and Mercy Yami in Malawi. These are women who started their own churches and exercise a healing and deliverance ministry.[249] The second are the "sisters". These are women who have Charismatic gifts and have been given the opportunity to minister those gifts in the church "without challenging the patriarchal base of the polity".[250] The third group is that of "first ladies", usually the pastors' wives who "serve as a nodal power point for mobilizing and deploying female evangelical power".[251] The women's fourth 'function' is that of "Jezebels". This comes from the idea that many Pentecostal pastors believe that "the enemy attacks a ministry by sending a woman in the guise of an active believer, but whose mission is actually to seduce the leader" and destroy their ministry. According to Kalu, by appealing to demonic attack in this way, the pastor involved can avoid taking personal responsibility for their sexual behaviour.[252]

This categorisation of some women as Jezebels indicates to Kalu that a patriarchal ideology lurks under Pentecostal theology.[253] Women fare even worse in some of the mainline churches like the Anglican and the Roman Catholic which would not ordain women as priests. Even though the trend is changing in different denominations in Africa and women are getting into more important and active roles, a solution has to be found to this structural oppression of women which persists. Kalu suggests the following solutions: first, he observes that changes in society and an increased level of education

[246] Ndungu, "The role of the Bible," 246.
[247] Kalu, African Pentecostalism, 148.
[248] Kalu, African Pentecostalism, 148. See also, Harris, Yoruba in Diaspora, 51.
[249] Kalu, African Pentecostalism, 148.
[250] Kalu, African Pentecostalism, 152.
[251] Kalu, African Pentecostalism, 153.
[252] Kalu, African Pentecostalism, 153.
[253] Kalu, African Pentecostalism, 163.

among women have translated into improved roles for women in African churches.[254] Women should build on this by advocating for more legal, economic and political power.[255] Second, Kalu notes that women often access power in the church through the exercise of their spirituality.[256] Women, Kalu suggests, should use this innate spirituality to fight against their oppression.[257] Thirdly, it is possible to make more of the feminine images in the Bible, such as the feminine images of the Holy Spirit and of God as the mother of Israel.[258]

Wider literature from outside Africa also supports the difference in emphasis I observed in how men and women understand the Holy Spirit. Whilst the treatment of women among Pentecostals and Charismatics has been complex and contradictory, the influence of the Holy Spirit in the thinking of the church has been to allow women more freedom. R.M. Griffith and D. Roebuck have pointed out that in classical Pentecostalism women were allowed to play prominent roles:

> because of the doctrinal emphasis on the third person of the Trinity, which enabled Pentecostals to view ministerial authority as rooted in the movement of the Spirit rather than in clerical office.[259]

They quote an article from 1906, which describes how:

> a young sister, 14 years old, was saved, sanctified and baptised with the Holy Ghost and went out, taking a band of workers with her, and led a revival in which one hundred and ninety souls were saved.[260]

Elizabeth Moltmann explores this from the socio-political dimension. In an article entitled "Becoming Human in Community" she justifies her belief that women feel particularly attracted to the Holy Spirit within the Trinity because of the need to oppose patriarchy: "In the long history of the patriarchal Church women were able again and again to breach the dominant structures in the power of the Holy Spirit."[261] In the same vein, Eunjoo Mary Kim explores how Asian women also find themselves marginalised in the Church that is "dominated by an institutionalised patriarchal system." In this situation, the

---

[254] Kalu, *African Pentecostalism*, 163.

[255] Kalu, *African Pentecostalism*, 163.

[256] Kalu, *African Pentecostalism*, 163.

[257] Kalu, *African Pentecostalism*, 163.

[258] Kalu, *African Pentecostalism*, 164.

[259] R.M. Griffith and D. Roebuck, "Women, Role of" in Stanley M. Burgess and Edward M. van der Maas (eds), *The New International Dictionary of Pentecostal and Charismatic Movements* (Grand Rapids: Zondervan, 2003), 1204.

[260] Griffith and Roebuck, "Women, Role of," 1204. See also, R. Kowalski, "The mission theology of early Pentecostals," *Journal of Pentecostal Theology* 19 (2010), 275.

[261] E. Moltmann and J. Moltmann, "Being Human in New Community," *Currents in Theology and Mission* 29.5 (2002), 269.

decisions of the women to become preachers "are often made by the intervention of the irresistible power of the Holy Spirit".[262]

Whilst the view that women have a special attraction to the Holy Spirit has wide agreement, not everybody links this with patriarchy. Some argue, instead, that it is possible that women have a natural spirituality which makes them open to the Holy Spirit. Anne Carr comments that "even with affirmations of equality between women and men . . . it seems clear that there are differences between the sexes in basic styles of understanding and relationship.[263] Thus there are probably differences in women's and men's spiritualities." Carr continues:

> Women's spirituality might be described as more related to nature and natural processes than to culture; more personal and relational than objective and structural; more diffuse, concrete, and general than focused, universal, abstract; more emotional than intellectual, etc.[264]

Whether this "feminist appeal to the Holy Spirit" is due to socio-political reasons or due to some innate spirituality among women cannot be discussed fully here. It will suffice to say that the difference in emphasis between women and men observed at Mount Zion is echoed widely in existing literature in Africa and around the world.

The Holy Spirit and the Bible

Under this final theme I discuss the two pattern theories on the relationship between the Holy Spirit and the Bible: 1) a relationship between the Holy Spirit and Biblical interpretation (hermeneutics), and 2) the Bible viewed as the source of the in-filling of the Holy Spirit and tool for the verification of inspired word.

Spirit-illumination

At Mount Zion, the church members believe that the Holy Spirit must be involved in order for one to get the intended meaning of Biblical texts. They believe that the Holy Spirit can give people different meanings to the same text and can even give a person a different understanding of the same text on different occasions.

The emphasis of the role of the Holy Spirit in Biblical interpretation can be found in the African Initiated Churches which preceded the African Pentecostal Churches.[265] For example, Francis Githieya describes how the Church of Holy Spirit (Arathi) of Kenya, which was founded in the 1920s, believed that:

---

262 E.M. **Kim**, "The Holy Spirit and new marginality," *Journal for Preachers* 25.4 (Pentecost, 2002), 26.
263 A. **Carr**, "On Feminist Spirituality," *Horizons* 9.1 (Spring, 1982), 97.
264 **Carr**, "On Feminist Spirituality," 99.
265 Anderson, *African Reformation*, p. 222.

the key to unlocking the truth of the scriptures came not from the mission churches but through their own study of the scriptures as illuminated by their experience of the Holy Spirit.[266]

The church's founder, Joseph Nganga, is said to have gone into seclusion in the early days of the church "to seek guidance from the Holy Spirit in his interpretation of the scriptures".[267]

In a similar vein, Omoyajowo shows how the members of the Cherubim and Seraphim of Nigeria rely on the Holy Spirit to give them the meaning of Biblical passages. The church's constitution states: "Believers shall study the Scriptures diligently relying on the power of the Holy Spirit of God to guide them to the correct and true meaning of the Scriptures."[268] Elsewhere, the church makes the statement that "A careful research and prayerful reflection of the Scriptures comparing Scripture with Scripture yields its beauty and its deep and hidden meaning . . . ."[269]

However, the link with the Holy Spirit in African Biblical interpretation is not universally made by African scholars. For example, **Justin Ukpong's** description of biblical interpretation in Africa does not refer to the work of the Holy Spirit. Ukpong, who writes from a Roman Catholic background, remarks that there is a discernable pattern in the way Africans interpret the Bible which is different from the "Western pattern".[270] The African pattern involves a direct encounter between the text and the African context.[271] He commends African scholars for giving greater recognition for the methodologies employed by the ordinary readers, a characteristic of which is the influence of their indigenous worldview. "The conceptual framework of interpretation is informed by African socio-cultural perspective" and their goal is to get the:

> theological meaning of the text in today's context, so as to forge integration between faith and life, and engender commitment to personal and societal transformation.[272]

Ukpong also remarks that in this African approach, there is no one absolute meaning of the biblical text to be recovered through historical analysis. Also, unlike in some Western-oriented interpretive approaches which consist of first recovering the meaning of the text through historical analysis and then applying it, Africans tend to have one process whereby the reader engages with the text based on his or her context.[273] Hence, while not specifically referring to the role

---

[266] Githieya, "The Church of the Holy Spirit," 233.
[267] Githieya, "The Church of the Holy Spirit," 233.
[268] Omoyajowo, *Cherubim and Seraphim*, 91.
[269] Omoyajowo, *Cherubim and Seraphim*, 91.
[270] Ukpong, "Developments in Biblical Interpretation in Africa…," 11.
[271] Ukpong, "Developments in Biblical Interpretation in Africa…," 11.
[272] Ukpong, "Developments in Biblical Interpretation in Africa…," 24.
[273] Ukpong, "Developments in Biblical Interpretation in Africa…," 24.

of the Holy Spirit in this process, Ukpong's descriptions cohere with much of the foregoing, especially with what Kalu referred to as the Pentecostals rejection of scholarly gymnastics in Biblical interpretation.[274]

The review of the work of Pentecostal ministers shows that they often specifically refer to the work of the Holy Spirit in biblical interpretation. In *Rhapsody of Realities*, the husband-and-wife team, Chris and Anita Oyakhilome, who at various times have ministered in Nigeria, South Africa and the United Kingdom, describe the same idea. In a chapter entitled "The Holy Spirit helps you understand God's word", Anita laments how people can spend hours reading the Bible without understanding what they are reading:

> Though they increase their mental knowledge, spiritual understanding eludes them. It's the Holy Spirit that gives understanding of the Scriptures, and without him all a man can do is "sense knowledge". When the Holy Spirit takes charge of your life, spiritual understanding is granted you.[275]

In another book, Chris Oyakhilome points out that one cannot receive the understanding of the scriptures or of "spiritual mysteries" through "intellectual knowledge" nor "from school or anywhere else in the world".[276] Rather, "it comes by the revelation of the Holy Spirit". He laments that in "the dark ages" it was said that "only the Pope and the priests could understand the Scriptures, and they kept God's people in darkness for hundreds of years".[277]

Similar ideas can be found in the writings of African Christians based in Britain. Albert Odulele of Glory House, London, writes:

> The Bible cannot be properly understood without the voice of God. Without God's voice there can be no real revelation. It is the Holy Spirit that takes the written word and makes it the revealed Word.[278]

Odulele refers to Jesus' words in John 16:13, which describe the Holy Spirit as the Spirit of Truth that would guide the disciples "into all truths" and adds, "The Holy Spirit will expound the scriptures to you.[279] He will rebuke error, correct flaws, instruct and guide you through the complexities of life."

This belief about the Spirit-illumination of the Bible is another idea commonly found in the wider Pentecostal movement. Anderson has pointed out that most Pentecostals rely on an experiential rather than a literal understanding

---

[274] Kalu, *African Pentecostalism*, xiii.

[275] C. Oyahilome and A. Oyahilome, *Rhapsody of Reality* (Lagos: Love world, 2006) – "Monday July, 2nd". (The pages of this book are indicated not by number but by date.)

[276] C. Oyakhilome, *The Seven Spirits of God – Divine Secrets to the Miraculous* (Lagos: Love world, 2006), 66.

[277] Oyakhilome, *The Seven Spirits of God*, 66. See also, Oyakhilome, *Seven things the Holy Spirit will do in you*, 33; and Adeboye, *God the Holy Spirit*, 5.

[278] Odulele, *Understanding God's Voice*, 80.

[279] Odulele, *Understanding God's Voice*, 81.

of the Bible and in that interplay between text and experience, they rely on the Holy Spirit:

> Pentecostals believe in spiritual illumination, the experiential immediacy of the Holy Spirit who makes the Bible "alive" and therefore different from any other book. They assign multiple meanings to the biblical text, preachers often assigning it "deeper significance" that can only be perceived by the help of the Spirit.[280]

F.D. Macchia has similarly noted how for Pentecostals, reading the Bible is "an event of the Spirit" because, through the ministry of the Spirit, they can enter the world of the Bible, without the usual hermeneutical difficulties of reading an ancient text in modern times.[281] Hence he notes that "the truth and authority of the Bible for Pentecostals have always been spiritually discerned".[282]

Hence, the view that the Bible needs to be illuminated by the Holy Spirit to be properly understood is found among African Pentecostal, the African Initiated Churches and the wider Pentecostal movement.

Holy Spirit and Biblical authority

At Mount Zion there was a dialectic relationship between the value the members and ministers put on the Bible and their reliance on the Holy Spirit. Whilst they believe that the Holy Spirit interprets the written words of the Bible to them and can spontaneously activate Biblical words in their memory as the need arises, they also believe that the Bible has its own independent authority. Not only does the reading of the Bible give the reader a greater sense of being filled with the Holy Spirit, but also the words and teaching in the Bible can act as an authority for evaluating claims of inspired words and actions.

Treating the Bible as a yardstick for measuring what is of God is a part of the longstanding relationship between African Christianity and the Bible. Some have traced this to the point in time when the Bible was translated to African languages. For example, David Barrett has claimed that scriptures in vernacular have greater power in communicating a religion than scriptures in *linguae francae* such as Swahili, Hausa, Arabic, French or English because the vernacular translation enables the ethnic group to get a stronger grasp of the doctrines.[283] In this way, Bible translation was part and parcel of the search for independence; in the course of time many churches broke from the mission churches and "many mission's dogma and practices have become reformulated and moulded in a more biblical pattern".[284]

---

[280] Anderson, *Introduction to Pentecostalism*, 226.
[281] Macchia, F.D., "Theology, Pentecostal" in Stanley M. Burgess and M. Edward van der Maas (eds), *The New International Dictionary of Pentecostal and Charismatic Movements* (Grand Rapids: Zondervan, 2003), 1204.
[282] Macchia, "Theology, Pentecostal," 1204.
[283] D. Barrett, *Schism and Renewal in Africa* (Oxford: Oxford University Press, 1968).
[284] Mbiti, *Bible and Theology*, 31.

Mbiti, who agrees with Barrett, points out that "the translation of the Bible into an African language provided a high degree of authority by means of which Christians can fashion their thinking and life".[285] He describes the authority of scripture for Africans as:

> an authority which penetrates deep into their spiritual, social, cultural and reflectional welfare. It gives them a form of liberation from ready-made and imported Christianity, a liberation to generate the kind of Christianity which more fully embraces the totality of their existence.

The Church of the Holy Spirit (Arathi) of Kenya is an example of an African church which has used the Bible in this way. Githieya notes that for the Arathi, the Bible was "a double-edged sword" in that it provided them with "a principled basis" for judging both the teachings of the Western missionary churches and the traditional African beliefs of their people.[286] Another example is the Celestial Church of Christ. Adogame observes that the members of the church see the Bible as the legitimate and final authority in all their practices, the source of all their knowledge, the foundation to belief and worship.[287]

Support for the view that reading the Bible can give the reader a greater sense of being filled with the Holy Spirit can be found in the writings of African Christians based in Britain. Taking the work of Albert Odulele, for example, in the book *Understanding God's Voice* he claims that to understand the role of the Bible in hearing God's voice, one needs to refer back to how the Bible was written in the first place. He quotes 2 Timothy 3:16, "All scripture is given by inspiration of God, for instruction in righteousness", and then writes:

> The scriptures were given by the Holy Spirit (to men) and the Bible is therefore the voice of God in written form. It stands to reason that the more of this written representation you know, the better equipped you become to hear him.[288]

He advises the reader that "Bible truths will wise you up to divine concepts" and will also, "introduce you to divine thought patterns that better prepare you for hearing him".[289] He points out that such things as love, forgiveness and self-sacrifice are not natural to human beings, but "the Bible imposes God's thoughts and ways upon rebellious human concepts".[290] The point here is that there is an ontological change that happens to a person through reading the Bible which makes him or her better able to hear God. This is the very effect Christians ascribe to the Holy Spirit.

---

[285] Mbiti, *Bible and Theology*, 32.
[286] Githieya, "The Church of the Holy Spirit," 231.
[287] Adogame, *Celestial Church of Christ*, 130. See also, Asamoah-Gyadu, *African Charismatics*, 79.
[288] Odulele, *Understanding God's Voice*, 80.
[289] Odulele, *Understanding God's Voice*, 80.
[290] Odulele, *Understanding God's Voice*, 80.

The same view is expressed by Sanusi who is also based in London. In a section of his book entitled "Holy Ghost and Boldness," he writes, "The Holy Ghost is the vehicle that transports boldness into the life of a believer. If you are born again, then you must desire to be regularly filled with the Holy Ghost through worship, Word study and praying in tongues."[291] Hence, he includes "word-study", that is, reading and studying the Bible, as one of three things that fills one with the Holy Spirit.

Odulele also affirms the importance of using the Bible as a yardstick, writing: "Judge every voice you hear by the Bible and determine if it is of God or not."[292] Indeed, he notes the dialectical relationship between the Holy Spirit and Bible (or "the Word), as he writes, "While the Holy Spirit unveils the Word, His utterances are conversely authenticated by the Word."[293] The great danger is the one who was called "serpent" in Gen 3:1 and who is "verbally active today as he was in the Garden of Eden". The serpent is "the chief of all liars" and is "out to deceive as many as he can". For this reason, God provided a safeguard: the Bible. Hence, "The most reliable way of ensuring that you respond only to God's voice is to compare what is said with the Bible. If it falls in line with the Scriptures, then in all probability it is God."[294] The thing to bear in mind, in Odulele's view, is that the Bible is "heaven's manual for an effective and successful life" and God "seeing that contradiction is the downfall of any kingdom" would not contradict the Bible, the very principles he has given".[295]

So, the literature suggests that the relationship I found at Mount Zion between the church and the Bible is common among Africans, both those in the continent and those in Britain. The relationship cuts across denominations and possibly goes back to the enthusiasm with which the Bible was received upon translation. From that view point, it can be said that Africans in general resist the prospect of anybody coming between them and their Bible and the concept of Spirit-illumination is the particular strategy employed by Pentecostals like those in Mount Zion in that resistance.

Something akin to being filled by the Holy Spirit through reading the Bible is also recognizable from wider Pentecostal literature. Andrew Davies informs that when ordinary Pentecostal read the Bible it is to "meet God in the text".[296] Hence, he writes, "Our common heritage, then, has taught us the miracle and the mystery of personal experience of God's presence, experienced and mediated through the biblical text among other ways."[297] He also states that

---

[291] Sanusi, *Goliath Killing Prayers*, 73

[292] Odulele, *Understanding God's Voice*, 80.

[293] Odulele, *Understanding God's Voice*, 80.

[294] Odulele, *Understanding God's Voice*, 82-83.

[295] Odulele, *Understanding God's Voice*, 41.

[296] A. Davies, "What does it Mean to Read the Bible as a Pentecostal," *Journal of Pentecostal Theology* 18 (2009), 223.

[297] Davies, "What does it Mean to Read the Bible as a Pentecostal," 221.

while Pentecostal readers bring their questions to the text, they are open to experience the power of the text to edify and inspire.[298]

These two ideas, namely, the Bible as yardstick and the source of in-filling resonate with ideas expressed in the Reformation and might suggest an undercurrent of Reformed tradition in Mount Zion. Regarding the in-filling of the Holy Spirit, the Reformers, in order to counteract the Roman Catholic Church's position that the Holy Spirit is "imparted" by "sacred ordination", made the case for the Bible to be recognised as also imparting the Holy Spirit.[299] Hence, The Augsburg Confession, which the Lutherans presented to the authorities asserted that the "Holy Spirit is imparted through word and sacrament as by instruments."[300] As regards the matter of yardstick, the Reformers mantra, *"sola scriptura"*, meant that scripture is the only source of knowledge of supernatural theology. For example, Calvin wrote that:

> in order that true religion may shine upon us, we ought to hold that it must take its beginning from heavenly doctrine and that no one can get even the slightest taste of right and sound doctrine unless he be a pupil of Scripture.[301]

He also described as God's plan that besides the common proofs of his presence in creation, the Scriptures would be "a more direct and more certain mark whereby he is to be recognized".[302]

In conclusion, African Pentecostals share with the wider Pentecostal movement the belief that reading the Bible fills the reader with the Holy Spirit. However, the tendency to treat the Bible as a yardstick with which we decide what is of the Spirit may be stronger among African Pentecostals than in the wider Pentecostal movement. It suggests that African Pentecostalism has its peculiarities. In this case, it might be showing the influence of the evangelical Christianity which spread through Africa before the current Pentecostal era.

Conclusion

The goal of this chapter is to gain further understanding of what has already been found in the case study.[303] I looked at literature from African Christianity, wider Pentecostal literature and other literature relevant to the study. The review showed that many of the patterns I observed at Mount Zion are widely shared by Pentecostals in general. The strong belief that the Holy Spirit enables worship and manifests sometimes in spectacular ways during worship, the little interest in explicitly referring to the Holy Spirit during worship, the belief that

[298] Davies, "What does it Mean to Read the Bible as a Pentecostal," 222.
[299] E. Schweizer, *The Holy Spirit* (London: SCM, 1981), 3.
[300] Cited in Schweizer, *The Holy Spirit*, 3.
[301] J. Calvin, *Institutes of the Christian Religion* (edited by John McNeil; Louisville, Kentucky: Westminster John Knox, 1960), 1.72.
[302] Calvin, *Institutes of the Christian Religion*, 70.
[303] Creswell, *Qualitative Enquiry and Research Design*, 30.

the Spirit makes biblical interpretation possible, the association of the Holy Spirit with empowerment, the sense of a special relationship between the Holy Spirit and women, and the belief that ministry is in the power of the Spirit and not by human ordination or training are some of the commonalities encountered. This is not to suggest that the Africans have necessarily received these from the worldwide Pentecostal movement, but rather that they *share* these with other Pentecostals.

Mount Zion and other African Pentecostals have been undoubtedly influenced by the African traditional cosmology in which their leaders, and most of their members, have been formed. This manifests in their Pneumatology in such ways as their very strong emphasis of the activities of the Holy Spirit in their daily life. I found that they gave stronger emphasis to this than do Pentecostals in general. The fact that Africans see the world as a spiritual theatre and life as spiritual warfare would incline these Africans to see the Holy Spirit as a spiritual fighter on their behalf in everyday issues. This retention of the African worldview is also possibly responsible for how many of their young people appear to have continued to maintain similar Pneumatology. They have not succumbed to the agnostic, secular view of life that is prevalent in the West.

Another important influence has been the Bible. One aspect of the Pneumatology I observed at Mount Zion is the view that any claim of spiritual revelation should be subjected to verification using the Bible. This view, which is more akin to evangelicalism than Pentecostalism, points to the special relationship Africans have with the Bible since it was translated to their native languages. Both Barrett and Mbiti have suggested that, as a result of the Bible being translated into native African languages, Africans developed a relationship with it as a book that gives them direct access to God. Another aspect of this is that most African countries experienced evangelical Christianity before the current Pentecostal period. Therefore, one finds among Africans beliefs about and attitudes to the Bible which resonate with the sixteenth century reformers. These two factors combine to give African Pentecostalism an evangelical underbelly, which filters into their Pneumatology.

Ironically, this history of the encounter of Africans with the Bible has given Mount Zion and many other African churches the confidence to challenge their African heritage in the name of the Bible. Their sense that the Bible has independent authority enables them to avoid being tied down by African philosophical ideas. This can be seen in their anthropology. Whereas Africans do not tend to dissect a human being into constituent parts and then give priority to the "spiritual" element; this is exactly what these African Christians do. Their idea that a human being is comprised of body, soul and spirit, and the sense of worthlessness they confer to the physical body resonates more with the writings of Paul (such as in Rom. 7:21 and Gal. 5:17-21) than with African traditional thinking.

Another area where this can be seen is in their idea of the deity of the Holy Spirit and its position within the Trinity. African Initiated Churches, which were the first group of African churches to break away from the churches founded by Western missionaries, often speak of the Holy Spirit as more or less the power of God. Their Pneumatologies show the strong influence of African traditional concept of God. If one imagines a continuum beginning from the concept of the Spirit as an agent of God and ending in the concept of the Spirit as God, it is fair to say that Mount Zion and the newer African Pentecostals have moved farther along towards seeing the Spirit as God. There is within this newer group a stronger insistence on the deity and personhood of the Holy Spirit. They are more likely to see the work of the Spirit as inner inspiration rather than visible possession. To them, the Holy Spirit is more of a person working alongside them in their daily activities, than a power that suddenly falls on them, particularly during worship, making them behave in strange ways.

CHAPTER 5

Deductive Empirical Study: Interviews

Having conducted an inductive study of a church (Chapter 3) and analysed the observations further with unrelated data using existing literature (Chapter 4), the next step is to apply the theoretical concepts to a new collection of data. As Van der Ven recommends:

> this testing must be done on a completely different set of empirical information, else one would end up in a vicious cycle, formulating hypotheses based on the examination of a set of information, and then testing them by means of the very same information set. That necessarily leads to spurious confirmation of hypothesis.[1]

Hence in this phase I am testing one or more of the pattern-theories on African Christians outside Mount Zion. This phase is deductive because it starts with a theory, which is then tested in the field. In a traditional deductive study the fieldwork would be preceded by a review of literature. In this empirical cycle approach, the preceding phases of the cycle serve that purpose.

Any one or more of the twelve pattern-theories can form the subject of **further investigation so there is an element of researcher's interest and choice. I** have chosen two areas covered by the twelve pattern theories on which to carry out further investigation. In what follows, I state the areas I have chosen and give reasons. I describe and explain the method I use. A total of four churches and thirty-two participants are studied in this phase. I provide the rationale for choosing the churches and the participants. Much of the chapter is devoted to describing my findings in the two areas being investigated. My hope is that over time other researchers will investigate all twelve theories.

Pattern Theories

The first of the two areas I investigate further relates to the nature of the Holy Spirit and specifically its place within the Trinity. At Mount Zion, I identified: *A belief that the Holy Spirit is a real person and related to the Father and the Son.* That relationship was seen as one of equality. The Holy Spirit was also clearly seen by the church as being divine. From the subsequent literature

---

[1] J.A. Van der Ven, *Practical Theology: An Empirical Approach* (Kampen: Kok Pharos, 1993), 115.

review, I observed that, compared to the African Initiated Churches, the new Pentecostal churches like Mount Zion are much clearer in their belief that the Holy Spirit is God. They are also more likely to see him as a person (not just the power of God) and to pray to him. I was intrigued by this and chose to investigate it further, to discover what other African Christians in different denominations believe about the Spirit's place within Trinity. Hence, the following three questions will be asked, a) whether the Spirit is seen as God, that is, the divinity of the Spirit, b) whether the Spirit is established in participants' understanding as a distinctive person, and not as a force or as a being subsumed within the Godhead, and c) whether the Spirit is seen as co-equal to both Father and Son.

The second area is the area of empowerment, that is, the view that the Spirit gives strength to believers in all aspects of life. At Mount Zion I found: *A link between the Holy Spirit and the empowerment of individual members.* Beyond this specific theory, I found that the idea of empowerment was very dominant in the Pneumatology of Mount Zion. The literature review also showed this to be the case among AICs and African Pentecostal Churches, in general. The theme of empowerment cut across such areas as their daily life, worship, ministry, and engagement with the Bible. Women are empowered to allow their natural ability and spirituality to come through and not be hemmed-in by patriarchal structures. Young people are also empowered to reject the prevailing youth culture by being assured that the Holy Spirit is part of an alternative reality to the secular worldview that is common in the West. This pervading nature of the theme of empowerment is why I want to investigate it further. I attempt to see the extent to which the theme of empowerment manifest in the whole Pneumatology of the Africans in the four churches studied in this phase. It should be noted that whilst my first choice for testing is a specific theory out of the twelve which arose from Phase One, my second choice covers many of the theories. I test the extent the theme of empowerment pervades the whole of their Pneumatology.

In choosing the cases to study, I use purposeful maximal sampling.[2] This is where one selects "cases that show different perspective on the problem".[3] In this regard, I will examine Africans in four congregations of different denominations. These are a Methodist church, a Church of England church, a Roman Catholic Church and an African Pentecostal church. Since Mount Zion is located in East London, I have chosen all four churches from within East London. By doing so, I have avoided (or minimized) the potential for the geographical location of the churches becoming a factor influencing the findings. In choosing whom to interview within each of these cases, I have also used purposeful sampling. I selected, mostly, interviewees who are likely to

---

[2] J. Creswell, *Qualitative Enquiry and Research Design: Choosing Among the Five Approaches* (London: Sage, 2007), 75.
[3] Creswell, *Qualitative Enquiry,* 75.

make meaningful contribution to the study, such as long standing members of the church/denomination who would have imbibed the denomination's theology over many years. I also ensured that men and women, of different age groups and from a variety of countries of origin, were interviewed.

It should be noted that at this phase of the study, the case study method is used in a different way from how it was used in the first phase. As has been offered by Yin, a case study can either be used in a way that starts off with a proposition and then data is presented to make the case — a deductive approach.[4] Or in a situation where the intention is to describe, one begins with a descriptive framework which is then used for organising the case study — an inductive approach.[5] The second approach involving the use of a descriptive framework is used in Phase One to describe what was found at Mount Zion. In the current phase, which is deductive, I use the first approach. So the data I present address the two areas of interest. However, rather than starting with proposition(s) I focus on the following questions: 1) How do the church members in the case studies understand the nature of the Holy Spirit, specifically, his divinity, personhood and co-equality? 2) How do they understand the Spirit's work, particularly his role of empowering believers? 3) Outside these two areas, what are the other significant aspects of their understanding of the Spirit? By including this third category, I can highlight a small number of important characteristics of their understanding which do not fall within the two specific areas being investigated.

East London Methodist Church

East London Methodist Church (E L Methodist) is located in one of the East London boroughs. This area shares many of the social-economic characteristics that have already been described. The church building stands in an inner, quiet road. Inside the building there are a number of large rooms and offices and the biggest room is used for church services. This room was very simply decorated. There was a raised platform in front with a lectern standing on one side, and an over-head-projector screen on the other. There were about ten rows of movable chairs on the lower level where the congregation sat. During the time I observed this church, the congregation ranged from fifty to sixty. The vast majority of people in the congregation were Africans, although there were Europeans and some people from the Caribbean. There were men, women and children. A majority of the congregation were in their 50s. I did not see anybody who looked in their 20s or 30s.

The church has services only on Sunday mornings. These are often led by the white European minister, whom I will call Geoffrey. Geoffrey led the singing, which was either projected on the screen or sung from a hymn book.

---

[4]   R. Yin, *Case Study Research – Design and Methods* (London: Sage, 1984), 103.
[5]   Yin, *Case Study Research*, 103.

He also preached the sermon. At other times, other lay preachers in the Methodist circuit came and led the service. I observed the church over a six-month period, during which I attended five services. During the same period, I interviewed eight members of the church. The list of pseudonyms and personal characteristics is given in the Appendix.

In my interviews, in addition to covering the same ground which I covered with the members of Mount Zion, I asked questions related to the two areas I am now focusing on, that is, the divinity of and empowerment by the Spirit.

The Holy Spirit within the Trinity

Most of the people I interviewed showed that they believed in the divinity of the Holy Spirit. For example, when I asked Gabriel, a Ghanaian man in his fifties, whether the Holy Spirit should be worshipped, he said:

> The Holy Spirit is God and we worship God. Therefore . . . it's like you are saying A is equal to B, B is equal to C, therefore A is equal to C. Therefore we have to worship him. It is as simple as that. The Holy Spirit is God. So whist we are worshipping God, we are worshipping the Holy Spirit.

Another member, Hannah, a Ghanaian woman in her forties, gave the following answer to the same question:

> Holy Spirit deserves to be worshipped because when you worship the Holy Spirit, you worship the Lord. You are not worshipping any other thing. You are worshipping God. You're worshipping the Father. You're worshipping the Son. You're worshipping the Holy Spirit.

More or less the same answer was given by another member, Dada, a Sierra Leonean man in his fifties. When I pointed out to him that some people see the Holy Spirit as a power or agent working for God, he rejected it. "I take God as the Holy Spirit. I do not regard the Holy Spirit as an agent. I regard the Holy Spirit as God. When I refer to the Holy Spirit, I am referring to God. . . . To me, the Holy Spirit is God himself." Similarly, Henrietta, a Ghanaian woman in her forties, said when I asked who the Holy Spirit is, "Holy Spirit is God."

Many of the interviewees also stated that they prayed to the Holy Spirit. One person, Hannah, in answering another question gave a description of how she would call on the Holy Spirit during difficult times:

> When you look and there is nobody to fall on, you tend to call [on] the Holy Spirit. And you say 'Lord, this is what I am going through'. Even though at the time you may not have the power to get through . . . but if you have the faith in the Lord and say, 'this is what I am going through Holy Spirit and I want you to lead me through' you can get the strength from there.

Ann, a Nigerian woman in her fifties, also described how one would pray to the Holy Spirit "to enlighten you, to guide you in whatever you do". This practice of praying directly to the Holy Spirit further supports that the church members saw the Holy Spirit as God.

Whilst their view regarding the divinity of the Holy Spirit was well established, there was a diversity of views on the issue of the Spirit as a distinctive person within the Trinity. To be sure, some of them specifically spoke of the formula, Father, Son and Holy Spirit. Hannah, for example, said, "Holy Spirit is a Guide. Holy Spirit is from God. When we pray, we say in the name of the Father, and of the Son and of the Holy Spirit." She also referred to Father, Son and Holy Spirit on two other occasions during the interview. Ann said something similar:

> Right from the beginning, I was made to understand that you cannot see the Holy Spirit but it is with us. Because I believe in the Trinity. That is, God the Father, God the Son and God the Holy Spirit. It's like you don't see God, but you believe God is with you. In the same way I know and believe in the Holy Spirit because I know of the three in one.

But not all those I interviewed showed such distinctiveness in their understanding. At times, the Spirit appears to be subsumed within the Trinity. Ebo, for example, gave me this description of the Holy Spirit:

> I see the Holy Spirit as the Creator, the omnipresence. The Holy Spirit manifests itself in many ways and depends on how you understand it and use it. We don't want to give it a name *per se*. People call it God, people call it Allah. The point is the recognition of a force outside us, stronger than us and within us, manipulating and directing our lives.

Dada, who converted from Islam late in life, also made a similar point. He said he thought of the Holy Spirit as "a divine power in charge of everything". He described how he had in the past been saved from accidents and had many near-misses and how he prays and gets answers. He attributed this to the Holy Spirit which he described as a "divine power there to protect us" and which punishes those who do wrong. When asked what the Holy Spirit does, he described how God has created many amazing things and said, "If God can take care of all of those, all the world, all the miracles that are happening, then God is capable of doing anything." Another participant describing the most important things the Holy Spirit does for a Christian talked about how he makes them sleep and wake up, go out and come back. She pointed out how some who were alive at last Christmas were now dead, but others are still alive because the Holy Spirit has made that possible.

One aspect of this lack of differentiation is the case of Elizabeth, a Nigerian woman in her sixties, who simply saw the Holy Spirit as Jesus. When I asked her who or what the Holy Spirit is, she said, "I can say it is Jesus because you can't see it. It's in us." She expanded this answer when I asked her whether the Holy Spirit should be worshipped. "Jesus is the Holy Spirit. . . . So if [you] really want to worship the Holy Spirit you worship Jesus, because he is the head. As far as you worship Jesus, you're worshipping the Holy Spirit. . . . Holy Spirit is Jesus."

Apart from this lack of distinctiveness, I also encountered in one interviewee, Ann, statements suggesting the Spirit was not a person to her. For example, she stated that "God is a Spirit which we refer to as the Holy Spirit", thereby suggesting that the Holy Spirit is none other than the nature of God as a spirit being. She also said during the interview, "The Holy Spirit is nothing but the power of God" and "The power of God is the Holy Spirit." This denies Spirit's personhood and merely sees him as an attribute of God.

Regarding equality, virtually everybody I spoke to saw the Spirit as equal to the Father and Son, perhaps because they had not significantly distinguished him from Father and Son in the first place. However, one person, Hannah, saw it in a different way. She saw the Holy Spirit more as subordinate, working as a route to God. She appeared to use "God" to refer to the Father. For example, on the issue of guidance, she said, "I feel the Holy Spirit around us every time. He guides you, just as God guides you." She later gave this illustration of how the Holy Spirit works, "As an African, I know you just can't go to a chief directly. You have to pass through a linguist before you go to the chief. You could pray directly to God, but I have been made to believe that you go through Jesus and the Holy Spirit to get to God." ("Linguist" here, as is common in West Africa, refers to the Chief's spokesman.) The view of subordination was more or less confirmed when I asked her whether the Holy Spirit deserves to be worshipped:

No, you can't worship the Holy Spirit. I only believe in worshipping God. Though there is three in one, you know, but, it's like God is the head. That is the way I see it. God is the head and Jesus and the Holy Spirit are the branches. So you can't do without the other. But you only have to worship God.

Empowerment by the Holy Spirit

The sense that the Holy Spirit gives power to their life as individuals and to their church was not much in evidence. But there was clearly the sense that they lived their daily life with the guidance and protection of the Holy Spirit. Ann said, "I feel the Holy Spirit around us every time. He guides you, just as God guides you." And Elizabeth, a Nigerian woman in her sixties, and Ebo, a Ghanaian man in his fifties, also described guidance as one of two most important things that the Holy Spirit can do for a person. Some described to me how the guidance happens. Henrietta described how the Holy Spirit prompts her through an inner voice she hears to go to church. "Without Holy Spirit you can't go to church, because the Holy Spirit is the one who can push you go, go, go, go and pray." She described how it is sometimes difficult to pray at home because of distractions. But when you go to church and meet other church members and the minister, you find you are able to follow the reading and the sermon. "That is the Holy Spirit as well."

This sense of a daily guide also appears in their tendency to use daily life experience to illustrate their point. Gabriel told me what happened to him when he came to Britain in 1988, not knowing anybody. An inner voice told him to travel to King's Cross and he did. For three days, he would go to the King's Cross area in the morning and sit on a park bench all day. Then his money started to run out. Eventually, a man approached him, who had been observing him for some days. The man worked at the local mini cab office. He had been wondering why such a well-dressed man was sitting on the park bench all day, like a tramp. Through this stranger, Gabriel met another man who had been his classmate in secondary school in Africa. And this classmate then helped him to settle into the country. He concluded, "To me if it had not been the Holy Spirit who had been guiding me to be going and sit at that place — listening to the inner voice and acting on it — I don't think I would be sitting here with you having this interview."

Dada gave the following description of what the Holy Spirit did for him on a ship:

> I remember one day, I was a trainee officer. We were discharging some cargo. And without thinking, I walked on the hatch-coaming which is a very, very dangerous thing to do. I lost my balance. I could have fallen into the hatch and died. But I don't know what happened, how I managed to regain my balance and jump down on the proper side. And God saved me.

He also described another incident in which he was a passenger on a motorcycle. The rider lost control so the interviewee jumped from the passenger seat. But he landed on the road in front of an on-coming lorry. What saved him was that the lorry did not get to him. He, however, continued to roll forward and ended up with his head wedged between the lorry's front wheel and the road. "That lorry could have rolled over my head," he said. "And I would have been history. I am very certain that divine intervention was involved in those things." Apart from these miraculous escapes, he also described how coming from a poor family, the fact that he managed to go to school, get scholarships to study overseas, get meaningful employment and now ended up owning a house in the United Kingdom was the work of the Spirit.

Other church members shared similar thoughts. Elizabeth, said the Holy Spirit was not only involved in "daily" life, but was involved "every minute, twenty-four seven." And Ann related the Holy Spirit to the feeling she sometimes gets, such as while waiting for a bus at a bus stop. While deciding whether to wait for a bus or not, the feeling would tell her what to do and that feeling usually turns out to be right.

Other significant characteristics

Even though the church members did not give much emphasis to the empowerment of the Holy Spirit, they clearly believed the Holy Spirit was involved in miracles. Hannah described something that happened once when she went to a Charismatic church. At the event, while the pastor was praying, the pastor said the Holy Spirit was telling him there was somebody in the gathering who had a bad knee and that the Holy Spirit was healing the knee. Hannah said that at the time she used to suffer from a very bad migraine:

I said to myself, this pastor, can't he see that there is somebody here with a migraine that he would ask the Holy Spirit to heal? As soon as I said that, as if he heard me, he said the Holy Spirit is telling him that there is somebody here who suffers from migraine... This is about ten years ago. The Holy Spirit is telling him that there is somebody here who suffers from migraine and that person is being healed.

She felt this was her and "claimed it". She said she has not suffered migraine since then and emphasised that it was not the pastor that healed her but the Holy Spirit and her faith.

Another area is that of vocation. Hannah also suggested that the Holy Spirit was involved in calling ministers to serve:

At the moment people follow money, for example. So if it is not Holy Spirit which has come through that person . . . you can say, oh, let me go and work and get more money. So you won't waste your time carrying Bible. But because of the Holy Spirit upon you, you forget about material things and follow Jesus Christ

Gabriel said that ministers were chosen by God. Even though many people would want to be ministers, it all depends on God. He pointed out that no matter how intelligent a person is, they still need God to give them something to share in their sermons. He said that training is important, but people still needed to be called by God in order to lead.

There was more emphasis on the Spirit's involvement at the initial stage of a person's vocational journey than the need for ministers to continuously rely on the Holy Spirit throughout their ministry. There was in that sense some regard for how ministers are equipped by their training in this church. In the same vein, they had more regard for the lectionary. For example, when I pointed out that at one of the services, the Holy Spirit was referred to only twice throughout the service, one person told me that it simply had to do with the lectionary. There was in that sense reasonable validity placed on such systemic things as training and time-tabling in this church.

Another important area is that of Biblical interpretation. The church members I interviewed believed that the Holy Spirit was involved in the interpretation of the Bible. Hannah, who attended a Pentecostal church in the past, gave this description of the Spirit's involvement in Biblical interpretation:

If the Holy Spirit is not involved in the reading of the Bible you are bound not to understand the meaning of what you are reading. You will read and you will not assimilate it. You will read it for the reading sake. But if the Holy Spirit is involved, you are bound to have more knowledge of what you are reading. The interpretation of it will be more clear. Putting it into practice will be more into you as well.

This was echoed by several other people. Ann supported the point that the Holy Spirit helps believers put what they have read into practice, by noting that the Spirit reminds you of what you have read. Dada, on the other hand, took it a step further by stating that the "Bible contains divine Spirit".

Summary

The purpose of this case study was to ascertain where the African members of E L Methodist stood regarding the Spirit's divinity, personhood and co-equality and also the extent to which they experienced him as an empowering figure in their personal and church life. The evidence showed that the African members, in general, saw the Holy Spirit as God and not merely an attribute of God. However, their sense of the unity of the God-head was sometimes so strongly expressed that the Spirit appeared subsumed within "God", thus losing the sense of the Spirit as a distinctive person. The church generally spoke of the Spirit on equal terms with Father and Son, although in one case, there was a clear sign of the subordination of the Spirit to the Father. There was not much emphasis on the empowerment of the Holy Spirit. Even though they clearly believed that the Spirit was involved in their daily life, did miracles in their life, and interpreted the Bible to them, there was not the sense that the Holy Spirit was the basis for measuring all else. So, for example, they had regard for the skills ministers acquire through training and for the order of readings and seasons already planned by the wider Methodist Church.

St Mary's Roman Catholic Church,

St Mary Roman Catholic Church (St Mary RC) is located on a quiet road in East London. The neighbourhood of the church shares the social-economic characteristics described in Chapter 3. The church is visible from a long distance away because it was built on the hilly part of the neighbourhood. The worship area inside the building is very bright with many rows of seats laid out. There was a slightly raised platform for the altar. Apart from the main worship area, there was a smaller chapel where weekday services were held. When I observed the services, this congregation ranged from seventy to one hundred people, often depending on whether it was the first or the second service of the day. The congregation was very mixed. There were large numbers of Africans, Asians and Europeans. I noticed that many of the Europeans spoke with an Irish accent. The congregation represented all age groups, although there were not many who appeared to be in their teens or 20s.

The church has two services on Sunday and one weekday morning service. This was often led by one of two white European priests, whom I will call James and John. Whoever was leading the service also appeared to lead much of the singing, although there was also a choir. The priests would also preach the sermon and preside over the communion. I attended five services at the church over a six months period. I noticed several references to the Holy Spirit during the service. At one of the services I attended, the priest began with the greeting, "In the name of the Father, and the Son and the Holy Spirit". One of the responsive prayers, "Kyrie", contained the following lines:

Father, who gave us life, save us from sin and strife
Lord have mercy.
Jesus who came to earth that we might have rebirth
Christ have mercy.
Spirit of God above, teach us the way to love.
Lord, have mercy.

The appointed prayer for the day (referred to as "The Collect" in many traditions) ended with the words, ". . . with the Holy Spirit, one God for ever and ever". Part of the Gospel acclamation read, "The Spirit of the Lord has been given to me. He has sent me to bring good news to the poor", which is a reference to Luke 4:18. The prayer said before the celebration of the Eucharist ended with the words, ". . . Father, Son and Holy Spirit". The Hymn before the Eucharist had a verse which read, "Anointed with the Spirit and with power." The Nicene Creed recounted belief in God, the Father, Jesus Christ and the Holy Spirit, who "has spoken through the prophets". Hence, in comparison with E L Methodist services that I attended as part of this study, the Roman Catholic service had many more references to the Holy Spirit or the "Spirit of God". These references were usually made within a Trinitarian formula.

During the six months of my study, I interviewed eight members of the church. As with the other case studies, I covered the same ground that I had covered with members of Mount Zion, and, also asked questions related to the two areas I focus on in this chapter, that is, the divinity of and empowerment by the Spirit.

The Holy Spirit within the Trinity

The focus here is on the divinity, personhood and co-equality of the Holy Spirit. It showed clearly that the church members saw the Holy Spirit in the context of the Trinity. Several people told me how for them God is Father, Son and Holy Spirit. Timothy, a Nigerian in his thirties, told me, "We believe in the Trinity, God the Father, God the Son and God the Holy Spirit. When you say [Holy Spirit] it means the third person in the Trinity." Another member, Nicky, a Nigerian in her twenties, said:

We are told that the Holy Spirit is the third person in the Trinity. When I think of the Holy Spirit, I actually just think of an invisible man, really. A supernatural being, you can't see him, but he is there.

Job, a man in his forties who came originally from Rwanda, said: "If you go back to the Trinity, there is God the Father, the Son and the Holy Spirit. And they have got their departments, if you like."

When asked why this Trinitarian formula Father-Son-Holy Spirit was commonly used in church service, Nicky explained that she did not really know:

> When we were in catechism then they tell you that you have to invite God, the Father, the Son and the Holy Spirit to come and be with us during prayers. That is how we grew up, that is what I grew up with, and that is the belief. Even if you want to say your Rosary or you want to just say a quick shout out to God, you start with "In the name of the Father..." I can't say precisely why, you know, but this is what I grew up with, this is my faith.

Bukky, a woman in her thirties whose parents are Nigerians, also made reference to the teaching she received as a child. "As a kid when you are doing your catechism they tell you, Oh, there are three Persons in one God, God the Father, God the Son, God the Holy Spirit, and you just recite that. I think as you get older, you start really to deepen into what that means."

Apart from the use of the word "Trinity", many of those I spoke to showed that they saw the Holy Spirit as God. Wamba, an Ivorian woman in her forties, who converted to Christianity from Islam about ten years ago, regarding worship, said that it was right to worship the Holy Spirit:

> The Holy Spirit deserves to be worshipped because when you say the Father, the Son and the Holy Spirit and when you believe that it is only one, so it deserves to be worshipped, like you worship God.

She also said that she prays to the Holy Spirit and remarked that people who say that they do not pray to the Holy Spirit do not understand who the Holy Spirit is:

> Because if you believe that the Holy Spirit is the same God, Father and Holy Spirit are the same person. So you cannot worship the Father, worship the Son and don't worship the Holy Spirit. It's about the meaning, who is the Holy Spirit for you. [Unless] you don't understand who the Holy Spirit is, there is no reason for you maybe not to worship the Holy Spirit. As I am concerned, I say I will worship the Holy Spirit like I would worship God the Father.

She also rejected any notion of the Holy Spirit as a kind of power working for God. The Holy Spirit, she said, is like a "delegate" because "God cannot be there" – meaning that the Father sends the Holy Spirit because he himself cannot come.

Nicky was similarly clear about the divinity of the Holy Spirit. She said that to ask what the Holy Spirit does is the same as asking what God does. "He does everything," She said. She also rejected the notion that the Holy Spirit is a power or agent working on God's behalf. "The Holy Spirit is God. We don't know how it is," she said. Regarding whether it is right to worship the Holy Spirit, she said, "if you can worship God that you don't see and you believe that the Holy Spirit is God, then why not." When asked whether she prays to the Holy Spirit she replied:

> I pray to God . . . when I pray I say something like 'come down Holy Spirit and fill the hearts of the faithful'. I call down the Holy Spirit when I want to pray. Maybe I don't say, 'Holy Spirit please do this, you know, but I say God and say Jesus and if three are one then I definitely pray to the Holy Spirit.

Job and Bukky also strongly affirmed the divinity of the Holy Spirit by saying that when one worships God, one is also worshipping the Son and the Spirit since the three are one. They also said that they pray to the Holy Spirit. Hence the indication was that the divinity of the Holy Spirit was firmly established in the minds of many of the participants at this church.

The participants, on the whole, did not see the Spirit as a mere power or force, thus establishing the Spirit's personhood. But the distinctiveness of the person of the Holy Spirit was not always clear. Much like I saw at the Methodist church, the Holy Spirit often appeared subsumed within the Trinity. One indication of this was the difficulty many of the participants had in attributing particular kind of work to the Holy Spirit. One person simply answered saying that to ask "what does the Holy Spirit do" is to ask "what does God do?"

There were also clear signs that many participants at this church saw the Holy Spirit as subordinate to the Father. For example, Kofi, a Ghanaian man in his fifties, who has attended St Mary RC for over twenty years, said the Spirit did not deserve to be worshipped. "We worship God, not the Holy Spirit. Although he works with God, and is part of the Trinity." He explained further using Jesus as an example:

> Jesus Christ is the link between us and God. He came to die for our sins. We don't worship Jesus, we rather worship God. We believe that Jesus came to atone for our sins. In that same way, we don't worship the Holy Spirit. We rather worship God.

Similarly, regarding whether people should pray to the Holy Spirit, he said, "I pray to God that he will bring down the Holy Spirit to guide me in what I do. But I don't pray to the Holy Spirit."

A similar view was expressed by other members of the church. Mubi, a Ugandan woman in her forties, said that the Holy Spirit is a gift from God and that only God the giver of the gift should be worshipped. Moses, a man in his twenties, who has roots in Ghana but has lived in Britain all his life and attended St Mary RC all his life, said the Holy Spirit did not deserve to be worshipped because he was sent by God. He also noted how Roman Catholics often ask Mary to intercede for them and said he found this unnecessary. "I wouldn't feel any need to go via the Holy Spirit or via Mary, to be honest." The same point was made by Timothy, who has been a member of the church for about four years. For Timothy, to worship the Holy Spirit or Jesus would mean singling them out and entail separating the persons of the Trinity. However, to worship the Father is right because the Father incorporates the Son and the Spirit into himself. He also said that anybody who prays to the Holy Spirit needed to be "enlightened" to understand the Trinity.

Empowerment by the Holy Spirit

I investigated the extent to which the Holy Spirit was seen as giving power to their individual and church life. Much as I found at E L Methodist, this did not come out in bold colours. There was not the sense the church members saw the Holy Spirit as a source of spiritual power for confronting issues of daily life. However, they clearly relied on the Holy Spirit in several other ways. One of these is guidance. There was very much the belief that the Holy Spirit guides believers through daily life. Nicky described this involvement in a person's daily life as one of the most important things the Holy Spirit does. For her, to ask whether the Holy Spirit is involved in daily life is like asking whether God is involved in daily life:

> You sleep and wake up, God is involved, and the Holy Spirit is involved. You get food to eat everyday, water to drink everyday, God is involved. You kneel down and you pray, he answers, he is involved.

Kofi also said guidance through day to day life is among the most important things the Holy Spirit can do for a person. He described how this happens: "Before you make a decision you might wonder, should I do it this way or that way. You begin to think which way is best. Then all of a sudden, you begin to think 'Ah, my mind tells me I should do this.' What is that mind which is telling you? As a Christian, I believe there is that Holy Spirit."

Another important area was protection. Moses described the Holy Spirit's involvement in daily life by recounting how he once received a message from God through the music he was playing on his iPod. "I needed some sort of answer. I was listening to my iPod, nothing related to anything Godly or Gospel. And then the message came through in a song. That is an example of the Holy Spirit working Magic!" Wamba also told me about the Holy Spirit's involvement in her daily life. She described how she would pray to ask the Holy Spirit to take control of her day and how the Holy Spirit has performed many miracles in her life:

> My life is full of miracles. Since I became a Christian, the Holy Spirit changed my life. The Holy Spirit saved me. I don't know, maybe if I was in my country I don't know if I will be alive again. So the Holy Spirit transformed me, my way to think, and my way to behave. So I will say the Holy Spirit bring me in this country.

Wamba, whose country of origin is Côte d'Ivoire, has experienced war and a high level of violence in the past decade, thus sees the work of the Holy Spirit as not only spiritual transformation but also in the practical sense of keeping her alive.

I was also struck by how many of the participants listed the building up of faith as one of the key works of the Holy Spirit. This was particularly significant because it was not specifically prompted by a question. Job described the role of the Holy Spirit as that of strengthening people in their faith. "Everybody has got a calling and the level of believing is quite different from individual to individual. And I think when we pray to the Holy Spirit we ask for having more faith." Mubi spoke along similar lines. She believed the most important thing the Holy Spirit can do for a person is to help them have faith and not give up.

> Sometimes we experience little downfall and sometimes that can sort of mask or get you think there is no God. But we are being guided by the Spirit. . . . You stumble you pick yourself up and you still carry on and still have that faith to say I must follow this path.

Kofi also described the work of the Holy Spirit as "enhancing our belief".

Even though taking the participants in this case study as whole, the sense of the Spirit giving spiritual power to individuals and to the church did not appear to be a major issue for them, one person stood out from the rest. Bukky, who in addition to her membership of St Mary RC also attended a weekly gathering of Charismatic Roman Catholics somewhere in London, spoke of the Holy Spirit with enthusiasm. She described how she would invite the Spirit at the beginning of her day and the Spirit would give her the ability to do several things. The Spirit enabled her to pray when she couldn't find the words, enabled her to discern more deeply what people were saying or doing at her work place and enabled her to discern all she needs to do during the day.

> The Holy Spirit gives you the power to do good, gives you the power of the knowledge of God. Because without the Holy Spirit, you won't really know who God is.

She told me that she believed Christians use less than a tenth of the power of the Holy Spirit.

She went on to describe how the Holy Spirit would enable even a shy person to evangelize, how the Holy Spirit is needed for "ministry to be powerful" and how it is the Holy Spirit that enables people to worship God. The central place the theme of empowerment had in her concept of the Holy Spirit also showed in the way she used the word "power" or "powerful". She described singing and worshipping with instruments as a "powerful way of praying", the view that Christians are in the dispensation of the Spirit as "a powerful thing" and the Holy Spirit as "a very powerful tool".

It was not only her thoughts about empowerment that differed from those of her fellow church members. Her treatment of other themes was also different. She described how she would pray for the Holy Spirit to open her mind and her heart before she reads the Bible. As a result, the "word" had transformed her life. "Now, without the Holy Spirit that word would not have that power to transform my life." She also described how the Holy Spirit can give different interpretations to different people:

> Without the Holy Spirit the word is just a word, but through the power of the Holy Spirit that word becomes effective and has that power to transform your life. Because the word speaks to you personally where you are.

That ability for the same text to have different meaning for different people was in her view "an example of the power of the Holy Spirit."

Other significant characteristics

Many of the participants saw the Holy Spirit not in the spectacular or the unusual but in the ordinary. When they were asked if the Holy Spirit was in the church, many contended that if he was not, the church would not be there. The very fact of gathering was a sign of the Holy Spirit. One person described to me the difficulties the church had with the building and how the congregation had pulled together to bring things round. Some others talked about the friendship and sense of community they experience in the church. This, they contended, was particularly significant, considering that the church members came from different ethnic backgrounds and continents. For example, Timothy said the Holy Spirit is active in their church, otherwise, there would be chaos instead of the order and understanding that currently exists between different nationalities. Timothy also described the peace of mind with which a Christian goes about his daily business as a sign of the involvement of the Holy Spirit. Mubi and Nicky both described how the Holy Spirit does "little" miracles as part of everyday life.

Only a few spoke of the Holy Spirit with excitement and a strong sense of intimate relationship with a person. One of them was Wamba, who converted from Islam ten years ago and had attended both a Methodist and a Pentecostal church for some years before becoming a Roman Catholic. She described the Holy Spirit as "another person after Jesus who is here to help us to teach us and to be with us". She went on to describe how the Spirit helped her to convert from Islam:

> In my life the Holy Spirit teach me a lot. As a Muslim it was very hard to become a Christian. This is like a testimony. When you are a Muslim, to say Jesus is the Son of God is very hard. And one day when I was reading my Bible in my bedroom, the Holy Spirit taught me why I should accept Jesus as the Son of God.

The passage she was reading at the time was John 1:1, which describes how the Word which was there in the beginning became flesh. "This verse was powerful for me, to understand why Jesus is Son of God." However, apart from Wamba and one or two other interviewees, the sense of the Holy Spirit as a person was not always evident in the thinking of other participants.

I also noticed that much like the Methodists, the Roman Catholics tend not to bring up the Holy Spirit without prompting; I often had to probe them to get a full response. In general, they gave short answers to my question and were often provisional in their answer, such as saying, "Well, yes and no" or "it depends on the individual".

Summary

The aim of this case study has been to find out the extent to which the African members of St Mary RC believe in the divinity, personhood and co-equality of the Holy Spirit and also to see the extent to which they believe the Holy Spirit empowers. The evidence shows that these African Roman Catholics see the Holy Spirit through the window of the doctrine of the Trinity. For many, this begins with the teaching they receive at Catechism (usually as children) but is constantly reinforced through the Trinitarian language and structure of the weekly church service. In spite of this, there exists a diversity of understanding of who the Holy Spirit is. The sense of the Holy Spirit as God (that is the divinity of the Holy Spirit) is established in the mind of most participants. There was some evidence of intimate relationship with the Holy Spirit for some members, but not for most. Also, some spoke about him as though he was subordinate to the Father. The sense of the Spirit as an empowering influence in their life was also lacking. Rather, much like the Methodists, they experienced the Holy Spirit as a guiding influence.

Two people stood out from the participants at this church. They spoke enthusiastically of the personal and empowering relationship they have with the Holy Spirit. It is noteworthy that of the two, one attended a Pentecostal church before becoming Roman Catholic and the other regularly attended a gathering of Charismatic Roman Catholics while still maintaining her membership of St Mary RC. This suggests that such Pentecostal or Charismatic influences (that is, whether inside or outside Roman Catholicism) shape belief about the Holy Spirit, making believers more likely to see the Spirit as a person. Another area of significance was the tendency to see the work of the Holy Spirit in less spectacular aspects of individual or church life. For example, the very fact of people gathering together from different backgrounds every Sunday to worship in the church was pointed to as a sign of the Spirit's work.

St John's Church of England

St John C of E is, like all the other churches, situated in East London. The immediate neighbourhood of the church has a very urban feel. There are several shops, a primary and secondary school, a pub and a bingo hall not far from the church. Like many other parts of East London, the area has grown in population recently, mostly due to immigration. The parish has large numbers of people of African or Caribbean origin, and many from Pakistan, India or Bangladesh. People of all ages and professions live in the parish of St John C of E, although there is a higher than average proportion of young families.

The diversity of background and age of those living in the area is reflected in the church membership. About fifty percent of the congregation is of African or Caribbean origin. The other fifty percent are mainly made of white British people. There are also a small number of people from Asia. Although there is a considerable Asian population in the area, many of the Asians are Muslims or belong to other faiths. There is also a good number of young families in the church. Regular church attendance is about 100. The church has two services on Sundays. There is the main service at 10.30 a.m. and an evening service at 6.30 p.m.

The services almost always followed the order in *Common Worship*.[6] At one of the services I attended, the leading minister began with this greeting: "In the name of the Father and the Son, and the Holy Spirit", to which the congregation responded, "Amen." After a few more prayers, including the "Confession", the music group led the congregation through a period of praise-singing. Five songs were sung consecutively during that period. Then the minister read the Collect, (i.e. the appointed prayer for the day based on the Anglican season). This prayer ended with the words ". . . through Jesus Christ our Lord, in the unity of the Holy Spirit, one God now and for ever. Amen." Later there were a number of Bible readings, including one from the Gospel. The vicar preached the sermon after this. A church member led the gathering through intercessory prayers. Many songs were sung at different points in the service, such as between the sermon and the Intercessions. The Eucharistic Prayer B was used from *Common Worship* which contained several references to the Holy Spirit.[7] At the end, the leading minister gave the final blessing "The blessing of God Almighty, the Father, the Son and the Holy Spirit be with you and remain with you always."

I observed the church for over a year, during which time I attended more than ten services. After that I started to interview the church members. I interviewed ten people, which includes one person in a leadership position in the church. I also collected several of the church's documents over that period, including a regular bulletin, and a parish profile.

The Holy Spirit within the Trinity

As in previous churches, the interest here is in the divinity, personhood and co-equality of the Holy Spirit. Many of those I interviewed affirmed the Spirit's divinity by saying they believed he deserved to be worshipped. Helen, a woman in her forties, who comes originally from Ghana and has attended St John C of E for six years said: "I know the Holy Spirit is from God and God is in the three persons so, definitely, he is to be worshipped." She also said she prays to the Holy Spirit. "At times when I'm praying, you don't even know what to say.

---

[6]   Archbishop's Council, *Common Worship* (London: Archbishop's Council, 2000).

[7]   Archbishop's Council, *Common Worship*.

So I ask for the guidance of the Holy Spirit to fill me so that I will know what exactly to say."

Jude, a man in his forties, who also comes from Ghana, when asked whether the Holy Spirit deserves to be worshipped, responded: "Yes. One hundred percent. I think the Holy Spirit deserves to be worshipped." He also said he prays to the Holy Spirit. "Because of what he has done for me in my life. I do pray every morning." Tunde, a Nigerian man in his thirties, who converted to Christianity from Islam, said the Holy Spirit deserved to be worshipped:

When you are worshipping God it is the same thing as if you are worshipping the Holy Spirit. Because whenever we say the Holy Spirit, it involves God and the Son that was sent to the world.

Apart from the issue of worship, other statements were made that showed the church members believed in the divinity of the Holy Spirit. Didier, an Ivorian man in his forties, spoke regarding the Holy Spirit as follows: "The Holy Spirit is God, our Lord, looking after us. It is our umbrella." Michael, a Nigerian man in his forties, who is part of the leadership team, rejected the idea that the Holy Spirit might be seen as a power that works on God's behalf, saying: "The Holy Spirit is God." He also said he prays to the Holy Spirit, "I pray to the Holy Spirit, I pray to God the Father, the Son and the Holy Spirit." Florence, a woman of Nigerian origin in her thirties, who leads one of the groups in the church, made statements of the Spirit's divinity a number of times. In describing the work of the Holy Spirit, she said:

The Holy Spirit reveals Christ to us. The Holy Spirit helps us and intercedes for us. . . . The Holy Spirit is peace and comfort, especially in the times of ups and downs and tribulations. It is the stillness of God I have in the innermost part of my being that makes me connect to God. The Holy Spirit is God.

When I asked her whether the Holy Spirit does miracles, she said yes, because God does miracles and "the Spirit is God". She also made a similar statement when I asked her whether the Holy Spirit could be seen as a power working for God, "No," she said, "the Holy Spirit is God."

It also came out strongly that the church members I spoke to often saw the Holy Spirit from the point of view of the Trinity. This is not surprising considering that many of the times the Holy Spirit is referred to during church services at St John C of E it was within the Trinitarian context. Abana, a woman in her thirties, originally from Ghana, said: "It's in the Bible, God the Father, God the Son and God the Holy Spirit. Three in one." Michael described him as "Third person of the Trinity" and Florence described him as "Third person of the Godhead." Tunde described how the words "in the name of the Father, and the Son and the Holy Spirit" are often uttered during church services and added: "So when you talk about the Holy Spirit, what comes to my mind is the God, and the Son that was sent to deliver us from sin." He also described how the Blessing is usually said at the end of the service with those same words: "Blessing of God Almighty, the Father, the Son and the Holy Spirit." To him this meant the Holy Spirit was being prayed to alongside Father and Son.

Tunde's reference to "the Son that was sent" resonates with something striking about the church members understanding of the Holy Spirit. At this church more than any other in this study, the Holy Spirit was very often associated with Jesus Christ. Apart from the kind of link made above by Florence when she says that "The Holy Spirit reveals Christ to us" there were others relating the Holy Spirit more closely with Jesus Christ. For example, Kunto said, "God is the Holy Spirit. Jesus Christ, God is the Holy Spirit." Helen said something similar when I asked her the relationship between the Holy Spirit and Jesus Christ:

> The Holy Spirit is Jesus Christ and Jesus Christ is the Holy Spirit. Because God brought him just to be a mediator between God and man, so that he will be on behalf of us human beings going to the Almighty. . . . I will call him a mediator. You can't get to God without going through Christ.

Something similar is seen in the answer given by Jude when asked whether the Holy Spirit deserves to be worshipped:

> I think the Holy Spirit deserves to be worshipped. As we say in one of our songs, we owe so much and he doesn't owe anything; he came to die on the cross just to take our debts away. So I think we need not pay him by money but by worship.

Both Helen and Jude began their comment with the Holy Spirit and ended talking about Jesus. It is fair to say that for many of the interviewees Jesus Christ and the Holy Spirit are so closely related that the divinity of the Holy Spirit was often being established by the divinity of Jesus Christ.

As I found in the other churches in this study, the church members rejected any notion that the Holy Spirit is merely a force or power and talked about him in personal terms. There was also the sign that, on the whole, they saw him as a distinctive person to whom specific acts can be attributed. However, one person described the Holy Spirit as "The same Triune God . . . just another aspect of God the Father." He explained further:

> I've got you in front of me, you might be a mathematician and a father . . . if I have a Maths problem I am calling on that aspect of you as a mathematician not as a father. If I've got parenting problem I come to you as a parent and say to you 'how do you do it'. So it's exactly that. It's just a different nature or aspect of God.

This description, which implies that the Holy Spirit is not a distinctive person, was not found in any other member of the church.

Regarding co-equality, the general view was that the Spirit was one with and therefore equal to the Father and the Son. However, as I found in both the Methodist and the Roman Catholic churches, a view was expressed which could be seen as the subordination of the Holy Spirit to the Father. Christopher, who came originally from Nigeria, and has been an Anglican virtually all his life, said he did not think the Holy Spirit deserved to be worshipped. He said, "You don't worship the Holy Spirit. It is only one God we have and to him we worship. We don't worship the Holy Spirit." He also made a similar point about Jesus:

> Do we worship Jesus? We worship God. We worship God through Christ. But not to worship Christ. . . . There was no place in the Bible he said we should worship him. He said we should follow him.

He also said he did not pray to the Holy Spirit and suggested that those who do may have an understanding built on wrong foundations.

Empowerment by the Holy Spirit

I investigated the extent to which the participants saw the Holy Spirit as giving power to daily life and the life of their church. I found that, on the whole, the sense that the Holy Spirit is a source of empowerment was stronger than I found in either the Methodist or the Roman Catholic. For a start, I found that the concept of the "indwelling of the Holy Spirit", which has been linked elsewhere with empowerment, was a key feature of their Pneumatology. Virtually everybody I spoke to indicated this in one way or other. Susan said: "What comes to my mind when somebody says 'Holy Spirit' is me being filled by the presence of God." Christopher gave a similar description: "Holy Spirit, as far as I know, is the Spirit of God that lives in us. It's that Spirit that tells us to do the Christ things." He also called him the "Spirit of discernment" helping Christians to distinguish good from evil:

> I think on the day of Pentecost, when they said the apostles were praying, the Holy Spirit came upon them. So that Spirit has been with us since then. As far as you identify yourself as a Christian, not by merely saying 'I go to church' — not a churchgoer — the Holy Spirit lives in you. The moment you give your life to Christ, the Holy Spirit resides in you and it becomes a part of you

Helen also described the Holy Spirit along similar lines. She described the Holy Spirit as the "Spirit of God" and said, "We Christians believe if you don't have the Holy Spirit then it means your belief in Christianity I don't think is genuine. That's what I believe. Because without the Holy Spirit you can't be a Christian." She also described how the Holy Spirit sometimes lifts her up from within:

> Certain times that I feel that I'm lonely, sad, or I've got some problems, if I begin to sing or start to pray. I am alone but, you feel within you, you've got something within you and I know as a Christian that is by the Holy Spirit.

The link between the indwelling of the Holy Spirit and empowerment by the Holy Spirit came out most clearly with Jude. He gave this description of the Holy Spirit:

> The Holy Spirit is a living Spirit. We don't see the Holy Spirit but I know the Holy Spirit liveth. It's something that dwells in us. You only feel it. It's like fire that burns in you. When you are in trouble or anything, you can see that something stands behind you and tells you that you've not lost everything. You've got something to move forward on. It's like the Holy Spirit to me. Something that pushes me [on] when I am falling down.

He also said that the Holy Spirit is "our backbone", adding: "Whenever we are in need of God's power we just ask and the Holy Spirit comes to lead us in whatever we want to have from God." He explained further:

> Without the Holy Spirit we can't stand. Just like an empty bag without anything in it. It just falls apart. The Holy Spirit, like I said, is something that boosts our spirit in us, something that boosts us. Even though we are falling, it makes us know that there is somebody in us which will always be there for us and keeps us moving.

Michael, similarly, described how the Holy Spirit sustains the believer. "No Christian can live without it . . . it is the oil for the Christian soul. Without it you will be lifeless and dead." By this he meant that even though the person would be physically alive, they would be spiritually dead.

In addition to giving power for daily life, as with the Methodist and the Roman Catholic churches, the Holy Spirit was also linked to guidance, protection, and miraculous events. Their strong sense that the Spirit indwells the believer made it easy for them to see the Spirit as having a role in the daily life of believers. Abana, in fact, indicated that the question of whether the Holy Spirit is involved in daily life is answered if one knows that the Holy Spirit lives in the Christian. Florence contended that Christians cannot separate their daily life from their walk with God, because "anything we are doing without God is a sin, so the Holy Spirit is very much involved in everyday life". She explained further the Spirit's role as a Guide:

> For me, as a Christian, the Holy Spirit is in everything. There is a song that says 'I need you every hour'. There is no other way I can explain it. The Holy Spirit is involved in my day to day activities. I listen to the Spirit of God within me for directions. I listen to the Spirit of God within me concerning each day as to what step to take. Even to the most minute things, I am dependent on the Holy Spirit.

One person described how, when she was in Africa, the Holy Spirit saved her from the hands of people who had planned to harm her using evil spiritual powers. When it was revealed to her that this spiritual attempt on her life had been made, she went to a Pentecostal church and the pastors laid hands on her. At that moment, she was "overtaken by something". It was a very long time before she recovered consciousness and through that incident the Spirit saved her from the spiritual attack. Another person told me how the Holy Spirit miraculously made her meet the man who later became her husband. This happened when she was still living in Africa. It had been her desire to marry a particular kind of person and she would stay up at night praying for that. And it happened. One day she visited a friend and this friend introduced her to a man at the house who met all she desired and that was it. "It just happened. I can't really explain it. I think it is a miracle. What happened was a miracle," she said.

Other significant characteristics

It was noticeable in this church how virtually all the people I spoke to have gone or still go to a Pentecostal church. Many had gone to Pentecostal churches in Africa, while some others still go to Pentecostal churches in this country. I noticed that they sang praise songs at the beginning of their service, just as I have noted Pentecostals do. They explained to me why they did this:

> Traditionally in the Church of England we always have [a] call to worship. We use a lot of praise and worship songs, basically, to prepare ourselves for the service and invite and welcome the Holy Spirit; to get people's attention centred on God . . . the songs we sing focus on Jesus and it just draws people near to God, prepares the atmosphere for the main service.

Another person made the following observation: "When you sing, it invites the Holy Spirit, as well and it gets people uplifted as well." This, in effect, means that these participants brought up the Holy Spirit without prompting.

The story of the Spirit's practical involvement to save a believer's life from spiritual attack alludes to the link between the belief that the Holy Spirit is involved in daily life and the African view of life as a spiritual theatre. One church member made that link more explicitly when discussing the actions of the Holy Spirit in daily life:

> Most things we do, whether good or bad, is guided by some sort of spirit. But the good one, mostly, is when the presence of the Holy Spirit is there. It prevents you from getting into problems or from harm. Sometimes when things happen, you hear some voices talking to you and urging you either not to do that thing or to go ahead. It's just that people have not realised that is the Holy Spirit talking to them.

This view that life is guided by good or bad spirits resonates with a typical African spiritual worldview.

The diversity of areas in which the church members saw evidence of the work of the Holy Spirit was remarkable in itself. The most common areas were in the singing and praising during the service. One person said that the Holy Spirit was in the worship because without the Holy Spirit it would not be possible to worship God. Another said she can feel it when the church sings or when somebody preaches. She could also see it in people's faces. Somebody else supported the point about the sermon. He pointed out that sometimes when you come to church intending to give £5 during the collection "due to the touch of the Spirit" during the sermon you give £20. He said the evidence of the Spirit's presence also lies in the physical development that has taken place in the church, such as the changes in furniture, and the increase in numbers in the church. "The church would not grow if the Holy Spirit is not there," he said. A number of people pointed to the ministry of the Vicar and the Vicar's wife as evidence of the presence of the Holy Spirit. Some pointed to the family atmosphere they experience in the church. Only one person referred to what could be seen as a supernatural experience. She described how she once felt the Holy Spirit overpowering her in the church, making her body tremble.

Summary

The divinity of the Holy Spirit, that is the view that the Holy Spirit is God, appears well established in this church. In answering questions many of the church members literally said those words, "The Holy Spirit is God". Virtually, all also believed the Holy Spirit deserved to be worshipped, thus establishing his divinity further. Many participants showed that they thought of the Holy Spirit in the context of the Trinity. This is understandable considering that Trinitarian language was prevalent in the service. The extent to which the Holy Spirit was related to Jesus Christ was striking. One church member took this relationship to the point of saying, "The Holy Spirit is Jesus Christ and Jesus Christ is the Holy Spirit." This further reinforced the sense of the divinity of the Holy Spirit, if one assumes the divinity of Christ, although a complete conflation of the two would undermine the personhood of the Holy Spirit. It is fair to say that most participants spoke of that link in terms of the Holy Spirit making believers become like Christ.

There was the commonly held view that the Holy Spirit lives in the believer. From that point of view, the participants believed the Holy Spirit was involved in their daily life. Much like the Methodist and the Roman Catholic, many Church of England participants expressed this as a guiding presence. But some also talked about the Spirit as an empowering influence, "moving them on" or "pushing them on" when they are flagging. Actual stories of things the Holy Spirit had done in their life also supported this point. There was a stronger sense of this at St John C of E than I found at either the Methodist or the Roman Catholic churches. It was pointed out how participants in this church brought up the Holy Spirit without being prompted. This could be because, as we noted, many of the church members have either in the past or at the present time belonged to a Pentecostal church or because St John C of E itself has a Pentecostal-style of worship.

Amazing Grace Pentecostal Church

Amazing Grace Pentecostal Church (Amazing Grace for short) was only a year old when I visited it. It was set up by an African couple, Ben and Benedicta Kangolo. The church met at a community hall in one of the liveliest parts of East London. The neighbourhood has a busy shopping street and shares many of the East London socio-economic characteristics I described earlier. The hall where the church met was off the main street. Amazing Grace had a long-term hire arrangement at the hall but paid them on a week by week basis. The church also sometimes used another smaller room for which they paid a lower fee. I was told that Amazing Grace had been moving from place to place in the past and the current location at the community hall was its first proper location since it started.

Amazing Grace had very few members. The regular membership was less than fifteen adults and at some of their services there were as few as five people present. The main church service was on Sunday morning, but they also had a prayer meeting on Thursday evenings. These meetings lasted for about an hour and half. The church's small membership and the fact that it is in its early stage of life offered me a different and complementary set of characteristics for my research, compared to Mount Zion. It was akin to watching the early years of a child. It is in line with my adopted sampling approach of "maximum variation".

The church was led by a Nigerian couple, Pastor Ben and his wife, Benedicta. They had been married for many years, and had three children. They had a ministry in Africa before coming to Britain five years ago. In many of their services I attended, Pastor Ben preached and Benedicta led the singing. Their children were also present and they participated actively in church services through singing and clapping. The rest of the membership was in similar family units, that is, a couple and two or three children. In this regard, there were often as many children as adults. This family-feel was important to the church and their sense of the kind of church God was calling them to be. Many of the members told me they like Amazing Grace because it was "a family church".

The church had a flat, organisational structure. Pastor Ben, a man in his early forties, was really in charge and he delegated responsibility as was necessary. Sometimes he gave people a long term role, like his wife who had the role of leading the music and another member who had the role of organizing the church's prayer life. This leadership style appeared to work and people were very keen to volunteer to do things or to be volunteered by others. Benedicta, who was in her late thirties, was also responsible for the Sunday school. Pastor Angelina, a woman in her forties, who was based at another church, came to lead the service and give the sermon whenever Pastor Ben was away on his personal business.

I visited the church a total of ten times over a period of one year. I attended both the Sunday services and the Thursday Prayer meetings. Both the services and the prayer meetings began with a short prayer, followed by praise-singing for about half an hour. The rest of the time was used for preaching and praying. Many of the prayer sessions involved the whole congregation praying at the same time. During such times, I heard some people praying "in tongues". Following the visits, I interviewed six adult members of the church.[8]

I also examined the church's documents, which are important because that material is a product of Africans, which are the subject of this study, unlike the material from the Methodist, the Church of England and Roman Catholic churches, produced by people of different ethnicity. Set out below are my findings regarding their belief about the divinity, personhood and co-equality of the Holy Spirit and how the Holy Spirit inspires or empowers the members.

The Holy Spirit within the Trinity

Statements from the participants showed that they saw the Holy Spirit as God. When Benedicta was asked whether the Holy Spirit was "a power that works for God," she said, "I think of the Holy Spirit as God, not just a power that works for God. Holy Spirit is God working here." And when she was asked whether the Holy Spirit "deserved to be worshipped," she said: "Definitely, because he is God. The Holy Spirit is God." Angelina, a visiting Pastor, said to me, "I do think the Holy Spirit is a power from God and is also God." Several members spoke of how they would pray to the Holy Spirit or see him as an object of worship. Bola, a Nigerian woman in her thirties, said:

> At my church back home [in Nigeria] we normally dedicate the first Sunday of the month [to the Holy Spirit]. We call it the Pentecost Sunday. And that day all the songs, all the praises, everything is about the Holy Spirit. In that perspective he is being worshipped.

She also said she prays to the Holy Spirit, although she does not pray to the Holy Spirit separately because God is Trinity.

By and large, the commonest way the participants tried to establish the divinity of the Holy Spirit was by reference to the Trinity. Angelina said that the Holy Spirit deserved to be worshipped because "Father, Son and Holy Spirit are one." When asked what she thought of the Holy Spirit she said: "When I think of the Holy Spirit, I think of God. Because I know that God is in three persons, the Son, the Holy Spirit and the Father." Yomi, a Nigerian man in his forties, who comes to the church with his family, told me his understanding of how the Holy Spirit works:

> If you look back at the Holy Trinity, God the Father, God the Son, God the Holy Ghost, which is the Spirit, they are all intertwined. . . . [Holy Spirit] is essentially part of God. Three in one.

And when asked whether the "Spirit deserved to be worshipped," he said: "the Holy Spirit is part of God. We say God the Father, God the Son, God the Holy Ghost...it comes back to the Trinity. So, yes."

---

[8]   See Appendix 3 for the breakdown.

All this coheres with what is stated in one of the church's documents, which is in fact the training manual of the wider group the Amazing Grace is part of. The documents state that the Holy Spirit is divine, not human, and support this with Bible passages on the divinity of the Father, the divinity of the Son and the divinity of the Spirit. Hence the document not only declares the divinity of the Holy Spirit, but does so within a Trinitarian framework.

Alongside this view of the divinity of the Holy Spirit, there was also a well-developed sense of the Spirit as a distinctive person. This was reinforced by a strong sense of a personal relationship with the Holy Spirit. Benedicta gave this description:

> In my day to day walk as a Christian, there is this helper that I feel with me wherever I go — that I feel nudging my spirit when I seem to be going astray — that I see putting this burden on me to praise and worship God when I wake up in the morning — that tells me, oh, you haven't read your Bible today. You know, just like that companion that is with me in everything that I do. That is how I visualise the Holy Spirit. That is who he is to me.

I was also told that many in the church experience the Holy Spirit during worship and the Spirit makes some church members speak in tongues. I witnessed this in some of the services. One person told me the world was in the dispensation of the Holy Spirit:

> I see the Holy Spirit as the God that is actually ruling now because, as Jesus said when he was leaving, that he will send the Comforter to the disciples. And on the Day of Pentecost, that is when the Spirit actually descended on them and it gives them the power. So he is the force that is actually ruling now. I am not saying God the Father and the Son are not working. It's like Trinity. They are all working hand in hand.

Hence, it is fair to say that the sense of the Holy Spirit as a distinct person was well established at this church, perhaps more than the other churches in this phase of the study.

Regarding equality, most of the participants spoke of the Spirit in a manner that did not suggest he was subordinate to the Father and the Son. However, as was found in the other churches in this phase of the study, signs of subordination remain. One person said, "We say there are three persons in God – God the Father, God the Son, God the Holy Spirit." And she went on to give the following description of the Trinitarian persons:

> We know that the God is there, the big God that I go and I worship. I know that Jesus came and he died for me and I've accepted him as my Lord and Saviour, which means I'm saved. Then in my day to day walk as a Christian there is this helper that I feel with me wherever I go.

One always has to make allowances for the language used in Trinitarian discussion because, as many of the participants themselves reminded me time

137

and again, the subject is too deep for them to capture in words. Nonetheless, the idea of God the Father as "the big God" that is worshipped suggests the subordination of Son and Spirit to the Father. That participant also said she did not think the Holy Spirit should be worshipped or prayed to.

Yinka, a Nigerian woman in her thirties, took a similar line, rejecting the idea that the Spirit might be worshipped or prayed to. She explained the reason behind this stance:

> The only person that deserves to be worshipped is God Almighty and Jesus Christ who was the Son of God. But the Spirit which is a body on its own, I don't think it needs to be worshipped, but is something that just descends when you do true worship.

The implication is that the Spirit could be an enabler or "validator" of worship, but should not be an object of worship.

Empowerment by the Holy Spirit

The evidence showed that the members of this church and their pastor believed that the Holy Spirit is the source of power for both their daily life and their church activities. One person described the Holy Spirit as, among other things, the "energy" God gives to Christians:

> When I think of the Holy Spirit, I think of God, because I know that God is in three persons — the Son, the Holy Spirit and the Father. And when I think of the Holy Spirit I think of the energy that he gives to Christians. I think of the support, I think of the friends that Christians have.

I heard several stories of how the Holy Spirit had showed his power through several life situations. For example, Pastor Ben told me how many years ago doctors told him his wife was medically not capable of having children, but he refused to accept their assessment. Eventually, the Holy Spirit gave him and his wife a miracle and they now have three children. "These days, I don't even believe anything is impossible," he said. I was told something similar happened to the whole church. Some time ago, a number of couples were trying for a child without success and Pastor Ben prayed about it. He asked God to show that the church was really a "family church" and following that prayer, the church was blessed with "a harvest of children". I also heard how a church member's immigration difficulties were suddenly resolved and he was called by the authorities and told, "Your papers are ready."

I heard how a church member was saved from being killed the day the London Underground was bombed. This was a man who worked on the London Underground, but on that day he had gone for a hospital appointment instead of going to work. His wife told me:

> I know there were believers on that train, but what made that appointment to fall on that day, and what actually made him not to be on that train, and what made

him not to be one of those with amputated limbs in hospital or even dead. To me I just say that is the work of the Holy Spirit.

They also described how the Spirit was showing his power in their life as a church. Pastor Ben told me that they would pray at the beginning of every service to ask the Holy Spirit to come and take control:

> In its entirety we believe in the presence of the Holy Spirit. When we are starting our service, we first of all ask God to bless us with the Spirit of God, that is, the Holy Spirit. And we ask the Holy Spirit to come and take control. And then, when we would have done that we start the service. We've prayed; we believe that the Holy Spirit is there with us.

Angelina described how she has witnessed the church members being empowered during the service to prophesy, discern and interpret "tongues". She also mentioned that the teaching at the church and the music often appear to be inspired by the Holy Spirit. And Benedicta, the Pastor's wife, said it was the power of the Holy Spirit that was keeping the church open. "If not for the Holy Spirit we would have packed up," she said. She described how the Holy Spirit helped them on Sundays, giving them the word to share and encouraging them to carry on worshipping. She also described how the power of the Spirit manifests itself in the work of Pastor Ben:

> When God wants to work miracles with us it is through the help of the Holy Spirit. For example, if someone is sick and the Lord wants to heal, it is through the Holy Spirit that the Pastor gets the word of God or word of wisdom that there is somebody sick and maybe calls people out to the front and lays hands on people.

She also described how the Holy Spirit gives "a word of knowledge", such as when a future evil event is predicted and prevented. Another example she gave of the power of the Spirit in ministry is when the Spirit reveals to you that somebody is not telling you the truth and, in some occasions, causing the person to break down and cry. Or when the Spirit gives you the words to say in a particular situation. Other members told me how the Holy Spirit "makes the impossible to be possible" and how the Spirit is "in charge and in control" of all things.

The church was not only intent on seeing their members grow in faith but also in their socio-economic status. Pastor Ben preached sermons with such titles as, "All things are possible" and "The journey to victory." He sometimes asked the congregation what they wanted the church to pray for in order for them to "move to the next level". One Sunday Pastor Ben prayed for the "spiritual progress and all round prosperity" of the church members. On another occasion he prayed that they would "grow" and "enlarge". On yet another occasion he described to them the characteristics of a "climber" as "Someone who succeeds in spite of physical, mental and spiritual limitations".

He urged them to be "climbers". One Sunday he asked them to prophesy for themselves: "Abundance, good report, breakthrough, enlargement of coast"; the understanding was that these were all things the Holy Spirit helped out in.

The sense that the Spirit was involved in daily life, which had been seen in the other churches, was also expressed with more vigour and confidence. One person said:

> The Holy Spirit is involved in my everyday life, everything I do, even at work, at play with the children, while cooking, whatever it is I'm doing, while driving, if I get into difficult situations, the Holy Spirit is all encompassing in my whole life because my Christianity is for my whole life.

Another church member said:

> If you have the Holy Spirit, you'll be able to know what to do and when to do it, when to move and when not to move. He is, kind of, instructing you, he's guiding you, telling you what to do. Because we are here, we cannot see God sitting beside us. We cannot see Jesus sitting there. But we can only feel them through the Holy Spirit.

The Holy Spirit was linked to the mystery of sleeping and waking up: "When one gets up in the morning, it is through the grace of God that one is even able to get up," one person said. I was also told the Holy Spirit revealed to a church member what topics will come out in her college examination so she would score high marks.

Other significant characteristics

I noticed that the church has a very strong sense of the spirit realm behind their understanding of the Holy Spirit. My analysis of Pastor Ben's sermon over a 12 month period gave strong indications of this. In these sermons he prayed against "spiritual barrenness", banished the "spirit of poverty" and commanded the "Spirits of Mammon, Complain and Unbelief" to die. Once he said:

> Spirit of defeat, doubt, every spirit that hinders me from believing the word of God or seeing impossibilities instead of possibilities, leave my life now, in the name of Jesus. Let fear die permanently today. Fear robs one of Victory. Fear is of the Devil. It destroys one's focus on the Lord. Get rid of fear out of your life today. Pray.

The implication was that for Pastor Ben, such things as poverty and barrenness were not caused merely by social, economic, biological or other physical conditions in or around a person but were due to what was happening in the realm of spirits. They were due to evil spirits, such the Spirit of Poverty and the Spirit of Barrenness. These evil spirits have to be fought and defeated.

Similarly, he referred in these sermons to the "Spirit of Counsel", the "Spirit of Evangelism" and the "Spirit of Worship" in the life of believers. Put against what we have already seen regarding the "evil spirits", there was a sense conveyed of a battle field where good "spirits" were fighting on the believer's side and evil "spirits" were trying to destroy him or her.

He often used apocalyptic stories in the Bible, such as the encounter between Daniel and a figure that was clothed in linen (Dan. 10, 11) in his sermon and prayers. In one prayer session he suggested that the same kind of conflict in the book of Daniel between the figure clothed in linen and the Prince of Persia was going on in the life of the members of his congregation. In another sermon, he talked about King Herod's attempt to kill Jesus (Matt. 2:1-7) and said: "Herod is a spirit that stops you from being fulfilled; a spirit troubled when you want to make a move; Herod is Destiny Destroyer; Destiny Breaker; loves to destroy leaders [so] that sheep may scatter."

Related to this concept of the spirit realm was the concept of the human spirit or what Pastor Ben called "the inner spirit of man". For example, Pastor Ben's reason for why they sing for a long period at the beginning of their Sunday service was that "Music has a way of bringing out the inner spirit of man to flow with what God intends them to hear for the day." Once when he was talking about fasting, he said the point of fasting was "To silence flesh and empower spirit". On another occasion he thanked God for having "activated a spirit in me to do the work he has called me to do".

This same idea of an "inner spirit of man" was present in the thinking of other members of the church. One of them said, "Sometimes I mean to travel somewhere and my spirit says, 'Don't', and I haven't, and then, for whatever reason it turns out to be the right decision." I also heard how people could be "guided by the spirit" to sense who they should avoid; "Even just by being in the vicinity of somebody, if the person is somebody you want to engage with or not to engage with, your spirit will tell you, no, you shouldn't." This sense of the spirit realm and an active human spirit was very strong in this church and formed the background for their thinking about the Holy Spirit.

I found that Amazing Grace had their doctrine of the Holy Spirit and the Bible intertwined. Time and time again I was told by their members and leaders that the Bible on its own was not worth much. One person said:

> If the Holy Spirit is not involved, you'll just read the Bible like a book, like every other novel. The Bible won't be different from picking up a newspaper or picking up a journal, or just picking up a text book written by somebody. But what makes the Bible unique when you read it is the Holy Spirit.

I heard how people would pray to ask the Holy Spirit to give them "interpretation and understanding" before starting to read the Bible. "So two people might read the Bible and might have different meaning depending on how they are filled with the spirit of God." Even an individual can have different understanding depending on what the Holy Spirit is doing:

> You can read the same Bible passage five times and get different understanding. It is the Holy Spirit that opens your eyes to see a different understanding of a

particular Bible passage and he is the one that helps you to relate it to whatever you are going through now or what another person is going through.

This, Pastor Ben told me, once happened to him when he was preparing his message for Sunday. He had asked the Spirit of God to "minister" to him before reading a very familiar passage and when he read it he said that the Holy Spirit showed him some new things about the passage. On that Sunday, when he preached the message, "a lot of people were really blessed."

For the church, the meaning in the Bible depended on what the Holy Spirit was doing in the life of the reader at that particular time. It is as though the Holy Spirit, knowing their situation, was drawing out from the Bible the interpretation that would have the right impact. Another dimension of this relationship between the Spirit and the Bible can be seen in the answer given by one of the members when I asked her whether the Holy Spirit was involved in the church. "Definitely," she said, "Everything they do is according to the Bible." In other words, adherence to biblical truth is itself a sign of the presence of the Holy Spirit.

Summary

Amazing Grace was a church that believed strongly in the divinity of the Holy Spirit. This can be seen not only in the way they talked about the Holy Spirit being part of the Trinity but also in the fact that most were comfortable with worshipping or praying to the Holy Spirit. The members also spoke of intimate experiences of the Holy Spirit in their daily life and during worship, suggesting that to them the Holy Spirit is a person. However, there remained in a minority of members the view that the Holy Spirit was subordinate to the Father, and in one case, the Son as well. This was also a church that believed strongly in the empowerment of the Holy Spirit. This theme was emphasized much more at Amazing Grace than in any of the other three churches studied in this phase. Members spoke about the Holy Spirit guiding them through life and away from trouble and working miracles in their life to meet life's many challenges. Because this was a church which was not shy of asking God for the material as well as spiritual prosperity of their members, the Holy Spirit was also understood as having a role in it.

At the background of these beliefs was a highly spiritualised way of seeing the world. It was common to see such things as doubt and fear as spirits plaguing the believer and to cast the urge to evangelize or worship or the wisdom to counsel as opposing spirits working on the believer's side. Complementary to this worldview was an anthropology that prioritized the spiritual aspect of the human being. They talked about an "inner spirit of man" that was helped by fasting and enabled by worship music to point towards God. The church's Pneumatology was intertwined with how it used the Bible. The Holy Spirit brings out the true meaning of biblical texts and often does this according to what he wants to achieve at a particular time with a particular person.

Concluding observations

It is important to point out that the various churches in this study are not samples that can be generalised over their respective denominations. So, what was observed at E L Methodist, for example, should not be taken as what would be observed in all Methodist churches in London or the United Kingdom. Rather, it is the views and beliefs of this particular group of Christians at this particular Methodist church. Beyond that, it would give us an indication of how this group of African Methodists might be similar or different from the group of African Anglicans and African Roman Catholics and African Pentecostals studied. From that point of view, it might be possible to discover how the differences observed are the influence of denomination and how the similarities might be the result of their shared African heritage. Even then, we have to tread carefully. Many of these Africans attend more than one church at a time or have attended another church recently. In particular, the vast majority of the participants attend or have attended a Pentecostal church. In that sense the association of individuals with a particular church will not always be clear cut.

Two out of the four churches in this study, the Anglican and the Roman Catholic, used written liturgy which guaranteed regular reference to the Holy Spirit. The other two, the Methodist and the Pentecostal, did not use written liturgy and during the time I observed them there were very few verbal references to the Holy Spirit. But the findings show that verbal reference during church service on its own does not guarantee a strong Pneumatology. Ironically, in the Pentecostal church, the fact that they have to do without a written liturgy (which would have guaranteed regular references to the Spirit) is to them a sign that they trust the Spirit. It was, indeed, at that church that the sense of intimate relationship with the Holy Spirit was strongest. Conversely, at the Roman Catholic Church, where the entire service is couched in Trinitarian language with several references to the Holy Spirit, I encountered the least intimate relationship with the Holy Spirit.

All four churches, in general, showed that the divinity of the Holy Spirit was well established in the minds of the participants. Most participants in all four churches saw the Holy Spirit as a distinctive person, sharing the Godhead with the Father and the Son. But there was a minority in all four churches who thought differently. Among the Methodists, somebody likened the Holy Spirit and Jesus to a palace aide that you would need to go through to see an African chief. Among the Anglicans, I encountered Christopher who was adamant that on no condition should the Holy Spirit or Jesus Christ be worshipped. Among the Pentecostals, one person referred to God the Father as "the big God that I go and I worship", and another thought the Holy Spirit should neither be worshipped nor prayed to because he is simply there to enable worship. Among

Roman Catholics, where this view was most common, it was best expressed by Timothy who said that to worship the Holy Spirit or Jesus would not be right because it would entail separating the Godhead, but to worship the Father is acceptable since, in his view, the Father incorporates the Son and the Spirit. The implication of his position is that neither the Spirit nor the Son incorporates the other two persons. There is the sense in which among this minority in all four denominations "God" means "God the Father", and the Son and the Spirit are subordinates.

In all four churches participants expressed the view that guidance through daily life was a key work of the Holy Spirit. In the Church of England church, for example, many people spoke about the Holy Spirit as a being indwelling believers and from that point of view they built their view of the Spirit's activities in daily life. Some of the Church of England participants also spoke of the Spirit as an empowering influence on them. This view that the Holy Spirit helps believers through daily life is facilitated by an African worldview which sees life as a spiritual battle and the world as a realm of spirits. This was verbalised by one or two people in the churches studied. This issue of how the African worldview might be affecting Pneumatology is one of the areas to be explored further in the next chapter. Among the Pentecostals, the issue of the Spirit's involvement in daily life was taken to another level. Participants at Amazing Grace spoke enthusiastically about how the Holy Spirit performs all manners of miracles in their day-to-day life and the church leader did not hesitate to link the Holy Spirit with the church members' desires for spiritual and material prosperity.

Looking at other areas outside the nature of the Spirit and the work of the Spirit to empower enabled me to detect additional denominational differences. I noticed that at the Methodist church there was regard for how ministers are equipped by their training and for the lectionary. They did not interpret reliance on the Holy Spirit as requiring them to disregard such things. At the Roman Catholic Church I could see that they often associated the Holy Spirit with the ordinary rather than the spectacular. I was told, for example, that the mere fact that people of different backgrounds gather weekly to worship in one place is the work of the Spirit. At the Church of England church I noticed there was much more diversity in where people saw the Holy Spirit working. The sermon, the songs, the physical development of the church, people's faces and the Vicar's ministry were some of the examples. Finally, at the Pentecostal church a spiritual worldview was much more evident. Several things were spoken of as "spirits", such as poverty, unbelief, counseling and evangelism. The human being was also spoken of as possessing an active spiritual dimension.

The finding from this research shows a picture too complex to be fully explained by denominational differences. Even though I have identified some emphasis in particular denominations, there are, firstly, some major similarities across all the denominations and, secondly, some cases of wide variations within the same denomination. This suggests that a variety of factors are involved and in the next chapter I attempt to give an account of these factors and how they determine the Pneumatology that I have encountered. I draw not only on the result of this phase of the study, but also on the work done at Mount Zion to discuss what, in effect, is the anatomy of African Pneumatology.

CHAPTER 6

The Anatomy of African Pneumatology

Chapter 5 completes the empirical cycle. Through that process I reached some conclusions on the specific theory and theme tested. In the present chapter, I draw on the whole study to reach wider conclusions on African Pneumatology. Just as a plant or an animal is made up of its parts, I identified in this study five factors that make up African Pneumatology. In that sense we can speak of this chapter as the discussion of "the anatomy of African Pneumatology". Crucially, I show that the factors I identified have their influence within Trinitarian boundaries or around a Trinitarian frame already adopted by participants (notwithstanding which version of the Trinity). A common answer I received to the question of who the Holy Spirit is was: "We have God the Father, God the Son and God the Holy Spirit." In that sense, the acceptance of the doctrine of the Trinity as a given is fundamental. This coheres with Colin Gunton's description of dogma as "that which delimits the garden of theology providing a space in which theologians may play freely and cultivate such plants as are cultivable in the space which is so defined."[1]

In this chapter, I show that the sense that dogma sets the boundary for theologising and theological understanding applies to this study. My proposition is that what the participants believed about the Holy Spirit is what they could accommodate within their doctrine of the Trinity. I show how the factors which shape their Pneumatology were negotiated within the Trinitarian boundary. I begin the chapter with a historical review of how Pneumatology has developed within the Trinitarian setting. After that, I will discuss how each of the five factors I identified affects participants' Pneumatology and show how the effects of the factors are negotiated within a Trinitarian frame. I end with a discussion of the role of dogma in this context.

The Spirit within the Trinity — A historical overview

The traditional sequence for naming the persons of the Trinity is Father, Son and Spirit. This sequence places the Holy Spirit as the third in a line of three; with the result that what Christians believe about the Holy Spirit tends to be worked out in the light of what they already hold to be true about the first and

---

[1] C. Gunton, "Dogma, the Church and the task of theology" in Victor Pfitzner and Hilary Regan (eds), *The task of theology today* (Edinburgh: T & T Clark, 1999), 1.

the second persons, that is, the Father and the Son. H. Van Dusen in the book purposely entitled *Spirit, Son and Father* makes that exact point.[2] He notes that Christian theology has been shaped by the traditional sequence, "Father, Son and Holy Spirit" and wondered how different it might be if the order was changed. He noted, for example, that The Grace which begins with the Son — "The grace of our Lord Jesus Christ, the love of God . . ." — has brought about a tendency towards a Christocentric theology.[3] He speculates that if the same is done with the Spirit, such as by starting with the Holy Spirit, so that the Grace begins "The fellowship of the Holy Spirit, and the grace of the Lord Jesus Christ . . ." and the Great Commission (Matt. 28:19) reads, "baptising them in the name of the Holy Spirit, and of the Son and of the Father" a similar inclination of theology towards the Holy Spirit might happen.[4]

But the reality has been that the Holy Spirit has been treated as the third in the line of three and this has shaped Pneumatology throughout history. In the first few centuries of the Christian religion, Christians took much time and energy to work out what to believe about the Father and the Son and only then did they turn to the Holy Spirit.[5] Much of the contention took place in the fourth century. Arians, who had argued against the full divinity of the Son because for them only the Father is ingenerate and everlasting and could not have communicated his essence to any other, saw the Holy Spirit as even less than the Son and more at the level of other creatures.[6] So what the Arians believed about the Father made it difficult for them to accept the full divinity of the Son, let alone that of the Holy Spirit.

A similar difficulty arose with the Homoeousians. Their contention centred on the term "begotten". Since the Father begot the Son (KJV Jn. 3:16), the Homoeousians "taught the likeness/similarity of the Father and Son".[7] But bringing the Holy Spirit into the equation was not so easy. F. Dunzl sums up the dilemma:

> Was the Holy Spirit to be said to be "begotten", like the Son? But in that case, the Son would no longer be the "only-begotten" or the "only" one, and there would be *two* Sons! If, on the other hand, the Spirit was unbegotten like the Father, one had to assume *two* unbegottens and that would mean *two* Gods. And if the Spirit was

---

[2] H. Van Dusen, *Spirit, Son and Father — Christian Faith in the Light of the Holy Spirit* (New York: Charles Scribner's Sons, 1958), 116.

[3] Van Dusen, *Spirit, Son and Father*, 4.

[4] Van Dusen, *Spirit, Son and Father*, 4.

[5] C. Braaten, "The role of dogma in church and theology" in Victor Pfitzner and Hilary Regan (eds), *The task of theology today* (Edinburgh: T & T Clark, 1999), 27.

[6] R.P.C. Hanson, *The Search for the Christian doctrine of God: The Arian controversy 318-381* (Edinburgh: T & T Clark, 1988).

[7] F. Dunzl, *A Brief History of the Doctrine of the Trinity in the Early Church* (translated by John Bowden; London: T & T Clark, 2007), 118.

derived from the Son, at the same time the Father would be "grandfather" of the Spirit — absurd speculation![8]

So perplexed were the Homoeousians that they settled on the view that the Spirit was neither God nor creature.[9] Odd as that may seem, it is important to recognise that this was a position they reached while trying to fit their view of the Spirit into what they already accepted about the Father and the Son.

The same phenomenon can be seen with the group in the East given the derogatory name "Pneumatomachi" (which meant "Assailants of the Spirit") and the Tropici in the West.[10] These were the two best known groups that contended against the divinity of the Holy Spirit. The Pneumatomachi accepted the divinity of the Son but not of the Holy Spirit.[11] The Tropici, similarly, argued that when the Spirit is said to be divine, this was really a figure of speech.[12] The Spirit, for them, was really not divine. But the motive of these groups is important to understand, because, as **Collin Gunton writes, "The** Tropici, like so many of the protagonists in this struggle, were resolute defenders of the unity of God."[13] All they were trying to do was to press their understanding of the Holy Spirit into what they already held to be true regarding the Father and the Son. Having begun from the point that there is only one God, and, in some cases, accepted the divinity of the Son reluctantly, bringing in another personality was too much for these groups.

Just as the difficulties of balancing out the dynamics within the Trinity forced some to take what many Christians now see as the wrong direction regarding the nature of the Holy Spirit, there are examples of the same process being used for the opposite argument. One example was the case put by Athanasius. Athanasius applied logic which used the unity and the relation of the persons of the Godhead to argue for the divinity of the Holy Spirit. Referring to the Tropici, he writes:

Why then do they say that the Holy Spirit is a creature, who has oneness with the Son as the Son with the Father? Why have they not understood that, just as by not dividing the Son from the Father they ensure that God is one, so by dividing the Spirit from the Word they no longer ensure that the Godhead in the Triad is one, for they tear it asunder, and mix with it a nature foreign to it and of a different kind, and put it on a level with creatures. On this showing, once again the Triad is

---

[8]   Dunzl, *A Brief History of the Doctrine of the Trinity*, 119.
[9]   Dunzl, *A Brief History of the Doctrine of the Trinity*, 118.
[10] Hanson, *The Search for the Christian Doctrine of God*, 761.
[11] Hanson, *The Search for the Christian Doctrine of God*, 761.
[12] C. Gunton, *Father, Son, and Holy Spirit: Essays Toward a Fully Trinitarian Theology* (London: T & T Clark, 2003), 82.
[13] Gunton, *Father, Son, and Holy Spirit*, 82.

no longer one but is compounded of two differing natures; for the Spirit, as they have imagined, is essentially different.[14]

Because the concept of "three-in-one" was already well established in Christian theology, Athanasius argued that it would not be a true triad if it was made of Creator and Creature:

What doctrine of God is this, which compounds him out of creator and creature? Either he is not a Triad, but a dyad, with the creature left over. Or, if he be Triad — as indeed he is! — then how do they class the Spirit who belongs to the Triad with the creatures which come after the Triad?[15]

Athanasius's point to his opponents is that if they accept that God is a Trinity, then they must accept that the Spirit is God with the Father and the Son, but if, on the other hand, they want to argue that the Spirit is a creature, then they have to state their position on God as a duality and not a Trinity. On this point, he sought to establish the divinity of the Holy Spirit by appealing to the unity of the Godhead and the accepted divinity of the Father and the Son.

The Ecumenical councils which were used to settle disputes in early Christianity give us further examples of the very same phenomenon. An important Council for the doctrine of the Holy Spirit was the Council of Constantinople in AD 381, where the dispute with the Pneumatomachi was settled. This Council took place after the place of the Son and his relationship with the Father had already been debated and settled in an earlier Council at Nicaea in AD 325. The words that emerged from the Council of Constantinople followed the line which had been argued by Basil of Caesarea (also called "Basil the Great"). The Council established the divinity of the Spirit by calling him "Lord" and describing him as giving life, following John 6:63, and as proceeding from the Father, following John 15:26. In using "proceeding" the Council avoided the conflict that would have arisen from using "begotten" which had already been used for the Son in Nicaea. The Council also avoided describing the Holy Spirit as "one being with the Father" as had been said regarding the Son in Nicaea. Instead, the Council described the Holy Spirit as "co-worshipped and gloried" with Father and Son. They avoided trying to establish the divinity of the Holy Spirit through his being and sought instead to establish it through worship by putting him at the same level as the Father and Son.[16] Hence, the final wording accepted by the church and used till today regarding the Holy Spirit were reached in such a way as to avoid conflict with established positions of the Father and the Son.

Apart from the divinity of the Holy Spirit, his personhood has also been subjected to a similar treatment. One of the contributions made to Trinitarian

---

[14] Athanasius, *The letters of St Athanasius concerning the Holy Spirit* (London: Epworth, 1951), 62-63.
[15] Athanasius, *The letters of St Athanasius*, 62-63.
[16] E.J. Fortman, *The Triune God* (London Hutchinson, 1972), 85.

149

discussion by Augustine of Hippo was the idea that the Holy Spirit is the love (or "charity") uniting Father and Son:

> Yet if the Word is more especially or appropriately named the wisdom of God, there may be a similar fitness in naming the Spirit charity; and this is confirmed by the language of 1 John 4. Charity is indeed the supreme gift, and Scripture is clear that the Holy Spirit is the gift of God. The Holy Spirit rightly may receive the name of charity, as proceeding from Father and Son and constituting the "communion" of both – for both are Spirit.[17]

This treatment of the Holy Spirit as the bond of love (*vinculum amoris*) between Father and Son has drawn both praise and condemnation. Cyril Richardson describes it as an aspect of Augustine's treatment of the Trinity which has remained unsurpassed.[18] Colin Gunton, on the other hand, sees it as undermining the distinctiveness and personhood of the Holy Spirit, leaving the Spirit with "inadequate economic hypostatic weight".[19] For Gunton this stems from Augustine's over-commitment to the unity of God and his "single-minded desire to fit the Spirit into his scheme".[20] Whatever value one attaches to this contribution by Augustine, it is yet another example of a theological attempt to find a place for the Spirit in a theological scheme after places for the Father and the Son have been worked out.

My intention here has not been to give a systematic description of the development of the doctrine of the Holy Spirit, but rather to give examples of how the doctrine has tended to develop through a process of negotiating with the entirety of the doctrine of God. In the discussion to follow, I will show that the African Christians who participated in this study were engaged in a similar process. They were negotiating within their doctrine of God for a secure place for the doctrine of the Holy Spirit.

Factors affecting participants' Pneumatology

I have identified five factors as influencing the participants' Pneumatology. These are their day by day experience, the Bible, their African worldview, the African traditional concept of God and the worldwide Pentecostal movement. In discussing these factors, I engage in a level of interpretation beyond what I have done so far in the study. I have so far employed what could be termed a "local" (or emic) interpretation which has enabled me simply to describe what is taking place. In this chapter the goal of the interpretation (known as etic) is to relate the findings to widely known concepts, theories or models.

---

[17] Augustine, *Later works*. Library of Christian classics 8 (London: SCM, 1955), 127.

[18] C. Richardson, "The enigma of the Trinity" in Roy W. Battenhouse (ed.), *A Companion to the Study of St Augustine* (Grand Rapids: Baker, 1979).

[19] C. Gunton, *The Promise of Trinitarian Theology* (London: T & T Clark, 1997).

[20] Gunton, *The Promise of Trinitarian Theology*, 50.

In that regard, it is worth recalling some of the points made in Chapter Two on methodology. I observed that interpreting religious experience into social scientific categories ends up, from a theological point of view, in a limited outcome. I cited the example given by Cameron *et al* in which spirit-possession is interpreted from an anthropological point of view as a means of attracting attention or expressing powerlessness. I also cited the work of the sociologist, Simon Coleman, who adopts the position of theological neutrality that results in the existence of God being an irrelevance. While these approaches might be appropriate for those disciplines, to me they seem totally inadequate for theology.

A related point has been made by Martin in his consideration of the "rescripting" of religious accounts.[21] He notes that Sociology sometimes proceeds on a line in which "evidence can be straight-jacketed by the imposition of misleading categories or tidied up and administered to serve the interest of global ontologies." He laments the use of "over-generalised concepts" for "corralling evidence" and how religious accounts are tucked into "standard package of characteristics" or subjected to "docketing and rapid disposal".[22] For Martin, it is important that people are allowed to speak of their own account and not treated as puppets that unwittingly emit "jabber" that can only be decoded by social investigators.[23]

I have already noted in Chapter 2 that the increasing rejection of Modernity is one of the socio-cultural changes behind this posture. Another important change is one which can be seen in Anderson's discussion of the theological education of Pentecostals.[24] Anderson laments the fact that the training of ministers tends to operate on a European model which is rationalistic. This is a model which divides the subject into clearly defined disciplines, rather than treating it in a holistic way. It deals in Enlightenment categories because it came out of a need to engage with Enlightenment ideas. He finds this model of training/thinking inadequate, not only because the Western world is moving past Enlightenment ideas, but also because the centre of gravity of worldwide Christianity is seen as having moved to the South, where people have a different way of seeing the world.[25]

In the light of the above, I have not so far and do not in this section deliberately rescript accounts derived from fieldwork to social-scientific categories. Rather, I conduct the discourse within a theological worldview as I have argued in Chapter Two. To be sure, it is possible to rescript religious

---

[21] D. Martin, "Understanding the Old Paradigm: Rescripting Pentecostal Accounts", Pentecostudies, 5.1(date), 18.

[22] Martin, "Understanding the Old Paradigm", 18, 19.

[23] Martin, "Understanding the Old Paradigm", 20.

[24] A. Anderson, "Pentecostal-Charismatic Spirituality and Theological Education in Europe in Global Perspective," Pentecostudies 2.1 (2004), accessed online.

[25] Anderson, "Pentecostal-Charismatic Spirituality."

accounts into a specific theological tradition, such as Pentecostalism.[26] But I do not do that either. Rather, I engage freely with any theological tradition which enhances the understanding of the findings.

Personal and communal experience of the Spirit

Experience was an area many of the participants relied on as the source of their knowledge of the Holy Spirit. For example, at Mount Zion, when I asked why the Holy Spirit was often not explicitly referred to during church services, some described how the ministers would normally pray to ask the Holy Spirit to come and take control of the church service or any activity going on, thus making the point that this was evidence of closeness to the Holy Spirit. One of the ministers, Pastor Sam, contended that what mattered was the immediate experience they had with the Holy Spirit, not explicit references. "He is working in us, He is living in us, He is directing. It is an ongoing thing. . . . As and when it is necessary to mention the Holy Spirit, you mention it," he said.

I also heard accounts such as the Spirit speaking to people and telling them what to do in particular situations. The Spirit told people when to go into business partnership with another person, secretly showed people things about the person sitting and talking with them and gave people words to say in conversations. Along with these came experiences of miraculous healing, such as the woman who was cured of arthritis, experiences of joyful worship services and experiences of insightful sermons and "words of knowledge". All these were attributed to the Holy Spirit. The diversity of ways in which the Spirit was experienced and the practical nature of some of the experiences made the Spirit "real" to them. Many participants in this church told me how much they experienced the Holy Spirit as a "real person". Similarly, many of the participants in the second phase of this study could also be seen relying on their experience as they grappled with the question of who the Holy Spirit is.

I noticed that participants had little difficulty fitting in their understanding of the Holy Spirit based on their experience of him alongside what they believed about Jesus. Many saw the two persons reinforcing each other's role. So they referred to both Jesus' affirmation of the place of the Spirit in the Trinity (such as in the command to baptise, Matt. 28:19) and the Spirit's role of revealing Jesus to believers. A small number went to the point of merging the two persons together. One person said, "The Holy Spirit is Jesus Christ and Jesus Christ is the Holy Spirit." Another person, responding to the question, who is the Holy Spirit said, "I can say it is Jesus, because you can't see it. It's in us." Regarding worship she said, "If [you] really want to worship the Holy Spirit you worship Jesus, because he is the head. As far as you worship Jesus, you're worshipping the Holy Spirit . . . Holy Spirit is Jesus."

---

[26] See, for example, M. Cartledge, *Testimony in the Spirit: Rescripting Ordinary Theology* (Farnham: Ashgate, 2010).

What the participants appear to be expressing, with the crudeness that one should expect of Christians with no theological training, is that the Holy Spirit is not a deity other than the one they already know as Jesus. They are happy to confer on him all that they already believe about Jesus. They do not need to worry whether they are neglecting him when it comes to worship because they worship him when they worship Jesus.

The ease with which some of them moved from the Holy Spirit to Jesus in their comments is another indication of how closely related the two persons are in their minds. For example, one person responding to the question whether the Holy Spirit deserves to be worshipped said:

> I think the Holy Spirit deserves to be worshipped. As we say in one of our songs, we owe so much and he doesn't owe anything; he came to die on the cross just to take our debts away. So I think we need not pay him by money but to worship.

The reference to dying on the cross obviously concerns Jesus, but is here used to answer a question about the Holy Spirit. On the whole, when the participants speak from their experience there appeared to be, for most of them, a relationship which was close and equal between Jesus and the Holy Spirit. This allowed them to confer on the Spirit all they already believed about the Son.

Regarding the Father, experience was much more problematic for some. I have already noted that in all the four churches involved in the second phase of this study, I encountered the view (albeit in a small minority of people) that the Holy Spirit was subordinate to the Father and should not be worshipped. In some cases this view was based on the participant's experience. For example, one person describing her experience of the Trinity said:

> We know that the God is there, the big God that I go and I worship. I know that Jesus came and he died for me and I've accepted him as my Lord and Saviour, which means I'm saved. Then in my day to day walk as a Christian there is this Helper that I feel with me wherever I go.

This is a clear description of the experience of the persons of the Trinity. However, in this participant's experience, the Father is "the big God" and the Spirit is "the Helper" that goes with them wherever they go. Little wonder that when I asked whether the Spirit deserved to be worshipped this participant said, "No." Another person who had earlier described to me how they experience the Spirit during worship said something similar. That participant said that "God Almighty" and Jesus Christ deserve to be worshipped. The Spirit did not, because the Spirit is "something that just descends when you do true worship." There is the sense in both these views that because they were experiencing the Father as "big" and "Almighty", the Holy Spirit ends up as a minor member of the Trinity. These views, though in minority, exemplify how the doctrine of the Holy Spirit is arrived at through negotiation with the believer's doctrine of the Trinity.

A comparison with other theological traditions shows that there is some restriction to the role experience is allowed to play. Many Christians would today accept that experience has a role as a source of theology, alongside the Bible, Tradition and Reason. This is now widely known as the Wesleyan Quadrilateral.[27] Liberation theologies of Latin America and Black people in the Diaspora have taken the role of experience to a different level. For example, Gustavo Gutierrez, a leading Latin-American Liberation theologian, described his work as, "a theological reflection born of the experiences of shared efforts to abolish the current unjust situation and to build a society freer and more human."[28] Similarly, the black theologian, James Cone, regarding experience, writes: "There can be no black theology which does not take seriously the black experience — a life of humiliation and suffering. This must be the point of departure of all God-talk which seeks to be black-talk." For these liberation theologians, the daily life experiences of poor people in Latin America or black people in the Diaspora are both the starting point of theology and the yardstick for measuring its success.

It is fair to say that the vast majority of African Christians I interviewed would not take the status of their experience and the communal experience of the church to the level of being both a starting point and a yardstick for their theology. In that sense, even though they give experience an important role, it is not a role without boundaries. In my view, the role the participants in this study give to experience is limited by the fact that at the back of their mind they have accepted the Trinity as a dogma that every aspect of their theology should fit into.

The Bible

It has already been noted that African Christians in general tend to rely heavily on the Bible.[29] This was found to be the case in this study. Many of the participants often used the Bible to make their case about the Holy Spirit. Many participants greatly valued the way the Holy Spirit opened up the meaning of this important book to them. I also heard how the Spirit can take you to a particular part of the Bible at a time of need to get the solution to your quest or strength to face your challenge. Studying the Bible, I was told, can enable you get filled with the Holy Spirit and enable you discern what is of the Spirit. This means that the believer needs to read their Bible regularly in order to maintain the right relationship with the Holy Spirit. In working out the nature and role of the Holy Spirit, participants drew on the Bible as a book with authority. An important passage to many participants across the denominations was John

---

[27] A. Outler, "The Wesleyan Quadrilateral in Wesley" Wesleyan Theological Journal 20.1, (Spring, 1985), 7-18.

[28] G. Gutierrez, Essential Writings (edited by J. Nickoloff; New York: Orbis, 1996), 28.

[29] J. Mbiti, Bible and Theology in African Christianity (Oxford: Oxford University Press, 1986), 32; A. Anderson, African Reformation: African initiated Christianity in the 20th century (Trenton, New Jersey: Africa World Press, 2001), 223.

14:16 where Jesus refers to the Holy Spirit as "another *paraclete*". Participants used this mainly to support the idea that the Holy Spirit is a person, just like Jesus is a person.

Reference was also made in one of the churches' manuals to Matthew 28:19: "Therefore go and make disciples of all nations, baptizing them in the name of the Father, and of the Son and of the Holy Spirit", to support that the Spirit is in the same position as the Father and the Son. Another manual described the Holy Spirit as follows: "the third person of the Trinity. He is a person, not an impersonal force or just an influence. He has all the attributes of a person. He has all the absolute and relative attributes of God." Hence, in addition to the knowledge they gain about the Holy Spirit through their personal and communal experience, participants are allowing the Bible, because of the authority they accord to it, to contribute in shaping their Pneumatology.

However, it is noticeable that the way the Bible is appropriated on this subject has been guided by the Trinitarian dogma.[30] This can be seen by comparing the way the participants and their churches use the Old and New Testaments with other more scholarly reading of the Bible. Biblical scholars tend to show the difference between Old and New Testament in the understanding of the Holy Spirit. George Montague in his description of the growth of the biblical tradition around the Holy Spirit pointed out how in the Old Testament the Spirit was seen as God's breath of life breathed in human beings and as inspiration for prophetic utterances, but "when we turned to the New Testament, beginning with the letters of Paul, we suddenly found the 'Holy Spirit' everywhere."[31] He notes that particularly in John's gospel, "the role of the Spirit as a distinct person emerges more clearly".[32] References to the "Holy Spirit" in the Old Testament are rare and when they occur, they are often references to the holiness of God rather than to the third person of the Trinity. It does not carry, as we find in the New Testament, the sense of a distinct person.

I noticed that the vast majority of Biblical references used by participants to support their view of the Holy Spirit came from the New Testament. For example, at Mount Zion the case for the personhood of the Holy Spirit is made with statements that the Holy Spirit speaks, commands people, guides, teaches, prays for believers, helps the weak, calls people to God's work, thinks and comforts. And these statements were supported with the following biblical references: Revelation 2:7, Acts 16:6-7, John 16:13, John 14:26, Romans 8:26, Acts 13, Romans 8:27 and Acts 9:31. The Old Testament which tends to refer to the "Spirit of God" understood as a force was more or less overlooked. When the Old Testament is referred to, it is usually read with the New Testament eyes. For example, I was told by some participants that when in Genesis 2:26

---

[30] See for example, O.Kalu *African Pentecostalism: An Introduction* (New York: Oxford University Press, 2008), 266.

[31] G. Montague, *Holy Spirit – Growth of the Biblical tradition* (New York: 1978), 367.

[32] Montague, *Holy Spirit*, 367.

God said: "Let us make man in our own image," that the use of "us" was a reference to the three persons in the Godhead. By focusing on the New Testament and adopting a New Testament understanding of the Holy Spirit, participants and their churches ensure that their Pneumatology fits within the dogma of the Trinity.

It must be said that reading the Old Testament with the New Testament eyes is not peculiar to African Christianity, but rather something Christians from different parts of the world commonly do. Also, it would be unfair to expect ordinary Christians to reflect the balance between the Old and New Testaments in the treatment of a theological issue, since ordinary Christians are not theologians or biblical scholars. The significant point I am making here is that these Christians and their churches are being influenced in their use of the Bible on this subject by the Trinitarian dogma. This adds to the complexity of African Christian hermeneutics. It has been described as "literalist", uncritical, experiential and Holy Spirit-directed.[33] Yet, in the subject of Pneumatology, this study finds that it is in most cases done within the theological boundary of the doctrine of the Trinity.

A comparison of what I found among these Christians with what one would find in the African Initiated Churches buttresses this point. The African Initiated Churches sit very lightly on the doctrine of the Trinity or have their own particular version of it so they are not so compelled to construct their doctrine of the Holy Spirit from the New Testament. This bias to the Old Testament is perhaps best seen in how comfortably their modus operandi sits within the Old Testament. As Anderson notes, AICs are often led by one dominant figure, regarded as "a man of the Spirit" and on whom, the followers believe, the Holy Spirit has come in a special way.[34] This figure usually has the persona of Old Testament prophets, which is why AICs are sometimes called "Prophetic" churches. The African prophets also tend to "proclaim" God's word and perform miracles much like the Old Testament prophets did.[35] Many of them set out to maintain continuity with that prophetic tradition by the use of such symbols as robes, staff, ropes and beards. With this Old Testament bias, it is not surprising that their Pneumatology does not emphasize the personhood of the Holy Spirit and quite often depicts him as a force or power acting in the world.

To summarize, the evidence from the case studies shows participants relying on the Bible for their understanding of who the Spirit is and what he does. This means that the Bible alongside experience shape their Pneumatology. But the

---

[33] R. Burgess, *Nigerian Christian Revolution: The Civil War Revival and its Pentecostal Progeny (1967-2006)*, (Oxford: Regnum, 2008), 29; D. Maxwell, "The Durawall of Faith: Pentecostal Spirituality in Neo-Liberal Zimbabwe," *Journal of Religion in Africa* 35.1 (2005), 9; Kalu, *African Pentecostalism*, 267.

[34] A. Anderson, *Moya* (Pretoria: University of South Africa, 1991), 105.

[35] Anderson, *Moya*, 106.

influence of the Bible, in my view, is itself restricted by what the participants have already accepted about the Trinity. This can be seen from the fact that on the issue of the personhood of the Spirit, the Old Testament which portrays the Spirit as more of a force than a person is overlooked.

The African worldview

It was pointed out in Chapter 4 that Africans have a worldview that emphasizes the spiritual. Also, Africans perceive space as if the spirit world is one dimension of it, alongside the earth and the sky. They believe deities live in the earth, the sky and the spirit world, and that spiritual forces were "imbuing the whole of the world of the living".[36] For the African, the universe is one in which all realms of life are sacralised; the three dimension of space are bound together and the visible and the invisible interweave.[37] Given this knowledge of the spiritual forces around them, people feel fearful. They fear the aggrieved spirits of dead relatives, powerful marine spirits and deities which can afflict humans with such detestable propensities as stealing and incest. This has been described by Kalu as a very religious worldview and by Asamoah-Gyadu as a "sacramental universe".[38] People have to seek higher spiritual powers for their protection because, "going through life is like a spiritual warfare."[39]

The evidence from this study suggests that this African worldview which sees spiritual forces in the whole of life and, consequently, sees life as spiritual warfare, does not only make churches that emphasise the work of the Holy Spirit attractive, but influences the way the Holy Spirit is understood. Participants in all the churches in this study spoke about the Holy Spirit as working with them not only during worship but in their daily life. An example of this is the participant at Mount Zion that said to me:

If I go down that corridor, [and] somebody says something to me, if I don't depend on the Holy Spirit I might say the wrong thing. So I need the Holy Spirit every second of every minute of every hour of every day.

Another person related it to business partnership, describing how the Spirit would tell you about a potential partner and whether or not to go ahead with the partnership.

At the Methodist church, the relationship I found between the church members and the Holy Spirit was that of a person that was always there guiding them through daily life. One person described how the Spirit led him to wait

---

[36] O. Kalu "Preserving a Worldview" in *Pneuma* 24.2 (Fall, 2002), 116.

[37] Kalu "Preserving a Worldview," 122; Adogame, "Engaging the Rhetoric of Spiritual Warfare," 503.

[38] Kalu "Preserving a Worldview," 122; J.K. Asamoah-Gyadu, *African Charismatics: Current Developments within Independent Indigenous Pentecostalism in Ghana* (Leiden: Brill, 2005), 440.

[39] Kalu "Preserving a Worldview," 122; Adogame, "Engaging the Rhetoric of Spiritual Warfare," 504.

day after day at a London Underground station so he could meet the person to help him settle into life in Britain. Another person told me how he was saved from having an accident on a ship that would almost certainly have led to his death. One of the participants said: "I feel the Holy Spirit around us every time" and another said the Spirit was involved in the life of Christians, "every minute, twenty-four seven." I found something similar among the Roman Catholic participants. One person put it this way, "You sleep and wake up, God is involved, and the Holy Spirit is involved. You get food to eat every day, water to drink every day, God is involved. You kneel down and you pray, he answers, he is involved." Another person identified him with the thoughts that come into your mind when you are making day to day decisions. Much the same was found among the Anglicans and at the Amazing Grace.

The strength of the belief that the Holy Spirit is active in daily life (not just in worship) and the extent to which it is widespread within each church and across all five churches in this study is in my view due to the influence of the African worldview. Because Africans in their traditional thought believe that the spirit world is interwoven with the material world and habitually relate daily life events to activities within the spirit world, the activities of the Holy Spirit also cut across the spirit and the material world.[40]

A comparison with Western Christians, for example, particularly those in the traditional denominations like Anglicans and Roman Catholics, would show a different emphasis in understanding the work of the Spirit. In much of Western Christianity, a close concept to what has been described here is the Spirit's work of sanctification, that is, the process of making the believer holy over time. But this is still short of the kind of active participation in daily life described here. Among Western Pentecostals, there is the idea of the empowerment of Christians by the Holy Spirit. However, this is often related to service and witness and not to everyday mundane matters. It is hardly comparable to the incident where the Spirit told a person to go and wait at a train station in order to meet the person to help them settle into the country or the situation where the Spirit discreetly gives a person information about a potential business partner sitting in front of them.

Having highlighted the influence of the African traditional worldview on African Pneumatology, it is important to note that African traditional worldview is quite similar to the worldview one finds in the Bible.[41] The interweaving of the world of deities/spirits and the world of humans can easily be seen in several biblical stories such as the appearance of God to prophets and leaders (e.g. Moses in Ex. 3, Joshua in Josh. 1:1-9 and Elijah in 1 Kgs 19) and acts of exorcisms by Jesus and his followers (e.g. Matt. 8:28-34, Lk 8:26-39 and Act 16:16-21). The dichotomy between the material world and the spirit world that is central to Western worldview today is alien to the Bible. More

---

[40] Anderson, *Moya*, 8.
[41] Anderson, *Moya*, 111

importantly, the similarity between the biblical worldview and the African traditional worldview means that it is impossible to determine categorically the extent to which the tendency within African Christianity described above should be attributed to the African worldview and not to the Bible.

Evidence that the African worldview has an influence on Christian belief can be seen in a study conducted by myself and published in 2008.[42] Working on the subject of Christology, I explored the extent to which the African worldview affects African Christians' ideas of who Jesus is. The study involved comparing how fifty Africans described Jesus to how fifty white Europeans described him. The result showed that of the six titles respondents had to choose from, Africans were more likely than the white Europeans to describe Jesus as a "Victor" or "Provider". On the other hand, the white Europeans were more likely than the Africans to describe him as "Teacher" or "Forgiver". The study argued that Africans see Jesus as "Victor" because they tend to see life as a spiritual battle and so need a warrior on their side.[43] A similar reason also lies behind the view that Jesus was a "Provider". To them, Jesus is able to drive away the evil spirits blocking the path through which the material things they need can get through to them. Both interpretations are possible because they make no distinction between the physical and the spiritual.[44]

Relating this to my proposition, namely, that what is believed about the Holy Spirit is what can be accommodated within the Trinity, I submit that the Holy Spirit is given free rein on the issue of acting or guiding in daily life because this does not threaten what the people already believe about the Father or the Son. The outcome here is the exact opposite to what was seen on the issue of worship. Whereas some felt that to worship the Holy Spirit would conflict with the position they have given God the Father in their mind, in the matter of daily life there is no such conflict.

African traditional concepts of God

Apart from the African worldview, African traditional concepts of God have an effect on how African Christians think of the Holy Spirit. Even though Africans do not all have the same concept of God in their traditional religion, there are significant similarities across the continent. Hence, Mbiti writes:

> It is remarkable that in spite of great distances separating the peoples of one region from those of another, there are sufficient elements of belief which make it possible for us to discuss African concepts of God as a unity and on a continental scale.[45]

---

[42] C. Chike, *African Christianity in Britain* (Milton Keynes: Author House, 2007).
[43] Chike, *African Christianity in Britain*, 223.
[44] Chike, *African Christianity in Britain*, 223.
[45] J. Mbiti, *Concepts of God in Africa* (London: SPCK, 1970), 30.

Similarly, Bolaji Idowu has pointed out that although there are local variations in African concepts of God, there is no need to exaggerate them because, "in spite of the variations, an unmistakable basic pattern stands out".[46]

The common attributes of God in traditional African thought include omniscience, omnipresence and omnipotence.[47] Mbiti, following the study of nearly three hundred peoples across Africa, found many examples of these across the continent. He observed that because of the high regard Africans have for wisdom, when they say that God is omniscient, "African people are placing him in the highest possible position"[48] The omnipresence of God is seen in the statements and names used for God across the continent. The Karanga, who live in the Zambezi area, refer to God as the "Great Pool". This name uses the image of the annual flooding of the Zambezi River and its tributaries to capture the sense that God "embraces everything within its presence".[49] Similarly, God's omnipotence can be seen in the beliefs and sayings of many African people-groups such as the people of Zanzibar, the Yoruba, the Ngombe, the Zulu, the Abaluyia, the Akan and the Ashanti.[50] The Yoruba name for God, Olodumare, means "the Almighty" because they believe that God is the most powerful being in heaven and on earth and is able to do all things.[51]

Idowu gives a fuller description of the supremacy of Olodumare.[52] He likens Olodumare to a monarch ruling over a kingdom which includes not only humans but other divinities. The world, humans, spirits and deities owe their existence to him since he brought them into being.[53] He may sometimes seem remote, but that is because he has delegated responsibilities to smaller divinities.[54] These other divinities have a limited "almightiness" which, if they try to overstep, the Creator, Olodumare, would quickly step in to suppress them. Idowu recounts a Yoruba myth in which one thousand seven hundred divinities conspired against Olodumare. But he defeated them by switching off the machinery of the universe, bringing everything to a standstill. The heavens withheld rain, rivers ceased to flow, and neither yam nor corn grew. The divinities confessed their conspiracy and asked for mercy and Olodumare, the Creator, forgave them. It is believed by the Yoruba that the one thousand seven hundred divinities still give annual tributes to Olodumare in acknowledgement of his Lordship.[55] Idowu sums up the position as follows:

[46] B. Idowu, *African Traditional Religion – A Definition* (London: SCM, 1974), 148.
[47] Mbiti, *Concepts of God in Africa*, 4-13.
[48] Mbiti, *Concepts of God in Africa*, 4.
[49] Mbiti, *Concepts of God in Africa*, 5.
[50] Mbiti, *Concepts of God in Africa*, 8-9.
[51] Mbiti, *Concepts of God in Africa*, 8.
[52] B. Idowu, *Olodumare – God in Yoruba belief* (S.l: Longman, 1962).
[53] Idowu, *Olodumare*, 49.
[54] Idowu, *Olodumare*, 49, 51.
[55] Idowu, *Olodumare*, 55.

Yoruba theology emphasises the unique status of Olodumare. He is supreme over all on earth and in heaven, acknowledged by all the divinities as the Head to whom all authority belongs and all allegiance is due.[56]

The belief that smaller deities exist alongside a Supreme God coheres with my personal experience of growing up in Africa. My ancestral hometown (i.e. where my parents and forebears come from) in the Igbo area of southeast Nigeria, until recently, have had three spiritual beings they depended on. These are Ani Isu, Igwe-ka-ani and Ugwu-owa. Each of these beings ("Alusi" in Igbo language) had a shrine and a priest who attends to matters related to them. The three shrines of these beings were positioned on the outskirt of the town, in such a way that each shrine stood between my hometown and one of the three neighbouring towns. The people believed that these beings purposely positioned themselves in this way to form a protective triangle round the town. Now, I was told that in addition to these three beings, the people always believed there was a fourth one that they did not see, which lived in the sky. This was called Eze-enu, which literally means the "king in the Sky". Whenever there was a village ceremony and sacrifices were made to the three protective beings, a sacrifice was also made to the unseen being in the sky. Although I have never heard it articulated in the village, what kind of relationship the three protective beings had to the Unseen one, this belief system coheres with the pattern widely held among Igbo people that a Supreme being (usually called "Chukwu" meaning "the big God") lived in the sky with mediating spirits between him and humans residing on earth.[57]

It is very likely that some aspects of these African concepts of God have found their way into Christianity. This likelihood is strengthened by the fact that Africans, particularly those who have a pre-Christian belief in a Supreme Being, tend to use the name of that Being to refer to God in Christianity. For example, Yoruba Christians, when they speak Yoruba, refer to God as Olodumare. So from a purely linguistic point of view, it would be difficult to separate totally the "Olodumare" of Christian theology from "Olodumare" the Monarch of Yoruba cosmology, standing in lordship above the pantheon of several other divinities.

A similar linguistic phenomenon was reported by some missionaries who were evangelising Hausa people in a community in Niger Republic of West Africa. They found that with the domination of the local language by Arabic, the Hausa Christians tended to use Arabic words for Christian concepts. So the Hausa word for God was Allah. But the use of this word meant the Hausa Christians retained much of the attributes associated with the word "Allah" in

---

[56] Idowu, Olodumare, 56.
[57] See, for example, R.A. Egwu, Igbo idea of the Supreme Being and the Triune God (Wurzburg, Echter, 1998), 58; C.O. Obiego, African image of the ultimate reality: an analysis of Igbo ideas of life and death in relation to Chukwu-God (New York: Peter Lange, 1984), 60.

161

Islam in their concept of God. The missionaries also found that Arabic words were used for other important Christian concepts such as sin, forgiveness and repentance with the result that these concepts retained heavy Islamic connotations for the Christian converts. As one of the missionaries noted, "It took us many years of poor communication to come to the realisation that we were talking about different things".[58] The Hausas who used to be Muslims (the missionaries acknowledge that this was a particular local variation of Islam) had an existing theological framework on the basis of which meaning was assigned to the words they used.

I suspect that a similar, although milder, phenomenon is present in the understanding of some of the participants in this study. The pre-Christian concept of God they have retained within their Christian beliefs is continuously reinforced by their use of African names for God within Christianity and the widespread belief that the God of African religion is the God of the Christian religion. This retention of the African concept of God might explain the readiness with which many of the participants in this study accept the divinity of both Jesus and the Holy Spirit, because they would be used to the idea of having many divinities. But, on the other hand, it may also account for why some spoke as if the persons of the Godhead were not equal. Ideas such as an all-powerful God that is Lord over smaller divinities, which exists in some parts of Africa, might lie behind that. Such ideas might have influenced the participants who identified the Father as "God" or the "the big God" and as a consequence, see the Holy Spirit as a subordinate, a kind of "Junior God".

In summary, it could be said that for this minority of people, they have conceived of the Father in such a way that the equality of the Holy Spirit with the Father is no longer accommodated. The fact that I found this view in all the denominations studied suggests that this is not a matter for a particular denomination, but consequence of something those holding such views have in common, such as the influence of African Traditional Religion.

The worldwide Pentecostal/Charismatic movement

Even though Christian history has seen forms of Charismatic Christianity, such as the New Prophecy (or Montanist) of the second century, there is hardly any doubt that there has been a phenomenal growth of Pentecostal and Charismatic movements in the past one hundred years. One of the best known revivals in this period was the Azusa street revival in Los Angeles, California, which dates back to 1906.[59] This was centred on the work of an African American man, Elder William J Seymour, the leader of the Apostolic Faith Mission at 312

---

[58] J. Corrie, *Mission Theology in Context* (Cheltenham: Open Theology College, 1998), 1.3.

[59] E. Blumhofer, *The Assemblies of God: a chapter in the story of American Pentecostalism* (Springfield: Gospel Publishing, 1989), 99.

162

Azusa Street.[60] Other revival movements which began about the same time, usually with no obvious influence from Azusa Street, are the Welsh Revival of 1904-1905, the Korean revival of 1907, the Indian revival which reaches back into the nineteenth century, and several indigenous African Pentecostal-type movements.[61] Since that period Pentecostalism has grown around the world. For these early Pentecostals, their worship which was often characterised by spontaneous audible prayer, people bursting into songs spontaneously, was "motivated directly by the Holy Spirit".[62]

The Charismatic Movement, which originally referred to the work of the Spirit to fill and empower Christians within the historic denominations but is now used more widely to refer to all manifestations of Pentecostal-type Christianity outside classical Pentecostalism, followed Pentecostalism roughly half a century later.[63] From that period, Charismatic Renewal movements which, as has been noted by Anderson, were already stirring in several of the historic denominations, gained momentum, penetrated deeper into virtually all Christian denominations and also spread more widely around the world.[64] Alongside the growth of Charismatic Renewal movements in the historic churches, the nondenominational Spirit-filled assemblies and networks also grew. An example of this was the Full Gospel Business Men's Fellowship International (FGBMFI) formed by the California millionaire Demos Shakarian in 1951, with which the preacher Oral Robert was associated.[65] Other examples include the numerous mega-churches in Asia, such as the KAG of David Yonggi Cho. What these Charismatic Movements have in common and also share with Pentecostals was "a personal encounter with the Spirit of God, enabling and empowering people for service".[66]

This worldwide Pentecostal and Charismatic movement has "global theological synergies".[67] This movement and its theology has been a source of influence on what Africans believe regarding the Holy Spirit. A major channel of this influence is the partnership and collaboration arrangements many African Pentecostal churches have with Pentecostal churches from other parts of the world. One such relationship, which was established early in the life of

---

[60] L.G. McClung, Jr., "Exorcism" in Stanley M. Burgess and Edward M. van der Maas, (eds), *The New International Dictionary of Pentecostal and Charismatic Movements* (Grand Rapids: Zondervan, 2003), 2; W.J. Hollenweger, *Pentecostalism: Origin and developments worldwide* (Peabody: Hendrickson, 1997), 20.

[61] A. Anderson, *Introduction to Pentecostalism* (Cambridge: Cambridge University Press, 2004).

[62] Blumhofer, *The Assemblies of God*, 142.

[63] Anderson, *Introduction to Pentecostalism*, 144.

[64] Anderson, *Introduction to Pentecostalism*, 149-55.

[65] Anderson, *Introduction to Pentecostalism*, 145.

[66] Anderson, *Introduction to Pentecostalism*, 9. 187.

[67] C. Clark, "Old wine in new wine skins," *Journal of Pentecostal Theology* 19 (2010), 144.

African Pentecostalism, was that which existed between the Nigerian preacher, Benson Idahosa, and Charismatic preachers in the USA.[68] Similar partnerships have led to the setting up of theological colleges and universities in Africa where the ideas and theologies of the foreign partners have found ready recipients. In the Diaspora, such influence comes through the non-African preachers that the African Pentecostal Churches invite as guest speakers to their services and conferences.

Less formal routes include the books written by the leaders within the worldwide movement that are bought and read by ordinary Christians, not necessarily in pursuit of a formal, theological qualification. Books by Western Pentecostal writers, such as Kenneth Hagin, Myles Munroe, Kathryn Kuhlman, Benny Hinn, Ben Carson, T.D. Jakes and the Korean writer David Yonggi Cho I have found to be commonly read by African Christians in Africa and elsewhere. Radio and television are yet other important media through which the worldwide Pentecostal and Charismatic movement are influencing African Christians. Particularly for Africans in the Diaspora, radio and television programmes have become a major source of Christian knowledge. In the past decade the multiplicity of channels provided by digital TV has brought dozens of Christian channels, many run by Western Pentecostal churches, to the living rooms of anybody willing to subscribe. Similarly, radio listeners in some areas, such as London where I live, get all-day service on Christian radio, featuring Pentecostal and Charismatic preachers from around the world. This coheres with the observations about the globalisation of Charismatic Christianity through the media, frequent international travel, including pilgrimages and the existence of a meta-culture.[69]

These sources shape not only what the African Pentecostals believe but also influence what African Christians from the historic denominations believe, because the latter group also access them. Considering that many African members of the historic churches tend also to go, if occasionally, to the African Pentecostal Churches as well, the importance of these sources becomes clearer. For the Africans, the effect would be to hold them theologically close to the worldwide Pentecostal/Charismatic movement. The Pentecostal/Charismatic tendency to "emphasise empowerment through the Spirit for witnessing and service" would reinforce the Africans' belief that the Holy Spirit empowers.[70] Also the focus on the work of the Spirit within the worldwide movement would reinforce among the Africans the idea that the Spirit is a distinctive person

[68] See, for example, I. Olofinjana, *20 Pentecostal Pioneers in Nigeria: Their Lives, Their Legacies* (Xlibris Corporation, USA, 2011), 1.98-113.

[69] S. Coleman, *The globalisation of charismatic Christianity: Spreading the Gospel of Prosperity* (Cambridge; Cambridge University Press, 2005), 66-69; A. Anderson, "New African initiated Pentecostal and Charismatic Churches in SA," *Journal of Religion in Africa*, 35.1 (2005), 84.

[70] V. Karkkäinen, V., *Pneumatology – The Holy Spirit in Ecumenical, International, and Contextual Perspective* (Grand Rapids: Baker Academic, 2002), 92.

within the Trinity, since the Pentecostal movement from its early days has been Trinitarian.[71]

This partly accounts for the difference between African Pentecostal Pneumatology and the Pneumatology of the AICs. The AICs, who are much less open to the influence of the worldwide church, are more likely than other African Christians to see the Holy Spirit as a kind of force or power which God sends.[72] The Nigerian Pentecostal preacher, Kenneth Onyeme was probably referring to the AIC when he noted in *The Holy Spirit Exposed* that "some Christian denominations claim that the Holy Spirit is not a person but rather the force of God". This prompts him to make this clarification, "the Holy Spirit is a person. . . . He is the third person in the Godhead. The Holy Spirit should be worshipped just as the Father and the Son. There is a need to know the Holy Spirit as a person and more intimately."[73]

Charismatic renewal movements within the historic denominations also have some influence. The effect of this can be seen on one of the participants at the Roman Catholic Church who regularly attended a Roman Catholic Charismatic renewal group. She gave responses quite similar to what I received at the Mount Zion Pentecostal church and very different from what I heard from most of the other Roman Catholic participants. She talked about getting power from the Holy Spirit to take her through the day and to do good things. She spoke of how the Spirit enables worship, evangelism and all other ministries. For her, the Holy Spirit gives different interpretations to the words of the Bible and activates the word within the reader to transform their life. Also, the sense of the Spirit as a person was well developed in her thinking. These statements were in sharp contrast to what was said by the vast majority of the other participants from her church, and thus shows the influence of the Charismatic fellowship she attends on her Pneumatology.

This emphasis of the personhood of the Holy Spirit and the work of the Spirit to empower, both of which are reinforced by the influence of the worldwide Pentecostal/Charismatic movement, are accommodated readily within the Trinity. This is because these two aspects do not threaten in any way what participants already believe about the Father or the Son.

---

[71] K.E. Alexander, "Matters of Conscience, Matters of Unity, Matters Orthodoxy: Trinity and Water Baptism in Early Pentecostal Theology and Practice," *Journal of Pentecostal Theology* 17 (2008), 51.

[72] See, for example, A. Adogame, "Engaging the Rhetoric of Spiritual Warfare: The Public Face of the Aladura in Diaspora," *Journal of Religion of Africa* 34.4 (2004), 500; A. Anderson, "New African initiated Pentecostal and Charismatic Churches in SA," *Journal of Religion in Arrica* 35.1 (2005), 85.

[73] K. Onyeme, *The Holy Spirit Exposed* (publishing details not stated, undated), 3.

The Trinity as dogma

As already stated, all the above factors operate within the boundary set by the doctrine of the Trinity. This is because the participants accept the doctrine of the Trinity as dogma, that is, the teaching of the church whose authority they recognise. Dogma has been unpopular inside and outside Christianity for centuries.[74] F. Meyrick (1883) remarked that at the individual level it is often associated with pomposity as it presents one person as superior to another. At the institutional level, the church can seem to be "erecting their peculiar opinions into dogma".[75] Two developments continue to make the debate about the place of dogma important in recent times. The first is the rise of postmodernity, which rejects metanarratives, looks at truth claims with suspicion and favours plurality of ideas, cultures and perspectives.[76] In that cultural/philosophical environment, dogmas and dogmatism are more unpopular than they have ever been.

The second, which is somewhat related, is the increased activities and influence of non-white people on social and religious matters. In the Christian context, Harvey Cox describes this as a "jarring inversion":

> From all directions of the compass new peoples are arriving at the feast of the Kingdom and many who were last are last no longer. Whereas once theology was manufactured at the centre for distribution in the provinces, the direction of the flow is now being reversed. It is the periphery which is now threatening, questioning, and energizing the centre.[77]

This also has consequences for truth and authority:

> Whereas the model once asserted that religious truth must be promulgated at the top and then "trickle down" through layers of hierarchy to the local level, now that vertical path has also been upended.[78]

The combined effect of these two developments is, as Cox notes, that black people, women, poor people, and non-Westerners are insisting that the prevailing theology which saw itself as all-inclusive was, in fact, narrow, provincial, white, male, Western and bourgeois. There is, from this point of view, a tendency among many to sit lightly on positions and dogmas arrived at without their input.

Even so, Christian dogmas have their defenders. Meyrick has suggested that dogmas can add "bone and flesh" to a Christianity which would be otherwise

---

[74] A. Meyrick, *Is Dogma a Necessity?* (London: Hodder and Stoughton, 1883), 1.
[75] Meyrick, *Is Dogma a Necessity?* 99.
[76] J.R. Middleton and B.J. Walsh, *Truth is Stranger Than it Used to Be* (London: SPCK, 1995), 165-71.
[77] H. Cox, *Religion in the secular city: Towards a postmodern theology* (New York: Simon and Schuster, 1984), 175.
[78] Cox, *Religion in the secular city*, 175.

166

"soft and yielding" leaving a Christian "all abroad in his views". Writing specifically about God, he notes that dogmatic enunciation by a trustworthy authority can support the process and correct possible error.[79] In such cases as with the doctrine of the Trinity, where truth cannot be reached through reasoning:

> Dogmatic enunciation is not only useful as subsidiary instrument of knowledge, but it is of primary value, necessary, and not to be dispensed with, if knowledge is to be had or imparted at all.[80]

Carl Braaten also defends the place of dogma in "churchly theology". He laments the way experience is becoming the source and norm of theology turning theology into "religious autobiography".[81] As it happens, Braaten recommends "the ancient Trinitarian dogma" as the paradigm for all theology. Similarly, Gunton, quoted at the beginning of this chapter also sees important roles for dogmas. However, for Gunton, dogma functions both to "delimit and realise theology's freedom."[82] For him, there should still be room, in spite of the boundary, to let the Holy Spirit guide the theological process. Hence even though dogma is the boundary of the garden of theology, the activities of theology may change both the territory and the character of the garden.[83]

Participants in this study were prepared to accept the Trinity as a dogma of the church without necessarily understanding or, in some cases, experiencing it. This seemed to happen early in their Christian life. Hence those participants who were less able to articulate what they believed about the Holy Spirit tended to be quick to use the Trinity in their answer. For example, the participant who started their answer with the Trinity and then asked for the question to be repeated had only been going to church seriously for a year. In that sense the dogma was performing an important function for these new Christians. It gave them solid parameters within which to develop and to negotiate what to believe about the Holy Spirit.

It is important that the position of the participants on this dogma is not taken out of proportion. It does not imply that they take the same position on other areas of their Christian life or other doctrines because that would be going beyond the scope of this study and was not investigated. I cannot, therefore, say that participants were given to being dogmatic. Rather, I can speak of their view on the doctrine of the Trinity. In that regard, I found that the authority of the doctrine as church dogma is a key factor in shaping participants' Pneumatology.

---

[79] Meyrick, *Is Dogma a Necessity?* 110.
[80] Meyrick, *Is Dogma a Necessity?* 110.
[81] Braaten, "The role of dogma in church and theology," 27.
[82] Gunton, "Dogma, the Church and the task of theology," 2.
[83] Gunton, "Dogma, the Church and the task of theology," 2.

Modern debates often set dogma against experience. But it is worth bearing in mind that where Christian dogma is concerned, these have evolved out of the experience of the whole church over a period of time. So when these African Christians accept the authority of an existing dogma, what they are doing is accepting a position which has crystallised out of the experience of their church and the worldwide church. In the case of the doctrine of the Trinity, this is particularly useful because it is one of the most difficult doctrines to figure out by oneself. Many people would be encouraged to see that the participants do not simply accept the doctrine and leave the matter there. Instead, many try over time to understand more fully what they have already accepted. Both aspects of this dynamic, that is, the acceptance of a teaching of the church before one fully understands it, and the attempt to understand it even after accepting it, are, in my view, signs of a mature faith. It shows they recognise the authority of the church and value the experience and wisdom of those who have gone before them, without neglecting their responsibility to understand and be able to articulate what they believe.

The foregoing also shows why the worldwide church over its history has consistently insisted that its members accept the doctrine of the Trinity. The boundaries the doctrine sets out are very important at an early stage of a person's faith. Since the doctrine also acts as a framework, it also ensures that the faith of members develops along lines taken by the church. In addition to the requirement on members, denominations also often make the doctrine pivotal when considering relationship with others. For example, the World Council of Churches describes itself as "a fellowship of churches which confess the Lord Jesus Christ as God and Saviour according to the scriptures, and therefore seek to fulfill together their common calling to the glory of the one God, Father, Son and Holy Spirit".[84] This reference to the Trinity was added some years later to the original formulation in order to include a "more explicit expression of the Trinitarian faith".[85] By uniting around this doctrine, Christians ensure that when they say "God" they are referring to the same being.

Bearing in mind these benefits, it is important for churches to find ways of teaching and reinforcing this doctrine to their members. I noticed that the reciting of creeds, which helps to keep the dogmas in the collective memory, was not a regular practice in any of the churches in this study. If creeds were recited regularly, it might remove some of the deviations from mainstream Christian beliefs that were encountered in this study. What is today known as the Nicene Creed, which, in fact, incorporates the agreements reached regarding the Holy Spirit in the later Council of Constantinople, includes the words:

---

[84] World Council of Churches official website: www.oikoumene.org/en/who-are-we.html, visited, (26th Nov 2010), 1.
[85] WCC website, 1.

168

We believe in the Holy Spirit,

The Lord, the giver of life,

Who proceeds from the Father and the Son,

Who with the Father and the Son is worshipped and glorified,

Who has spoken through the prophets.

This would have removed many of the doubts among participants regarding whether the Holy Spirit should be worshipped. The Athanasian Creed, which is rarely used in worship nowadays, also makes clear statements about the equality of the persons.

Whosoever will be saved: before all things it is necessary that he hold the Catholick Faith . . .

The Godhead of the Father, of the Son, and of the Holy Ghost is all one: the Glory equal, the Majesty coeternal . . .

In this Trinity none is afore [i.e. before], or after other: none is greater, or less than another;

But the whole three Persons are co-eternal together, and co-equal.

So that in all things, as is aforesaid: the Unity in the Trinity, and the Trinity in Unity is to be worshipped.[86]

Such a clear statement of co-equality would directly challenge any belief within the congregations that the Holy Spirit is subordinate to the Father or the Son.

Conclusion

This chapter has been about crystallising a position from the fieldwork and the literature review that have been carried out. The most prominent thread I found was the extent to which doctrine of the Trinity influenced their Pneumatology. My proposition is what the participants believe regarding the Holy Spirit is what can be accommodated within the Trinity. This often means negotiating with what they already believe regarding the Father and the Son. In the process of understanding this negotiation process, I described the influence of five factors on what the participants believe about the Holy Spirit. These are their personal experiences of the Holy Spirit, their African worldview, the Bible, the beliefs about God in African religion and the worldwide Pentecostal /Charismatic movement.

The participants' acceptance of the doctrine of the Trinity as a teaching of the church they will stick to sets both the framework for their negotiation of Pneumatology and the boundaries of what they can accept. It also commits them to the unity of the Godhead and the divinity and personhood of the Holy Spirit. Even though participants relied heavily on both their personal experiences and their church's experience, the indication was that they did not let Experience on its own become a yardstick for what to accept. Their

---

[86] *Book of Common Prayer* (Cambridge: Cambridge University Press, 2004), 27-28.

experience of the Godhead had two effects. On the one hand, they could accommodate the close relationship it showed between the Son and the Spirit, but on the other hand, for a small number of the participants, their experience of worship made it difficult for them to see the Spirit as God. This is most sharply described by the participant who saw the Father as the person to be worshipped and the Spirit as that which enables one to worship.

The relationship with the Bible was another area where the phenomenon was on display. The New Testament clearly describes the Spirit as a person and this is absorbed by the participants in their understanding. However, even though a careful reading of the Old Testament shows that the Holy Spirit is not presented as a person, this is ignored by participants (as probably other Christians) because it falls outside the boundary of their doctrine of the Trinity. The sense of the Holy Spirit as ever-present which is promoted by the African worldview is unrestricted because it does not threaten what is believed regarding the Father or the Son. Similarly, the sense that the Spirit empowers is unhindered because it does not detract in any way with what is believed about the other Trinitarian persons.

Some participants had difficulty is in the area of equality of the persons. Possibly due to the effect of the concepts of God in African traditional religion, a small minority could not bring themselves to think of the Holy Spirit as being equal to the Father. Even though they say that they believe that God is three in one, often when they say "God" they are referring to the Father. For them only the Father should be worshipped. The fact that this is an age-old problem going as far back as the time of the early Church Fathers means that this is not a peculiarly African phenomenon.

The way in which the acceptance of the Trinity as the teaching of the church sets the boundaries for the operation of all the other factors shows why the church has over centuries taken this doctrine very seriously. However, some of the responses from the participants show that a dogmatic approach to the doctrine of the Trinity is not sufficient to promote an adequate understanding. Although most of the participants appeared to have grown to the point where the Trinity was no longer just a dogma but something they experienced in their life, some would still need the help and encouragement of their church in this regard.

The evidence from the interviews and the other sources, such as my observations and documents, show some similarities and variation across the denominations. Apart from the Roman Catholics, the participants, in general, give the most weight to the Bible and to Experience. The Roman Catholics, more than any other church, gave weight to Tradition usually in the form of what they had been taught in Catechism in early life. Reason was also important to the participants not only in the sense that they sought to give coherent explanation in their answers, but by the way some would advance an argument because it made sense. One example of this was the argument that for people from a variety of ethnic backgrounds, ages and walks of life to gather

170

weekly at one location to worship peacefully indicated the presence of the Holy Spirit. The point was a logical one, namely, that nothing but the power of God and the special qualities of the Holy Spirit could make that possible.

But on the whole, even though denomination had some effect, it did not **determine the participants' Pneumatology. The effect** of denomination is best understood in terms of how each church combined or allowed their members to combine the six factors that have been listed. This meant that there was a variation in what participants within each denomination believed, with the widest variation occurring among the Roman Catholic participants. The denominational picture is also complicated by the complex pattern of church attendance. Many members of the historic churches simultaneously belong to an African Pentecostal church and many members of the African Pentecostal church were former members of the historic churches. It is fair to say that on the doctrine of the Holy Spirit, the six factors identified run deeper within Africans than the denomination they happen to belong to at a particular time.

CHAPTER 7

Conclusion

The aim of this study has been to find out how African Christians living in Britain think of the Holy Spirit. The hope is to add to existing knowledge of African Christianity and to promote mutual understanding between African Christians and their counterparts from other parts of the world. In the fieldwork, I adopted the pattern of an empirical cycle, which meant an inductive study followed by a deductive one. The inductive phase of the study, which was conducted at Mount Zion, gave rise to twelve pattern theories. Among the key ones was how little verbal mention the Holy Spirit received in church services. But I also found that the church's mid-week teaching included lessons on the Holy Spirit. Also, church activities included speaking in tongues and flexibility in liturgy. Interview of the church members showed that they thought much about the Holy Spirit not only during church services but in their daily life. This meant that the lack of mention of the Holy Spirit did not mean the Holy Spirit was being neglected. Rather, it was more a matter of having a relationship with the Holy Spirit that is so close that they often took his presence for granted. They also suffered the pitfall of not having a written liturgy which would ensure the mentioning of the three persons.

Another key feature of the church was the central place given to the Bible. It was very intriguing to see how in their minds the Holy Spirit and the Bible interacted. On the one hand, they believed the Holy Spirit interpreted the true meaning of the Bible to believers. This meant that the same passage could have different meanings to different people or even to the same person at a different time. On the other hand, they believe that the Bible was to be used to ascertain what was truly of the Spirit. Many members of this church were aware of the dangers of leaving the church totally open to claims of Spirit guidance and hence believed strongly that the Bible should act as a yardstick for checking what is of the Spirit. Many of the church members also believed that reading the Bible makes the believer become filled with the Holy Spirit. This pride of place given to the Bible resonates with what one finds among African Christians of various denominations. So the African roots of these Christians is possibly a factor here. Secondly, evangelical Christianity swept through much of Africa before Pentecostalism arrived, further strengthened the role of the Bible in the faith of African Christians. The result is that churches like Mount Zion are neither simply Pentecostal nor simply evangelical but a blend of the two traditions.

A third pattern to highlight is the belief that the Spirit empowers the believer in all they do. This was expressed with such force at Mount Zion that it is possible to see empowerment as the theme that runs through the whole life of the church. They see the Spirit as empowering their worship, which is why they pray for the Spirit to come before they start; they see the Spirit as empowering their ministers, which is why they are happy to have some spontaneity in their selection and training of ministers. It is also the same reason why women and young people have ministering roles within the church. They see the Spirit as empowering daily life which is why they often pray for the progress and prosperity of their members. This stress on the empowering work of the Holy Spirit is shared with non-African Pentecostal churches. What is different with Mount Zion and other African Pentecostal churches is the extent to which this empowerment has to do with daily life. This aspect, in my view, is the influence of their African worldview — one in which the material world and the spirit world interweave and daily occurrences are habitually explained by means of what is happening in the spirit world.

The final area to highlight is the strength with which the church emphasised the personhood of the Holy Spirit. A review of literature around this subject showed that this is an area of some difference between the new generation of Pentecostal churches in Africa and in the Diaspora compared to the first generation of African charismatic churches, the AICs. Whilst churches such as Mount Zion emphasized the inner inspiration of the Holy Spirit more than his visible possession of believers, the AIC did it the other way round. The reason behind this is that the African Pentecostal Churches compared to the African Initiated Churches are much more linked with other Christians around the world and have taken on board and held firmly the teaching of the church regarding the Trinity. The doctrine of the Trinity in which God is believed to be three persons in one, helped them to conceive of the Holy Spirit as a person walking alongside them in their daily life, rather than an impersonal force **implementing God's will in** the world.

Having established how the Spirit is seen in this one church, the next stage was to see the extent to which this view was widespread among African Christians as a whole. The best view would come from studying Christians from a variety of denominations. I chose participants from a Methodist church, a Roman Catholic Church, a Church of England church, and a Pentecostal church. On average, eight people were interviewed in each church, making a total of thirty-two for the four churches. Since this stage of the research is deductive, that is, trying to ascertain the extent to which participants in these churches conformed or differed from the pattern theories derived from Mount Zion, it meant that I could not investigate all twelve pattern theories. I chose to investigate two, 1) the relationship between the Holy Spirit and the other two Persons of the Trinity and, 2) the empowerment of believers by the Holy Spirit.

Results from interviews showed that the vast majority of participants from all the denominations believed in the divinity and personhood of the Holy

Spirit. The fieldwork also showed that, in general, participants saw the Holy Spirit as an active participant in their daily life. Unlike at Mount Zion, where participants saw the Spirit as a source of empowerment, participation at the historic churches saw the Holy Spirit mainly as guiding believers through daily life. This suggests that neither Pentecostalism on its own nor the African worldview on its own accounts for the belief among Africans that the Holy Spirit empowers Christians for daily life. Rather, it is the two factors combined.

In the true nature of an overarching inductive study, the position evolves from the study rather than being its starting point. Perhaps a different position might have crystallised for a different researcher. What crystallised for me from the study was the way participants used the doctrine of the Trinity as a backdrop when answering questions about the Holy Spirit. Hence the proposition was: what is believed about the Holy Spirit is what can be accommodated within the Trinity. A short historical review showed that this very much cohered with what had happened in the early Church as the doctrine of the Holy Spirit was being agreed on. The Church, having dealt with the person of Christ, when it turned to the person of the Holy Spirit in the fourth century, found that it always had to take account of what it had already believed about the Father and the Son. For example, it could not say that the Spirit was begotten by the Father because it had already described the Son as the "only begotten", so it said the Spirit "proceeded" from the Father.

Something similar happened with the participants in this study. The participants had to negotiate five factors, which I identified as the main ones shaping their Pneumatology. These were:

1) their experience, both personal and communal, of the work of the Holy Spirit reinforced their belief of who the Spirit is and how he works,

2) what the Bible said about the Holy Spirit and the experience of the text being interpreted by the Holy Spirit gave rise to a close relationship,

3) the concepts of God in Africa, such as the idea of the Supreme Being as one who rules over a pantheon of divinities, probably created the sense of subordination of the Holy Spirit with some participants,

4) the African worldview in which the material and the spiritual were interwoven possibly gave rise or strengthen the belief that the Holy Spirit acts in daily life, not just in worship or in overtly Christian ministry, and

5) the worldwide Pentecostal movement which influences Africans through the media and other routes had the effect of supporting the Trinitarian nature of their belief.

These factors had to be negotiated within boundaries or around a framework formed by the doctrine of the Trinity. Unlike in the early Church when the doctrine was still being worked out, the participants in this study had already accepted the Trinity as a settled dogma of the worldwide Church and they continuously reminded themselves of the accepted formula, three persons in one God. It was on that basis that they tried to work out what they could accept about the Holy Spirit. This meant, for example, that the Old Testament was read with New Testament eyes, because the latter was more in consonance with the doctrine of the Trinity than the former. But it also meant that those who had **a hierarchical Trinitarian structure in which the Father is "the big God"** could not contemplate worshipping the Spirit. That Trinitarian structure resulted in their sense of the Holy Spirit as a kind of junior God.

One may ask, what is African about this Pneumatology? The answer lies both in such specific elements as the influence of the African worldview and African concept of God, but also in the way all the constituting elements are put together. Whereas Pneumatology from other regions of the world might be biblical or experiential etc., the combination of these factors as described above, would be unique. It could also be asked, how does life in the Diaspora put its stamp on African Pneumatology. The answer to this question lies in the point already made about the time it takes for an African to significantly replace his African worldview with a Western, rationalistic one. This period was estimated at twenty years, provided the person concerned is constantly interacting with Western Europeans. For those who attend an African led and populated church, the time would be much longer. The implication is that for many there is no significant difference in their Pneumatology compared with people in Africa.

Methodology

I have followed the work of van der Ven in two ways. I, broadly, used the empirical cycle to structure my fieldwork. Also, in reaching this position and in **all my analysis, I adopted an "intradisciplinary" approach to interpretation. I** did not attempt to rescript my findings into social scientific categories. That approach, I find, tends to force theologians to engage in social scientific discourse and thus limits them to what social scientists are professionally allowed to say about religious concept. What I have done, instead, following the work of van der Ven, is to integrate the methods, concepts and techniques that I have used, which have been developed within the social sciences, into theology. I have treated them as tools of theology, thereby retaining my theological goal and worldview.

Recommendation for Practice

The two areas of empowerment and Trinitarian relationship raise two important points for Christian practice. Taking empowerment first, it has been pointed out above that Pentecostals emphasize empowerment for daily life and as part of that some Pentecostals focus on how the Spirit can help believers prosper materially. Whilst this link between the spiritual and the material has been explained as rooted in the African worldview, and one also ought to note an **immigrant people's need for encouragement in living in what is sometimes a** harsh socio-economic environment, there are dangers here. A relationship with

God that is simply about what one stands to gain materially would fall short of the faith exemplified by Jesus Christ, who went from place to place giving rather than receiving, serving rather than being served (Mk 10:45). Christians who get used to such a way of relating to God may also find it difficult to play a full part in their society, because they would have imbibed a selfish outlook to life and would not care much about making society better for all. It is important that Christian ministers and scholars continue to highlight these dangers.

The second area relates to the role of the Trinity as a dogma of the Church. **In this liberal age, "dogma" can be a dirty word. But this study has shown that,** in reality, many Christians willingly accept the doctrine of the Trinity as a teaching of the Church even if they do not understand it. This study thus shows that there is still a place in the Church for dogmas, that is, statement of what the Church believes which they expect their members to accept. But, on the other hand, the study also shows that dogmas on their own are not enough for most Christians. Many would expect that over time they would come to understand through reasoning or personal experience the wisdom of the Church behind the dogmatic statement. This is where more should be done by churches. A possible way forward is to use creedal statements during services regularly and have teaching programmes, inside and outside church services, to explain these statements. Alongside these, churches should also show in their own way that they are living by the Holy Spirit.

Areas for Future Research

This work opens up many areas for future research. The twelve pattern theories identified from Mount Zion are particularly important in this regard. For example, future research could be devoted to ascertaining how widespread is **the difference between men's relationship with the Holy Spirit and women's** relationship with the Holy Spirit. Also, future research could be devoted to finding out what changes occur among young Africans or second generation immigrants in the understanding and relationship with the Holy Spirit as their hold on the African worldview wanes.

Appendix 1: Consent Form

Research project on the understanding of the Holy Spirit

The following information is provided for you to decide whether you wish to participate in the present study. You are free to decide not to participate or to withdraw at any time without affecting your relationship with any other parties, such as the church or the university.

The research project investigates how the leaders and members of churches in Britain understand the person of the Holy Spirit by means of participant observation of worship, interviews and analysis of publicly available church information. At this stage in the research, I begin to conduct interviews in order **to hear 'first hand' what people think and understand about who the Holy Spirit** is and what the Holy Spirit does. The interviews are recorded in order to assist my analysis.

Please do not hesitate to ask any questions either before or after the interview. My finding will be shown to the church management before I use it. However, your name will not be associated with the research findings in any way, and your identity as an interviewee will only be known to the researcher.

There are very low risks associated with this study. Yet, it is hoped that your participation will be a source of encouragement to you and one that deepens your understanding and knowledge of the Christian faith.

Please sign your consent with full knowledge of the nature of the project and its procedures. A copy of this consent form will be given to you to keep.

Print name . . . .

Signature of Interviewee. . . . .

Date . . . .

By Revd Chigor Chike

Appendix 2: Interview Protocol

Date:

Time of interview

Place:

Interviewee:

(Give a brief description of project)

Context

1   Can you describe me your role in this church?

2   How long have you been involved with this church?

3   What do you like about the church?

4   Are there any principles that guide you at work? If so, what are they based on?

5   I have noticed the singing of praise songs during church services. Is there any reason behind this?

6   **I have noticed that the ministers… (sentence to be completed based on** an observation in the church)…What is the reason behind this?

        I am now going to ask you questions about the Holy Spirit

7   **When I say "Holy Spirit" what comes to your mind?**
       Who/what is the Holy Spirit?

8   What does the Holy Spirit do?

9   Is the Holy Spirit involved in daily life?
       How?

10   Do you think the Holy Spirit is involved in this church?
       In what ways?

11   Is the Holy Spirit involved in
       a) the reading of the Bible?
       b) in miracles?
       c) in the work of ministers?

What things do you associate with the Holy Spirit?

12   In your view, what are the two most important things the Holy Spirit can do for a human being?

13   **I have noticed during church services..... Why is this?**

Question on specific positions

14   Do you think of the Holy Spirit as a power that works for God?

15   Do you think the Holy Spirit deserves to be worshipped?

16   Do you pray to the Holy Spirit?

17   How do you think of the Trinity?

18   What is the relationship between Holy Spirit and Jesus?

Thank the interviewee for participating in the interview and assure them again of confidentiality.

Appendix 3: **Participants' pseudonyms and personal characteristics**

(Pseudonym) Mount Zion

Pseudonym	Age range	Gender	Country of Origin
Michael	31-40	M	Ghana
Evelyn	31-40	F	Ghana
P. Lara	41-50	F	Nigeria
P. Kenneth	41-50	M	Ghana
P. Christy	41-50	F	Caribbean
Momo	41-50	M	Nigeria
P. Abasi	41-50	M	Nigeria
Liz	41-50	F	British/Caribbean
Eva	61-70	F	Caribbean
John	21-30	M	Kenya
Geoff	18	M	British/Nigeria
Daya	20	F	Zimbabwe

(Pseudonym) East London Methodist Church

Pseudonym	Age range	Gender	Country of origin
Gabriel	51-60	M	Ghanaian
Ann	51-60	F	Nigerian
Hannah	41-50	F	Ghanaian
Elizabeth	61-70	F	Nigerian
Dada	51-60	M	Sierra Leone
Ebo	51-60	M	Ghanaian
Henrietta	41-50	F	Ghanaian
William	41-50	M	Ivorian

Bibliography

Adeboye, E., *Divine Encounter* (Lagos: Church Media Services, 2003).

—. *God the Holy Spirit* (Lagos: Christ the Redeemer's Ministries, 1997).

—. *Holy Spirit in the Life of Elijah* (Lagos: Christ the Redeemer's Ministries, 1997).

—. *Holy Spirit in the Life of Peter* (Lagos: Christ the Redeemer's Ministries, 1999).

—. *Jesus, Lord of the Universe* (Lagos: Alpha Press, 2002).

—. *Showers of Blessing* (Carrollton: One Hour Books, 2003).

—. *The Water and the Fire* (Apapa: F. and J. Publishing, 1999).

Adekunle, S., *Crossing your Jordan* (London: Sword of the Spirit Evangelical Outreach, 2007).

—. *Risk for Returns* (Ibadan: Victory, 2005).

Adesogan, E., *Christian Discipleship* (Jos: NIFES, 1998).

Adogame, A., "African Christian Communities in Diaspora" in Ogbu Kalu (ed.), *African Christianity: An African Story* (Trenton, New Jersey: African World Press, 2005), 494-514.

—. "African Instituted Churches in Europe, Continuity and Transformation" in Klaus Koschorke (ed.), *African Identities and World Christianity in the Twentieth Century* (Wiesbaden: Harrassowitz Verlag, 2005), 225-244.

—. "A Home Away from Home: The Proliferation of Celestial Church of Christ in Diaspora-Europe," *Exchange* 27.2 (1998), 141-160.

—. "Betwixt Identity and Security: African New Religious Movements and the Politics of Religious Networking in Europe," *Nova Religio: The Journal of Emergent and Alternative Religions* 7.2 (2003), 24-41.

—. *Celestial Church of Christ* (Frankfurt: Peter Lang, 1999).

—. "Claiming the Continent for Christ: The Civic Role of Christian Church Outreach Mission International in Global Contexts" in Katharina Kunter and Jens Holgar (eds), *Changing Relationships Between Churches in Europe and Africa: The internationalisation of Christianity and Politics in the 20th Century* (Wiesbaden: Harrassowitz, 2008), 225-40.

—. "Clearing New Paths into an old Forest: Aladura Christianity in Europe" in Jacob K. Olupona and Terry Rey (eds), *Orisa Devotion as World Religion: The Globalisation of Yoruba Religious Culture* (Madision: Wisconsin University Press, 2007), 247-262.

—. "Engaging the Rhetoric of Spiritual Warfare: The Public Face of the Aladura in Diaspora," *Journal of Religion of Africa* 34.4 (2004), 493-421.

—. "I am Married to Jesus! The Feminization of New African Diasporic Religiosity," *Archives de Sciences Sociales des Religions* 143 (September, 2008), 129-148.

—. "To be or not to be? Politics of belonging and African Christian Communities in Germany" in Afe Adogame and Cordula Weisskoeppel (eds), *Religion in the Context of African Migration*, (Bayreuth: Bayreuth University, 2005), 95-112.

—. "Mapping Globalization with the Lens of Religion: African Migrant Churches in Germany" in Armin Geertz and Margit Warburg (eds), *New Religions and Globalization, Empirical, Theoretical and Methodological Perspectives* (Aarhus: Aarhus University Press, 2008).

—. "Partnership of African Christian Communities in Europe," *International Review of Mission* 89.354 (2000), 291-298.

—. "Raising Champions, Taking Territories: African Churches and the Mapping of the New Religious Landscape in Diaspora" in Theodore Louis Trost (ed.), *The African Diaspora and the Study of Religion* (New York: Palgrave Macmillan, 2007), 21-46.

—. "Spiritual Terrorism Beyond Borders: African Pentecostalism, Cultural Synthesis within Local-Global Space" in Afe Adogame, Magnus Echtler and Ulf Vierke (eds), *Unpacking the New: Critical Perspectives on Cultural Syncretization in Africa and Beyond* (Wien: Lit Verlag, 2008), 305-330.

—. "The Quest for Space in the Global Spiritual Marketplace: African Religions in Europe," *International Review of Mission* 89.354 (2000), 400-409.

—. "Up, Up Jesus! Down, Down Satan! African Religiosity in the former Soviet Bloc — the Embassy of the Blessed Kingdom of God for All Nations," *Exchange: Journal of Missiological and Ecumenical Research* 37.3 (2008), 310-336.

—. "Who Do They Think They Are? Mental Images and the Unfolding of an African Diaspora in Germany" in Adogame et al (eds), *Christianity in Africa and the African Diaspora: The Appropriation of a Scattered Heritage* (London: Continuum, 2008), 248-264.

Aggrey-Solomon, D. and S. Aggrey-Solomon, *The Courtship that Leads to Marriage* (Accra: Blessed Publications, 2003).

Agyin-Asare, C., *Power in Prayer — Taking Your Blessings by Force* (publishers not stated, 2001).

—. *The Impact of Prayer — How to Win the Invisible War* (His Printing Hoornaar, 2001).

Akanle, G., *Satan-Proof Your Children* (London: Emmanuel House, 1999).

Akanni, G., *Becoming Like Jesus — God's Key to Abundant Living* (Gboko, Nigeria: Peace House, 2001).

—. *The Resurrection and the Life Is Here* (Gboko, Nigeria: Peace House, 2002).

Akosa, C., *Fresh Anointing* (Enugu: El' Demak, 2003).

Akoto-Bamfo, K., *Breaking the Power of Despair* (London: Alivia Media, 2002).

Albrecht, D.E., "Pentecostal Spirituality: Looking Through the Lens of Ritual," *Pneuma* 14.2 (Fall, 1992), 107-125.

Alexander, K.E., "Matters of Conscience, Matters of Unity, Matters Orthodoxy: Trinity and Water Baptism in Early Pentecostal Theology and Practice," *Journal of Pentecostal Theology* 17 (2008), 48-69.

Amanor, A. Pentecostal and Charismatic Churches in Ghana...", *Journal of Pentecostal Theology* 18 (2009), 123-140.

Amoo-Guttfried, K., *Beginnings — The Philosopher's Stone* (London: Solid Rock, 2003).

Anderson, A., "A 'Failure in Love' Western Missions and the Emergence of African Initiated Churches in the Twentieth Century," *Missiology* 29.3 (July, 2001), 275-286.

—. *African Reformation: African initiated Christianity in the 20th century* (Trenton, New Jersey: Africa World Press, 2001).

—. *An Introduction to Pentecostalism* (Cambridge: Cambridge University Press, 2004).

—. *Moya* (Pretoria: University of South Africa, 1991).

—. "New African initiated Pentecostal and Charismatic Churches in SA," *Journal of Religion in Africa* 35.1 (2005), 66-92.

—. "Pentecostal-Charismatic Spirituality and Theological Education in Europe in Global Perspective," *Pentecostudies* 2.1 (2004), (web journal).

—. "Varieties, Taxonomies, and Definitions" in Allan Anderson et al (eds), *Studying Global Pentecostalism* (London: University of California Press, 2010), 13-24.

Anyahamiwe, E., *The Flesh of God* (Publisher's location not stated: Voice of the Church, 2003).

Archbishop's Council, *Common Worship* (London: Archbishop's Council, 2000).

Armstrong, C., "Embrace Your Inner Pentecostal," *Christianity Today* 50.9 (2006), 86-89.

Asamoah-Gyadu, J.K., *African Charismatics: Current Developments within Independent Indigenous Pentecostalism in Ghana* (Leiden: Brill, 2005).

—. "An African Pentecostal on Mission in Eastern Europe: The Church of the Embassy of God in the Ukraine," *Pneuma: The Journal of the Society for Pentecostal Studies* 27.2 (2005), 297-221.

—. "'Born of Water and the Spirit' – Pentecostal/Charismatic Christianity in Africa" in Ogbu Kalu (ed.), *African Christianity: An African Story* (Asmara, Eritrea: African World Press, 2007), 339-357.

Ashimolowo, M., *31 Pillars of Divine Favour* (London: Mattyson Media, London).

—. *Breaking Barriers* (London: Mattyson Media, 2000).

—. *Divine Understanding*, Audio Tapes Set (London: 2007).

—. *No More Excuses for Failure* (London: Mattyson Media, 2001).

—. *Obeying Devine Signal Matthew* Ashimolowo (London: Media Ministries, 2007).

—. *Prevailing Prayer Against Spirits of Wickedness* (London: Mattyson Media, 2002).

—. *So You Call Yourself a Man* (London: Mattyson Media, London, 2003).

Augustine, *Later works*. The library of Christian classics 8 (London: SCM, 1955).

Athanasius, *The letters of St Athanasius concerning the Holy Spirit* (London: Epworth, 1951).

Ballard, P. and J. Pritchard, *Practical Theology in Action* (London: SPCK, 1996).

Barrett, D., *Schism and Renewal in Africa* (Oxford: Oxford University Press, 1968).

Bauer, W., *Orthodoxy and Heresy in Earliest Christianity* (Mifflintown: Sigler, 1996).

Becker, F. and W. Geissler, "Searching for pathways in a Landscape of Death: Religion and AIDS in East Africa," *Journal of Religion in Africa* 37 (2007), 1-15.

Bediako, K., *Theology and Identity* (Oxford: Regnum, 1992).

—. *Jesus in Africa: The Christian Gospel in African History and Experience* (Carlisle: Editions Cle and Regnum Africa, 2000).

Behrend, H., *Alice Lakwena and the Holy Spirits: War in Northern Uganda 1985-1997* (Oxford: James Carrey, 1999).

Bhaskar, R., *Possibilities of Naturalism: A Philosophical Critique of the Contemporary Human Sciences* (Harvester Wheatsheaf, Hemel Hempstead, 1989).

—. *Reclaiming Reality: A Critical Introduction to Contemporary Philosophy* (London: Verso, 1989).

Blair, C., "Women's Spirituality Empowered by Biblical Story," *Religious Education*, 87.4 (Fall, 1992), 532-544.

Blamiress, H., *A Defence of Dogmatism* (London: SPCK, 1965).

Blumhofer, E. "Azusa Street Revival" www.christiancentury.org, viewed 18th Nov. 2010.

—. *The Assemblies of God: a chapter in the story of American Pentecostalism* (Springfield: Gospel Publishing House, 1989).

Bompani, B., "Religion and Development from Below: Independent Christianity in South Africa," *Journal of Religion in Africa* 40 (2010), 307-330.

Book of Common Prayer (Cambridge: Cambridge University Press, 2004).

Braaten, C., "The role of dogma in church and theology" in Victor Pfitzner and Hilary Regan (eds), *The task of theology today* (Edinburgh: T & T Clark, 1999), 1-22.

Bryman, A., *Social Research Methods* (Oxford: Oxford University Press, 2004).

Bullock, J.L., "A Conversation with Robert Wuthnow and John Milbank," *Theology Today* 57.2 (July, 2000), 239-252.

Burgess, R., *Nigerian Christian Revolution: The Civil War revival and its Pentecostal Progeny (1967-2006)* (Oxford: Regnum, 2008).

—. "Nigerian Pentecostal Theology in Global Perspective," *Pentecostudies* 7.2 (2008), 29-63.

Burrell, D.B., "An Introduction to Theology and Social Theory; Beyond Secular Reason," *Modern Theology* 8.4 (October, 1992), 319-329.

Burrow, R., "Personalism and Afrikan Traditional Thought," *Encounter* 61.3 (Summer, 2000), 321-348.

Butin, P.W., *Revelation, Redemption and Response – Calvin's Trinitarian Understanding of the Divine-Human Relationship* (Oxford: Oxford University Press, 1995).

Calvin, J., *Institutes of the Christian Religion* (edited by John McNeil; Louisville, Kentucky: Westminster John Knox, 1960).

Cameron, H., et al, *Studying Local Churches* (London: SCM, 2005).

Cargal, T.B., "Beyond the Fundamentalist-Modernist Controversy: Pentecostals and Hermeneutics in a Postmodern Age," *Pneuma* 15.2 (Fall, 1993), 163-187.

Carr, A., "On Feminist Spirituality," *Horizons* 9.1 (Spring, 1982), 96-103.

—. "Providence, power and the Holy Spirit," *Horizons* 29.1 (Spring, 2002), 80-93.

Cartledge, M., *Charismatic glossolalia: An Empirical-Theological Study* (Farnham: Ashgate, 2002).

—. *Encountering the Spirit: The Charismatic Tradition* (Maryknoll: Orbis, 2007).

—. "God, Gender and Social Roles: A Study in Relation to Empirical Theological Models of the Trinity," *Journal of Empirical Theology* 22.2 (2009), 117-141.

—. *Practical Theology: Charismatic and Empirical Perspectives* (Carlisle: Paternoster, 2003).

—. *Testimony in the Spirit: Rescripting Ordinary Theology* (Farnham: Ashgate, 2010).

Chike, C., *African Christianity in Britain* (Milton Keynes: Author House, 2007).

—. "Proudly African, proudly Christian," in *Black Theology: an International Journal* 6.2, (London: Equinox, 2008), 221-240.

Church, J.E., *Quest for the Highest* (Cape Town: Oxford University Press, 1981).

Clark, C., "Old wine in new wine skins: West Indian and New West African Pentecostal Churches in Britain and the Challenge of Renewal," *Journal of Pentecostal Theology* 19 (2010), 143-154.

Corbetta, P., *Social Research: Theory Methods and Techniques* (London: Sage, 2003).

Coleman, S. "Anthropological Strand" in Cameron et al (eds), *Studying Local Churches* (London: SCM Press, 2005), 44-54.

—. *The globalisation of charismatic Christianity: Spreading the Gospel of Prosperity* (Cambridge; Cambridge University Press, 2005).

Cone, J., *God of the Oppressed* (New York: Orbis,1997.)

Conn, J.W., "Women's Spirituality: Restriction & Reconstruction," *Cross Currents* 30.3 (Fall, 1997), 293-308, 322.

Cook E.D., "Epistemology" in S.B. Ferguson and D.F Wright (eds), *New Dictionary of Theology* (Leicester: Inter Varsity Press, 1988), 225-226.

Corrie, J., *Mission Theology in Context* (Cheltenham: Open Theology College, 1998).

Cox, H., *Religion in the secular city: Towards a postmodern theology* (New York: Simon and Schuster, 1984).

Creswell, J., *Qualitative Enquiry and Research Design: Choosing Among the Five Approaches* (London: Sage, 2007).

—. *Research Design: Qualitative and Quantitative Approaches* (London: Sage, 1994).

Daneel M.L., "African Independent Church Pneumatology and the Salvation of all Creation," *International Review of Mission* 82.326 (April, 1993), 143-166.

—. *Zionism and Faith-Healing in Rhodesia: Aspects of African independent churches* (Paris, Mouton, 1993).

Davies, A., "What does it Mean to Read the Bible as a Pentecostal *Journal of Pentecostal Theology* 18 (2009), 216-229.

De Groot, A., *Methodology: Foundations of Inference and Research in the Behavioural Sciences* (Paris, Mouton, 1969).

Denscombe, M., *The Good Research Guide* (Buckingham: Open University Press, 1998).

—. *The Good Research Guide* (Buckingham: Open University Press, 2007).

De Vaus, D., *Research Design in Social Research* (London: Sage, 2001).

Deya, G., *Dangerous Prayers to Break Satan's Force* (Eastbourne: Stock, 2003).

—. *The Stronghold of Generational Curses* (Eastbourne: Stock, 2003).

Dickson, K., "Continuity and Discontinuity Between the Old Testament and African Life and Thought" in Kofi Appiah-Kubi and Segio Torres (eds), *African Theology en Route* (Maryknoll, New York: Orbis, 1997), 95–108.

Dorgan, M., "The Holy Spirit," *The Living Pulpit* (January-March, 1996), 8-9.

Dorman, D.A., "The Purpose of Empowerment in the Christian Life," *Pneuma* 7.2 (Fall, 1985), 147-165.

Driver, G.H., "What has become of the Doctrine of the Holy Spirit?" *Bibliotheca sacra* 93.369 (Jan-March, 1936), 26-40.

Dunzi, F., *A Brief History of the Doctrine of the Trinity in the Early Church* (translated by John Bowden; London: T & T Clark, 2007).

Dwane, S., "In Search of an African Contribution to a Contemporary Confession of Christian Faith," *Journal of Theology for Southern Africa* 38.1 (March 1982), 19-25.

Economic and Social Research Council, *Research Ethics Framework* (Swindon: Economic and Social Research Council, 2005).

Egwu, R.A., *Igbo idea of the Supreme Being and the Triune God* (Wurzburg, Echter, 1998),

Eia, J., *My Faith as an African* (Maryknoll, New York: Orbis, 1988).

Elias, J.H., "Authority" in *New Dictionary of Theology* (Leicester: Inter Varsity Press, 1998), 64-66.

Elebute, T., *Open Heaven — Your Covenant Heritage* (Lagos: International Christian Faith Mission, undated).

Elisha, P.M., *Effective Kingdom Living — A Prophetic Perspective* (Nairobi: Kings Script, 2004).

Emmanuel, O., *Maximizing Opportunities* (Lagos: Olumide Emmanuel Ministries, 2001).

Geotz, P. (ed.), *Encyclopaedia Britannica* (Chicago: Encyclopaedia Britannica Inc), 15th edition, Vol. 26, (1985).

Engebretson, K., "Young People, Culture, and Spirituality: Some Implications for Ministry," *Religious Education* 98.1 (Winter, 2003), 5-24.

Erdman, D., "Liberation and Identity: Indo-Hispano Youth," *Religious Education* 73.1 (1983), 76-89.

Eze, C., *Yes, Lord — Achieving Success Through Hearing From God* (Lagos: Consarcs, 2002).

Fagerberg, D.W., "A Theology of the Liturgy," *Liturgical Ministry* 14 (Fall, 2005), 169-179.

Fashole-Luke, E., "The Quest for African Christian Theologies" in G.H. Anderson and T.F. Stransky (eds), *Third World Theologies* (New York: Paulist/Eerdmans, 1976), 135-150.

Ferguson, D.S., *Biblical Hermeneutics: An Introduction* (London: John Knox, 1986).

Fishman, W., *The Streets of East London* (Nottingham: Five Leaves, 2006).

Fomum, Z.T., *The Way of Victorious Praying* (Mumbai: Crossroad Communication, 1988.)

Fortman, E.J., *The Triune God* (London: Hutchinson, 1972).

Frank-Briggs, E., *Unbreakable Laws of Father* (London: Emmanuel House, 2001).

Fryer, P., *Staying Power* (London: Pluto, 1994).

Geach, K., *Axiology: A Theory of Values* (Walton-on-Thames: Ken Geach, 1976).

Gerloff, R., "African Christian Diaspora in Europe: Religious and Cultural Aspects" — paper presented at the *IAMS Conference in Malaysia*, 31 July–7 August, (2004).

—. "An African Continuum in Variation: The African Christian Diaspora in Britain" in *Black Theology in Britain: A Journal of Contextual Praxis*, 4, (2000), 275-280.

—. "Editorial," *International Review of Mission* 89.354 (2000), 275–280.

—. "Theology on Route: The Inner Dynamics of the Black Church Movement in Britain," *Mission Studies* x.1&2, 19&20 (1993), 134-147.

—. "The Significance of the African Christian Diaspora in Europe," *Journal of Religion in Africa* 29.1 (1999), 115-120.

Gerring, J., *Case Study Research: Principles and Practice* (New York: Cambridge University Press, 2007).

Gill, R., *Theology and Social Structure* (Oxford: Mowbray, 1977).

—. *Theology and Sociology: A Reader* (London: Geoffrey Chapman, 1987).

—. *The Social Context of Theology* (Oxford: Mowbray, 1975).

Girling, B., *East End Neighbourhoods: Images of London* (Stroud: Tempus, 1940).

Githieya, F.K., "The Church of the Holy Spirit — Biblical Beliefs and Practices of the Arathi of Kenya, 1926-50" in Thomas Spear and Isaria N. Kimambo (eds), *East African Expressions of Christianity* (Oxford: James Currey, 1999), 231-243.

Grabe, P.J. "The Pentecostal Discovery of the New Testament Theme of God's Power and Its Relevance to the African Context," *Pneuma* 24.2 (Fall, 2002), 225-242.

Greene, C., *Christology and Atonement in Historical Perspective* (Cheltenham: Open Theological College, undated).

Griffith, R.M. and D. Roebuck, "Women, Role of" in Stanley M. Burgess and Edward M. van der Maas (eds), *The New International Dictionary of Pentecostal and Charismatic Movements* (Grand Rapids: Zondervan, 2003), 1203-1209.

Grundmann, C.H., "Inviting the Spirit to fight the Spirits: Pneumatological Challenges for Mission in Healing and Exorcism," *International Review of Mission*, 94.372 (January, 2005), 51-73.

Gunton, C. "Dogma, the Church and the task of theology" in Victor Pfitzner and Hilary Regan (eds), *The task of theology today* (Edinburgh: T & T Clark, 1999), 1-22.

—. *Father, Son, and Holy Spirit: Essays Toward a Fully Trinitarian Theology,* (London: T & T Clark, 2003).

—. *The Promise of Trinitarian Theology* (London: T & T Clark, 1997).

Gustafsson, M., "Workers for Christ: A Study of Young People in a Costa Rican Mega Church," *Swedish Missiological Themes* 93.4 (2005), 505-534.

Gutierrez, G., *Essential Writings* (edited by J. Nickoloff; New York: Orbis, 1996).

—. *The Power of the Poor in History* (New York: Orbis, 1983).

—. *The Theology of Liberation* (New York: Orbis, 1973).

Hagin, K., *Listen to your heart* (Tulsa: Rhema Bible Church, 1992).

Hanson, R.P.C., *The Search for the Christian Doctrine of God* (Edinburgh: T and T Clark, 1988).

Harris, H., *Yoruba in Diaspora: An African Church in London* (New York: Palgrave Macmillan, 2006).

Hinn, B., *Welcome Holy Spirit* (Lagos: Thomas Nelson, 1997).

Hollenweger, W.J., *Pentecostalism: Origin and developments worldwide* (Peabody: Hendrickson, 1997).

—. "The Black Roots of Pentecostalism" in A. Anderson and W. Hollenweger (eds), *Pentecostals After a Century: global perspectives on a movement in transition* (Sheffield: Sheffield Academic, 1999), 33-44.

Hudson, D.N., "Singing a New Song in a Strange Land" in Keith Warrington (ed.), *Pentecostal Perspectives* (Carlisle: Paternoster, 1998), 177-203.

Hunter, J., "What is Modernity? Historical Roots and Contemporary Features" in Philip Sampson et al (eds), *Faith and Modernity* (Carlisle: Regnum, 1997), 12-28.

http://neighbourhood.statistics.gov.uk; viewed 13th April, 2009.

Idowu, B., *African Traditional Religion – A Definition* (London: SCM, 1974).

—. *Olodumare – God in Yoruba belief* (S.I: Longman, 1962).

—. *Towards an Indigenous Church* (London: Oxford University Press, 1965).

Igwara, O., "My Spirituality: A Spirituality of Love" *Black Catholics Speak* (London: Catholic Association for Racial Justice, 1991), 50–58.

Ikenga-Metu, E., "The Revival of African Christian Spirituality: The Experience of African Independent Churches," *Mission Studies* 7-2.14 (1990), 151-171.

Jenson, R.W., "Liturgy of the Spirit," *Lutheran Quarterly* 26.2 (May, 1974), 189-203.

Jehu-Appiah, J., "The African Indigenous Churches and the Quest for an Appropriate Theology for the New Millennium," *International Review of Mission* 89.354 (2000), 410–420.

Johnson, J.A., "A Brief Oneness Pentecostal Response," *Pneuma* 30 (2008), 225-226.

Kalilombe, P., "My Life, Faith and Theology" in *Black Catholics Speak* (London: Catholic Association for Racial Justice, 1991), 59–78.

—. "Race Relations in Britain — Possibilities for the Future" in Paul Grant and Raj Patel (eds), *A Time to Speak* (Birmingham: CRRU, 1990), 37–45.

Kalu, O., *African Pentecostalism: An Introduction* (New York: Oxford University Press, 2008).

—. "Church Presence in Africa" in Kofi Appiah-Kubi and Segio Torres (eds), *African Theology en Route* (Maryknoll, New York: Orbis, 1979), 13–22.

—. "Preserving a Worldview," *Pneuma* 24.2 (Fall, 2002), 110-137.

Kayanja, R., *The Patience Patient* (Kampala: Publishing, undated).

Kärkkäinen, V., *Pneumatology – The Holy Spirit in Ecumenical, International, and Contextual Perspective* (Grand Rapids: Baker Academic, 2002).

Kay, W. and L. Francis, *Drift from the Churches* (Cardiff: University of Wales Press, 1996).

Kihiko M.K., *Resolving Church Splits* (Nairobi: Kings Scripts, 2004).

Kim, E.M., "The Holy Spirit and new marginality," *Journal for Preachers* 25.4 (Pentecost, 2002), 26-31.

Kiranga, J., *The Ultimate Weapon in Spiritual Warfare* (Nairobi: Men of Concerns, 2004).

Kisseadoo S.V.A., *Faith for Our Times* (Accra: Asempa Publishers Christian Council of Ghana, 2005).

Kiuna, A.W., *Created for Dominion* (Nairobi: Jubilee Christian Church, Nairobi, 2005).

Kollman, P., "Classifying African Christianities, Part Two: The Anthropology of Christianity and Generation of African Christians," *Journal of Religion in Africa* 40 (2010), 118-148.

—. "Classifying African Christianities, Past, Present and Future: Part One," *Journal of Religion in Africa* 40 (2010), 3-32.

Kowalski, R., "The mission theology of early Pentecostals," *Journal of Pentecostal Theology*, 19 (2010), 265-291.

Kraft, C.H., "Spiritual Warfare" in Stanley M. Burgess and Edward M. van der Maas (eds), *The New International Dictionary of Pentecostal and Charismatic Movements* (Grand Rapids: Zondervan, 2003), 1091-1096.

Kudanjie, J.K. and R.K. Aboagye-Mensah, *Christian Social Ethics* (Accra: Asempa Publishers Christian Council of Ghana, 1992).

Kumuyi, W.F., *ABC of Ministering Healing and Deliverance* (Lagos: Life, 2003).

—. *God's 3 Fold Invitation* (Lagos: Life, 1995).

—. *Joy in All Circumstances* (Lagos: Life, 2003).

—. *The Essentials of Christian Living* (Lagos: Zoe, 1985).

Lindhardt, M., "'If You Are Saved You Cannot Forget Your Parents': Agency, Power, and Social Repositioning in Tanzanian born-again Christianity," *Journal of Religion in Africa* 40 (2010), 240-272.

Lema, A.A., "Chaga Religion and Missionary Christianity on Kilimanjaro: The Initial Phase, 1893–1916" in T. Spear and I. Kimambo (eds), *East African Expressions of Christianity* (Oxford: James Currey, 1999), 39-62.

Loewen, J., "Which God Do Missionaries Preach?" *Missiology* 14.1 (January, 1986), 3-19.

Macchia, F.D., "Theology, Pentecostal" in Stanley M. Burgess and M. Edward van der Maas (eds), *The New International Dictionary of Pentecostal and Charismatic Movements* (Grand Rapids: Zondervan, 2003), 1120-1141.

Maddox, G., "The Church and Cigogo: Fr Stephen Mlundi and the Church in Central Tanzania" in T. Spear and I. Kimambo (eds), *East African Expressions of Christianity* (Oxford: James Currey, 1999), 150-166.

Madugba M.U., *Dealing with Evil* (Port Harcourt: Spiritual Life Outreach, 2003).

—. *Elders at the Gate* (Port Harcourt: Spiritual Life Outreach, 2002).

Malcolm, L., "Recovering Theology's Voice: Radical, Orthodoxy," *Christian Century* 29 (Oct. 2000), 1074-1079.

Mannheim, K., "Theology and Sociology of Knowledge" in R. Gill (ed.), *Theology and Sociology* (New York: Cassell, 1996), 79-90.

Martin, D., "Undermining the Old Paradigms: Rescripting Pentecostal Accounts," *Pentecostudies* 5.1 (2006), 18-38.

Martin, K.C., "A Spirit-Empowered Ministry," *Brethren Life and Thought* 20 (Winter, 1975), 45-51.

Martinson, R., "Spiritual but not religious: Reaching an invisible generation," *Currents in Theology and Mission* 29.5 (2002), 326-340.

Matynes, B., *Bridges to Miracles* (Lagos: Brodaxe, 1999).

Maxwell, D., "The Durawall of Faith: Pentecostal Spirituality in Neo-Liberal Zimbabwe," *Journal of Religion in Africa* 35.1 (2005), 4-32.

Mbiti, J., *African Religions and Philosophy* (Oxford: Heinemann, 1990).

—. *Bible and Theology in African Christianity* (Oxford: Oxford University Press, 1986).

—. *Concepts of God in Africa* (London: SPCK, 1970).

Mbogori, E., *Overcoming Bereavement — The Art of Dealing with Personal Loss* (Nairobi: Faith Institute of Counselling, 2002).

McClung, L.G. Jr., "Exorcism" in Stanley M. Burgess and Edward M. van der Maas (eds), *The New International Dictionary of Pentecostal and Charismatic Movements* (Grand Rapids: Zondervan, 2003), 624-628.

——. "Try to get people saved: Azusa 'Street missiology'" in Grant McClung (ed.), *Azusa Street and beyond* (Gainesville: Bridge-Logos, 2006), 1-22.

McGrath, A., *Christian Theology* (Oxford: Blackwell, 2001).

Mettle, H., *God's Zero Theory* (Accra: Rev Hansen Mettle, 2004).

Menzies, R.P., "Luke's Understanding of Baptism in the Holy Spirit: A Pentecostal Dialogues with the Reformed Tradition," *Journal of Pentecostal Theology* 16 (2008), 86-101.

Meyrick, A., *Is Dogma a Necessity?* (London: Hodder and Stoughton, 1883).

Middleton, J.R. and B.J. Walsh, *Truth is Stranger Than it Used to Be* (London: SPCK, 1995).

Milbank, J., *Theology and Social Theory* (Oxford: Blackwell, 1993).

——. *The World Made Strange* (Oxford: Blackwell, 1997).

Moila, M.P., "God's Kingship and Value Systems in Pedi Christianity," *Journal of Theology in South Africa* 116 (July, 2003), 101-119.

Moltmann, E. and J. Moltmann, "Being Human in New Community," *Currents in Theology and Mission* 29.5 (2002), 326-340.

Moltmann, J., *The Trinity and the Kingdom of God* (San Francisco: Harper and Row, 1981).

Montagu, G., *Holy Spirit – Growth of the Biblical Tradition* (New York: 1978).

Mpagi, P.W., *African Christian theology in the contemporary context* (Kisubi: Mananum, 2002).

Mosala, J., "African Traditional Beliefs and Christianity," *Journal of Theology for South Africa* 43.1 (June, 1983), 15-24.

——. *Biblical Hermeneutics and Black Theology in South Africa* (Grand Rapids: Eerdmans, 1989).

Munroe, M., *The Most Important Person on Earth: The Holy Spirit, Governor of the Kingdom* (Nassau: Bahamas Faith Ministries International, 2007).

Mwaura P.N., "Gender and Power in African Christianity" in Ogbu Kalu (ed.), *African Christianity: An African Story* (Trenton: African World Press Incorporated, 2007), 359-388.

Nathan, R., "African-Caribbean Youth Identity in the United Kingdom," *International Review of Mission*, 89.354 (2000), 349–353.

——. "African Christians United in a Unified Europe," *International Review of Mission*, 89.354 (2000), 299–303.

Ndakwe, P., *Are Africans Cursed by God?* (Nairobi: Kings Script, 2005).

Ndungu, "The role of the Bible" in Gerald O. West and Musa Dube (eds), *The Bible in Africa: Transactions, Trajectories and Trends* (Leiden: Brill, 2000), 236-247.

Newell, S., "Devotion and Domesticity: The Reconfiguration of Gender in Popular Christian Pamphlets from Ghana and Nigeria," *Journal of Religion in Africa* 35.3 (2005), 297-223.

——. "Pentecostal Witchcraft; Neoliberal Possession and Demonic Discourse in Ivorian Pentecostal Churches," *Journal of Religion in Africa* 37 (2007), 461-490.

Ng'ang'a J., *Freedom From Caged Life* (Nairobi: Neno Evangelism Centre, 2005).

Nieswand, B., "Enacted Destiny; West African Charismatic Christians in Berlin and the Immanence of God," *Journal of Religion in Africa* 40 (2010), 33-59.

Nthiga, F., *A Woman of Noble Character — Who Can Find?* (Nairobi: Faith Anointed Books International, undated).

Nyamu, P.K., *The Holy Spirit — His Baptism* (Nairobi: International Bible Society, 1984).

—. *The Holy Spirit — His Baptism* (Nairobi: Revival Springs Media, 2000).

Obiego, C.O., *African image of the ultimate reality: an analysis of Igbo ideas of life and death in relation to Chukwu-God* (New York: Peter Lange, 1984).

Odeyemi, E., *What is the Church? — A Pentecostal Perspective* (Lagos: Christ the Redeemer's Ministry, 2000).

O'Donovan, W., *Biblical Christianity in African Perspective* (Carlisle: Paternoster, 1996).

Odulele, A.A., *Eternity Unveiled* (London: OVMC, 2005).

—. *Living by Faith — Move Your Mountains* (London: OVMC, 2003).

—. *Prosperity of the Soul* (London: OVMC, 2007).

—. *Understanding God's Voice* (London: OVMC, 2003).

Oduyemi, G., *Holy Living* (Lagos: Bethel, 1995).

Oduyoye, M.A., *Daughters of Anowa: African Women and Patriarchy* (Maryknoll, New York: Orbis, 1995).

—. *Hearing and Knowing: Theological Reflections on Christianity in Africa* (Maryknoll, New York: Orbis, 1986).

—. "The Value of African Religious Beliefs and Practices for Christian Theology" in Kofi Appiah-Kubi and Segio Torres (eds), *African Theology en Route* (Maryknoll, New York: Orbis, 1979), 109–116.

Ofoegbu, M., *Family Liberation Prayers* (Lagos: Holy Ghost Anointed Book Ministries, 2000).

—. *Pray Down Money* (Lagos: Holy Ghost Anointed Book Ministries, 2003).

Oginde, D., *Possessing Your Possessions* (Nairobi: Cana, 2002).

Oha, E., *Potential for Excellence* (Enugu: El 'Demak, 2002).

Ojo, M., "The Charismatic Movement in Nigeria," *International Bulletin of Missionary Research* (July, 1995), 114-118.

Okorocha, C., "The Meaning of Salvation: An African Perspective" in W.A. Dyrness (ed.), *Emerging Voices in Global Christian Theology* (Grand Rapids: Zondervan, 1994), 59–92.

Olofinjana, I., *20 Pentecostal Pioneers in Nigeria: Their Lives, Their Legacies* vol. 1 (Xlibris Corporation, USA, 2011).

—. *Reverse in Ministry and Mission: Africans in the Dark Continent of Europe* (London: Author House, 2010).

Oludoyi, D.S., *Dare to Dream* (London: Emmanuel House, 2003).

—. *It's Ok To Walk Away* (London: Shinning Light Group, 2005).

Olukoya, D.K., *Dealing with Unprofitable Roots* (Lagos: The Battle Cry Christian Ministries, 1999).

—. *Meat for Champions* (Lagos: Mountain of Fire and Miracles Ministries, 1999).

—. *Satanic Diversion of the Black Race* (Lagos: Mountain of Fire and Miracles Ministries, 2001).

—. *Slaves Who Love Their Chain* (Lagos: Mountain of Fire and Miracles Ministries, 1999).

—. *The Lord Is a Man of War* (Lagos: The Battle Cry Christian Ministries, 2001).

—. *When God Is Silent* (Lagos: Mountain of Fire and Miracles Ministries, 2001).

Olson, R.E., "Confession of a Post-Pentecostal Believer in the Charismatic Gifts," *Criswell Theological Review* 4.1 (Fall, 2006), 31-40.

Omoyajowo, J.A., *Cherubim and Seraphim – The History of an African Independent Church* (New York: Nok, 1982).

Onwuchekwa, E., *Perilous Times and Its Consequences* (Enugu: Computer Edge, 2002).

Onyeme, K., *The Holy Spirit Exposed* (publishing details not stated, undated))

Ormerod, N., "A Dialectic Engagement with the Social Sciences in an Ecclesiological Context," *Theological Studies* 66.4 (December, 2005), 815-840.

Oshun C., "Encountering Aladura Spirituality in Britain." Paper presented at the *Africa Religious Diaspora Conference*, Tetley Hall, University of Leeds, UK 7–11 (Sept, 1997).

Outler, A., "The Wesleyan Quadrilateral in John Wesley" *Wesleyan Theological Journal* 20.1, (Spring, 1985), 7-18.

Owolabi, M., *Which God?* (London: Bible Christians, 2000).

Owusu-Ansah, K. and B. Owusu-Ansah, *The Secrets of the Anointing that Breaks Every Yoke* (Kumasi: Great Expectations Worship Centre, 2003).

Oyakhilome, C. and A. Oyakhilome, *Rhapsody of Reality* (Lagos: Love world, 2006).

Oyakhilome, C., *Seven things the Holy Spirit will do in you* (Lagos: Love World, 2004).

—. *The Seven Spirits of God – Divine Secrets to the Miraculous* (Lagos: Love world, 2006).

Oyedepo, D., *Dynamics of Holiness* (Lagos: Dominion, 1997).

—. *Long Life Your Heritage* (Lagos: Dominion, 1986).

—. *Showers of Blessing* (Lagos: Dominion, 1997).

—. *The Miracle Seed* (Lagos: Dominion, 1985).

—. *Understanding Financial Prosperity* (Lagos: Dominion, 1997).

Ozoko, D., *More Than Conquerors* (Enugu: Computer Edge, 2004).

Para-Mallam, G., *Getting Into Scripture — A Fresh Approach to Re-Discovering Biblical Truth* (Jos: NIFES, 1996).

Parratt, J., *A Reader in African Christian Theology* (London: SPCK, 1987).

—. *Reinventing Christianity* (Grand Rapids: Eerdmans, 1995).

Parrinder, G.E., *African Traditional Religion* (London: Sheldon, 1962).

Patton, M.Q., *Qualitative Research and Evaluation Methods* (London: Sage, 2002).

Pauw, A.P., "Who or what is the Holy Spirit?" *Christian Century* 113.2 (Jan. 17, 1996), 48-49, 51.

Payne, G. and J. Payne, *Key Concepts in Social Research* (London: Sage, 2004).

Pinnock, C.H., "The Work of the Spirit in the Interpretation of Holy Scriptures from the Perspective of a Charismatic Biblical Theologian," *Journal of Pentecostal Theology* 18 (2009), 157-171.

Pobee J.S., *Towards an African Theology* (Nashville: Abingdon, 1979).

Poythress, V.S., "Linguistic and Sociological Analyses of Modern Tongue Speaking," *Westminster Theological Journal* 42 (1979), 367-388.

Ramirez, D., "A Historical Response," *Pneuma* 30 (2008), 245-265.

Reno, R.R., "The Radical Orthodoxy Project," *First Things* 100.1 (February, 2000), 37-44.

Richardson, C., "The enigma of the Trinity" in Roy W. Battenhouse (ed.), *A Companion to the Study of St Augustine* (Grand Rapids: Baker, 1979), 235-256.

Robinson, E.B., "Youth With A Mission" in Stanley M. Burgess and Edward M. van der Maas (eds), *The New International Dictionary of Pentecostal and Charismatic Movements* (Grand Rapids: Zondervan, 2003), 1223-1224.

Robson, C., *Real World Research* (Oxford: Blackwell, 2002).

Sampson, P., "The Rise of Postmodernity" in Philip Sampson, Vinay Samuel and Chris Sugden (eds), *Faith and Modernity* (Oxford: Regnum, 1994), 29-57.

Sanusi, L., *Goliath Killing Prayers — How to Overcome Every Giant of your Life* (No Publisher address: Oraworld, 2003).

Schweizer, E., *The Holy Spirit* (London: SCM, 1981).

Seamone, D.L., "Body as Ritual Actor and Instrument of Praise: Verna Maynard's Experience as Praise Leader in the Kitchener Church of God," *Journal of Ritual Studies* 12.1 (Summer, 1998), 18-26.

Seidman, I., *Interviewing as Qualitative Research* (New York: Teacher College, 2006).

Setiloane, G., "Confessing Christ Today: From One African Perspective: Man and Community," *Journal of Theology for Southern Africa* 12 (September, 1975), 29-38.

Shea, F.X., "Reason and the Religion of Counter-Culture," *Harvard Theological Review* 66 (1973), 95-111.

Shepperd, J.W., "Worship" in Stanley M. Burgess and Edward M. van der Maas (eds), *The New International Dictionary of Pentecostal and Charismatic Movements* (Grand Rapids: Zondervan, 2003), 1217-1220.

Simotwo, J.M., *Towards Christian Maturity and Excellence* (Nairobi: Global Harvest and Management, 2000).

Smith, J., "Teaching a Calvinist to Dance — in Pentecostal worship, my Reformed theology finds its groove," *Christianity Today* 52.5 (May, 2008), 42-45.

Smith, S., "The Holy Spirit and Mission in some Contemporary Theologies of Mission," *Mission Studies* 17.2-36 (2001).

Soane, C. and A. Stevenson (eds), *Concise Oxford English Dictionary* (Oxford: Oxford University Press, 2006).

Society for Pentecostal Studies, "Oneness-Trinitarian Pentecostal: Final Report, 2002-2007," *Pneuma* 30 (2008), 203-224.

Somerville W. and B. Cooper, "United Kingdom: Immigration to the United Kingdom" in Uma A Segal, Doreen Elliott, Nazneen S. Mayadeas (eds), *Migration Worldwide: Policies, Practices and Trends* (New York: Oxford University Press, 2010), 124-137.

Stake, R.E., *The Art of Case Study Research* (London: Sage, 1995).

Stringer, M., "The Worship and Action of the Local Church; Anthropological Strand" in H. Cameron et al (eds) *Studying Local Churches* (London: SCM, 2005), 89-98.

Stoddart, E., "Spirituality and Citizenship: Sacramentality in Parable," *Theological Studies* 68 (2007), 761-779.

Stortz, M.E., "Purpose-Driven or Spirit-Led: A Spirituality of Work or the Work of the Spirit," *Word and World* 25.4 (Fall, 2005), 403-412.

Sturge, M., *Look What the Lord Has Done* (Bletchley: Scripture Union, 2005).

Swinton, J. and H. Mowat, *Practical Theology and Qualitative Research* (London: SCM, 2006).

Takenaka, M., *God Is Rice* (Geneva: World Council of Churches, 1986).

Takon, R., *Knowing and Developing Your Spiritual Gifts* (Lagos: Frontline Services, 1998).

Tetteh, L., *Benefits of the Anointing* (London: LT Media Ministries, 2002).

—. *Count Your Blessings* (London: LT Media Ministries, 2002).

—. *Do Miracles Still Happen?* (London: World Miracle Outreach, 1999).

Turner, H.W., *African Independent Church II — The life and faith of the Church of the Lord (Aladura)* (Oxford: Clarendon, 1967).

—. *Profile Through Preaching* (London: Edinburgh House, 1965).

Ukah, A., *A New Paradigm of Pentecostal Power: A Study of the Redeemed Christian Church of God in Nigeria* (Trenton: Africa World, 2008).

Ukpong, J., "Developments in Biblical Interpretation in Africa: Historical and hermeneutical Directions" in Gerald O. West and Musa Dube (eds), *The Bible in Africa: Transactions, Trajectories and Trends* (Leiden: Brill, 2000), 11-28.

Vander-Puije, K., *The Release Procedure* (Accra: Great Eagle, 2004).

Van der Ven, J.A., *Practical Theology: An Empirical Approach* (Kampen: Kok Pharos, 1993).

Van Dusen, H., *Spirit, Son and Father — Christian Faith in the Light of the Holy Spirit* (New York: Charles Scribner's Sons, 1958).

Van Schalkwyk, A., "On Healing, Spirituality and Culture: The Stories of Afrikaans Women and African's Women Theology," *Journal of Theology for South Africa* 124 (March, 2006), 4-18.

Vernooij, J., "Pentecostalism and Migration — The Dutch Case." Paper for the *IAMS Assembly in Malaysia* (2004).

Vickers, J.E., "The Making of a Trinitarian Theologian: The Holy Spirit in Charles Wesley's Sermons," *Pneuma*, 31 (2009), 213-224.

Wagura, P.M., "Karl Rahner's Theology: A Basis for Searching for an African Christianity," *African Ecclesial Revuew* 40.1 (Feb, 1998), 2-11.

Walvoord, J.F., "Contemporary Issues in the Doctrine of the Holy Spirit," *Spiritual Renewal* (April, 1973), 117-125.

Ward, K., "The armies of the Lord: Rebels and the State in Northern Uganda 1986-1999," *The Journal of Religion in Africa* 31.2 (2001), 187-221.

——. "Ugandan Christian Communities in Britain," *International Review of Mission* 89.354 (2000), 320–328.

Waritay-Tulloch, R., *Emotional Rollercoaster* (London: Christ Temple, 2001).

——. *The Power of the Word in Your Mouth* (London: Christ Temple, 2001).

World Council of Churches official website www.oikoumene.org/en/who-are-we.html, visited, (26th Nov 2010).

Wright, N.T., *The New Testament and the People of God* (London: SPCK, 1992).

Yin, R., *Case Study Research – Design and Methods* (London: Sage, 1984).

Young, M. and P. Willmott, *Family and Kinship in East London* (London: Routledge and Kegan Paul, 1957).

General index

ND - #0096 - 090625 - C0 - 229/152/12 - PB - 9781842278413 - Gloss Lamination